DAWA

Dawa

The Islamic Strategy for Reshaping the Modern World

Patrick Sookhdeo

Isaac Publishing

Dawa: The Islamic Strategy for Reshaping the Modern World

Published in the United States by Isaac Publishing
6729 Curran Street, McLean, Virginia 22101

Library of Congress Control Number: 2014951766

ISBN: 978-0-9916145-3-0

Book design by Lee Lewis Walsh, Words Plus Design

Printed in the United States of America

…if the ummah *is united in this lofty and honourable aim, namely to dominate all other nations, fostering them and pruning their souls…*[1]

—Muhammad Rashid Rida

The aim of the Islamic movement is to bring about somewhere in the world a new society wholeheartedly committed to the teachings of Islam in their totality and striving to abide by those teachings in its government, political, economic and social organizations, its relation with other states, its educational system and moral values and all other aspects of its way of life. Our organized and gradual effort which shall culminate in the realization of that society is the process of Islamization.[2]

—Jaafar Sheikh Idris

"Islamisation" has its own logic. It appropriates more and more space and leaves no room for societies to grow organically and in synch with the rest of the world. Secular culture is a victim and women bear the brunt of this.[3]

—Jugnu Mohsin

Islam wishes to do away with all states and governments anywhere which are opposed to the ideology and programme of Islam… Islam requires the earth – not just a portion, but the entire planet.[4]

—Sayyid Abul A'la Mawdudi

…the Kuffar [unbelievers, non-Muslims] are not allowed to establish a ruling system on earth because the earth belongs to Allah and only his righteous slaves are allowed to inherit it.[5]

—Muhammad Qasim

Men never do evil so completely and cheerfully as when they do it from religious conviction.[6]

—Blaise Pascal

CONTENTS

A Note on the Spelling of Arabic Words

Arabic words are spelled in a variety of ways when transliterated into languages that use other scripts. This book mostly uses the shortest and simplest English spellings. For example, the Arabic word for "Islamic mission" is written in this book as *dawa*. It is exactly the same word that other authors writing in English may spell as *dawah* or *da'wa* or *da'wah* or *daawa* or *daawah*. The Arabic term stayed the same when it moved into Turkish, but in Urdu it has become *dawat* and in the Malaysian language *dakwah*.

This rule also applies to names of people, places and organisations. For example, Mecca is spelled by some authors as Makka or other variations.

A Note on Quranic References

Quranic references are given as the *sura* (chapter) number followed by the number of the verse within the sura. All are from A. Yusuf Ali's *The Holy Qur'an: Text, Translation and Commentary* (Leicester: The Islamic Foundation, 1975) unless otherwise stated. Verse numbers may vary slightly between different translations of the Quran, so if using another version it may be necessary to search in the verses just before or just after the number given here to find the verse cited.

FOREWORD

The meeting of Islam and modern liberal societies is perhaps the most important story of our time. Yet despite eruptions of political and media interest in the matter (when someone is beheaded, or bombs detonated in some Western capital) there appears to be little or no will or desire to find out what is happening or why. Despite growing public concern, the posture of Western governments and much of the media remains an adamant refusal to connect the dots and a misguided, if understandable, desire simply to wish for the best.

Thirteen years ago, it might have been possible to excuse a widespread ignorance about the issues under discussion in this book. If the President of the United States, or Prime Minister of Great Britain, had been asked in the aftermath of 9/11 whether they could explain any principles of sharia law, Islamic banking or apostasy laws in Islam we might have forgiven their floundering. But all these years later, such an ignorance of basic Islamic doctrines and essential Islamic history is unforgivable. It is possible of course that our political leaders do now understand these issues. But if they do then it is curious that they continue to act as though they do not, giving in time and again to the most abrasive forms of Islam, conceding these to be the centre-ground and thus accomplishing the significant double-disaster of appeasing the radicals within Islam and cutting the legs from under any progressives.

Patrick Sookhdeo's work – and this new work in particular – stands as a powerful warning and corrective to these trends of wilful blindness. It explains why people act as they act, what propels them and what they are hoping to achieve. He performs this task not as a polemicist or politician, but as a historian, a scholar and somebody deeply committed to explaining the truth.

Anybody who seeks to learn about Islam and in particular about its inter-actions with other faiths and cultures has one author they must turn to first: Patrick Sookhdeo. It is not often that one can say this about a book, but the more people who read this book the safer in the long-term our societies will be.

Douglas Murray
July 2014

Douglas Murray is an award-winning journalist and author, associate member of the Henry Jackson Society think-tank and associate editor of *The Spectator* magazine.

PREFACE

Islam is a missionary religion. Its followers are required to try to teach their beliefs to others, in order to convince them and persuade them to convert. In this respect, Islam resembles another world religion, Christianity, and also a number of groups that have grown out of those two religions, such as the Ahmadiyyas, Jehovah's Witnesses and Mormons.

Such freedom of expression is a basic human right, as is the freedom to change one's religion. These freedoms are set out in Articles 19 and 18 respectively of the Universal Declaration of Human Rights, adopted by the General Assembly of the United Nations in 1948.

Article 18.

Everyone has the right to freedom of thought, conscience and religion; this right includes freedom to change his religion or belief, and freedom, either alone or in community with others and in public or private, to manifest his religion or belief in teaching, practice, worship and observance.

Article 19.

Everyone has the right to freedom of opinion and expression; this right includes freedom to hold opinions without interference and to seek, receive and impart information and ideas through any media and regardless of frontiers.

All missionaries should be free to proclaim their message, and all their hearers should be free to accept or reject that message. Probably the best way to ensure a level playing field for missionary activity is by means of a common secular space in which followers of all religions and none can co-exist and propagate their respective beliefs by peaceful and lawful means.

Sadly, missionaries of all religious traditions have not always limited their methods to prayer, preaching and persuasion, but have sometimes used completely unacceptable methods, including force. Such abuses must be condemned, but they do not alter the fact that all human beings have the right to share their beliefs with others and to follow the religion of their choice.

The first three centuries of Christianity saw the faith spread rapidly in a hostile environment without the use of sword, political power or any other kind of coercion, but simply by the proclamation of the message. This expansion happened despite the fact that the Christians faced innumerable sufferings and persecutions. It is a sad reflection on Christianity that this state of affairs did not continue.

In the post-Constantine era, when Christianity had gained political power, it used this power – and the sword too – to further its mission. Indeed, in various times and places, Christian mission became associated with some of the worst human rights abuses ever recorded. These included the conquest, forcible conversion and massacre of Saxons by the Frankish king Charlemagne in the 8th century, the expulsion and execution of Jews and Muslims by the Spanish Inquisition from the 15th to the 17th centuries, and the harsh persecution of the indigenous peoples of Goa and Sri Lanka by the Portuguese in the 16th century and after.

The principle of *cuius regio eius religio* (whose realm, his religion) did great damage to the cause of religious liberty. This principle was enshrined in the Peace of Augsburg (1555), which brought an end to armed conflict between Catholics and Lutherans in the Holy Roman Empire. It allowed each ruler to make the religion of his people either Catholic or Lutheran (other forms of Protestantism were not permitted). Although individuals who could not subscribe to the prince's religion were allowed to leave his territory with their families and goods, this principle effectively thus tied Christian practice to state power.

In more recent times, particularly during the Western colonial period, some Christian missions and missionaries were closely allied to the expansionist policy of their respective countries of origin. After the end of colonialism, certain American missions and missionaries in the latter half of the 20th century continued to view their work as including the spread of democracy. Even today, some missions and missionaries still link the Christian faith with Western political power.

However, there have always been notable exceptions to this attitude. Even when it was prevailing strongly, there emerged individuals and organisations in recent centuries who saw Christianity and Christian mission as based more on New Testament principles and on the example of the first three Christian centuries as well as the mission of Jesus himself, who rejected the sword and earthly, temporal powers. For such individuals and organisations, Christian mission was devoid of political and economic domination. Many such found themselves caught in a head-on conflict with their own governments. Such missions and movements have always existed throughout Christian history and have played no small part in a counter-movement opposing church and state power. Islam, on the other hand, has from its inception embraced the sword. Many Muslims were proud of the fact that Muhammad was a military general. The early Muslim call (*dawa*) issued by Muhammad carried with it an implicit threat.

In contrasting Christian mission with Islamic mission, it is important to see what were the pattern, model and aim of each religion and its founder. In this way we can avoid the trap of contrasting the best practice of one with the worst practice of the other. We should consider what is authentic in each religion. Yes, there have been innumerable times when Islam has sought to propagate its message through trade and preaching and through the quality of the Muslims' lives, and some Muslims and Muslim organisations still do so today. In this it is not dissimilar to early Christian mission. But the question remains: is this normative in Islam?

This book is an attempt to address the issue of Islamic mission. It is about how Islam uses its social calling to bring about transformation. It is therefore an exploration into political Islam and the way in which it has impacted the world, from the beginning of Islam but particularly in the modern era.

Patrick Sookhdeo
May 2014

— 1 —

INTRODUCTION

We are living in a time of rapid Islamic growth. This undeniable fact is true in two senses. Firstly, the number of Muslim people is increasing, partly due to a high birth rate and partly because non-Muslims are converting to Islam. (Relatively few Muslims choose to leave Islam, for reasons that we shall see later.) Secondly, Islamic principles are impacting and influencing societies across the globe, both Muslim-majority societies with a historic Muslim cultural heritage and non-Muslim-majority societies with Judeo-Christian, Hindu or other heritages.

Islamic sources, theology and history teach that all Muslims must engage in Islamic outreach or mission, known as *dawa* (literally "call" or "invitation"). In *dawa*, non-Muslims are called or invited to accept Islam as the true and final religion. Conversion takes place when a non-Muslim recites the Islamic creed (*shahada*): "There is no god but Allah and Muhammad is the messenger of Allah." Muslims call this "reversion" rather than "conversion", because they believe that every human being was a Muslim at birth, after which some went astray and followed other religions.

In this missionary aim, Islam resembles other missionary religions and sects. But there are two very important differences between, say, Christian mission and Islamic mission. The first is that most Christians are happy to see mission as a two-way process, with each faith having the freedom to propagate its message and try to convince others. Muslims, however, see *dawa* as a one-way street; only Islam has the right to propagate itself. They reject all Christian mission endeavours and seek to suppress them and smear them as aggressive, deceitful and evil.

The other key difference is that *dawa* is more than just the call to an individual to accept Islam. It also includes "the commanding of good and forbidding of wrong", both in Islamic societies and in non-Muslim-majority contexts. This means that the aims of *dawa* include establishing an Islamic state under sharia for Muslims and dominating non-Muslim nations so as to bring them under command of "the good", which is Islam.[7] The aim is to convert whole societies and their structures and create Islamic states or at least enclaves ruled by Islam. These will serve as models to show non-Muslims the power and benefits of Islam, as well as serving as bases from which to work for further expansion. After the non-Muslim-majority states have been converted to Islam, they will be integrated into the global *umma* (all Muslims worldwide). As Khurram Murad, a British Islamic scholar, explained:

> …there is the goal of bringing the same West to Islam, which would necessary mean that it would become part of the Muslim Ummah.[8]

Muhammad Abduh (1849-1905), who is regarded as the most prominent Muslim reformer of the 19th century,[9] held that the first duty of the Islamic *umma* is the mission to call all other nations to the good, which is Islam.[10] Indeed, according his disciple Rashid Rida (1865-1935), who interpreted Abduh's teachings, "the umma … is created for the da'wa in non-Muslim free countries".[11] The second duty, according to Abduh and Rida, is that of calling all Muslims themselves to obey God's law afresh and apply it to their specific context.[12]

This teaching highlights the fact that *dawa* is not just aimed externally at non-Muslims so as to enlarge the *umma* and widen Islam's religious and political dominion. Rather, there is also an internal *dawa* that targets Muslims to teach them the basics of Islam and strengthen their commitment to it.

The Arabic word *dawa* appears in the Quran and is understood by Muslims as a divine command. Islamic teaching about *dawa* is based on these Quranic passages and also on references in Islam's second most important written source, the *hadith*, and on the example of Muhammad and of early Islamic history. The Quran and *hadith* show that *dawa* was a main activity of Muhammad; this fact is very significant because of the Islamic doctrine that

Muslims should model their behaviour on Muhammad's example. Teaching on *dawa* was developed by Quranic commentary (*tafsir*), sharia and Islamic theology. Although not traditionally listed amongst the "pillars" of Islam (its five compulsory duties), many Muslim scholars stress that all Muslims must engage in *dawa*. *Dawa* is not just the duty of individual Muslims, but also the duty of Muslim states, which are responsible for converting non-Islamic states to Islam, following Muhammad's model.

> Dawa literally means "call" and in Islamic terminology "an invitation to Islam", and it is the *raison d'etre* of the existence of the Muslim ummah... It would not be incorrect to say that Islam means dawa – for dawa is essentially the fulfilment of Islam.[13]

CONVERSION, ISLAMISATION AND JIHAD

In recent decades, Islamists have re-discovered the Islamic principle of *dawa*. Islamic mission agencies are energetically engaging in an effort to convert individuals to Islam using literature, TV and every kind of media and method. Islamists are also driving a major project to Islamise society and culture, including converting institutions and state structures to conform them to sharia. Through well-funded, imaginative, bold and long-term strategies, they are already seeing much success. These strategies have been discussed openly by Muslims in many of their publications over the last few decades. Now, however, these Muslim writings, at least those in English, are becoming very hard to get hold of. They are disappearing from libraries and from the internet. The book of resolutions and recommendations[14] from the key Muslim World League conference in Mecca in 1975, for example, seems to be available to non-Muslims now only as one copy in the library of a small and obscure American college.

Some Islamists are willing to engage in violent jihad to facilitate or speed up their *dawa* work, whether it be converting individuals or Islamising society. The ultimate aim of jihad is to impose Allah's rule worldwide, and the practice can be supported theologically by certain interpretations of the Islamic sources. Violent jihad is by its nature very obvious and easy to spot. The majority of non-Muslims, whether ordinary citizens or senior government officials, are concerned only about violent jihadi activity; they do not recognise the non-violent conversion and Islamisation activities that permeate their societies. This lack of understanding and failure to recognise the substance and scope of the challenge, let alone the Islamic doctrines and strategies behind it, is not a matter of chance. In fact, disinformation and deception (*taqiyya*) are considered legitimate strategies in the Islamic cause, according to sharia and according also to the model of Islamic sacred history.

There is a sense in which violent Islam should be somewhat less of a worry to those in Muslim-minority contexts than more subtle conversion and Islamisation activities, just because it is impossible not to notice. The more discreet tactics that form part of the overall Islamist endeavour to establish Islamic rule in every level of government and society throughout the world might be considered a greater cause for concern. Daniel Pipes, for one, a noted academic and commentator on Islam and the Middle East, argues that non-violent methods are more effective than violence and therefore that "non-violent Islamists pose a greater threat than the violent ones".[15]

Whether the visible or the invisible is the more dangerous, there is no doubt that the three overlapping spheres of activity of contemporary Islamism – conversion, Islamisation and jihad – pose an urgent challenge. The advance of Islam within a society is very difficult to reverse by peaceful means. Islamists may utilise democratic methods to gain political power and then ban elections as un-Islamic. They may use freedom of speech to promote their viewpoint and then, having gained political power, pass laws to prohibit any criticism of what they are doing. Laws based on a common secular space, laws that enable religions to co-exist and be propagated freely by their respective missionaries, would not exist in an Islamised society. Sharia's rules, compiled in the Middle Ages and unchanged since the 10th century, would not provide a level playing field and would not try to. Although derived from a religion, Islamism bears many of the hallmarks of a totalitarian ideology that drastically re-shapes society and then puts a complete stop on any further change.

Of course, only a small percentage of Muslims are involved in the process described above. Like the majority of ordinary people in the world, most Muslims do not desire conflict but simply want to live out their lives in tranquillity. There are also Muslims who are liberal, progressive or secularist. Some interpret their scriptures spiritually, symbolically or eschatologically, rather than as a literal call to conquer non-Muslims and even to use physical warfare.

However, the combined weight of Islamic theology and history, the Islamic resurgence since the 1970s, and the oil money that helped Islamism to become increasingly dominant, mean that in the early 21st century it is the aggressive, literalist voices that have become the loudest in most Muslim-majority societies and states, while more tolerant views are supressed and marginalised, and these voices are having an increasingly powerful influence in Muslim-minority contexts too. A wise and timely response is needed.

HARMONY AND HOPE

The aim of this book is to raise awareness of the Islamist strategy and tactics. It is not to create fear or enmity. Not only is it important to remember the difference between active Islamists and moderate Muslims, but also we must acknowledge that Islamists are motivated by a sincere desire to obey what they believe Allah's commands to be. So great is their commitment that many are willing to sacrifice their own lives in his service. And we must recognise the difference between Islamists as our fellow human beings and the beliefs or ideology that they follow.

How then should we respond? The Christians of Sabah, Malaysia, have seen their percentage of the population greatly reduced in the space of a generation, through a multi-faceted campaign of conversion and Islamisation. In January 2014, as they protested against a clever trick that had led 64 illiterate Sabahan Christians to become Muslims without even realising it, Perpaduan Anak Negeri (an organisation representing Christians in Sabah), stated:

> Rest assured we do not see Muslims, and those who become Muslims by choice, as our enemies. We have always embraced them as our brothers and sisters. In Sabah, we are one big family with Christians and Muslims living in peace and harmony side by side even within the same family. But we want to make it very plain that for the past 50 years we have been in Malaysia,* we have been facing threats from extreme political Islam to systematically eradicate our cultural heritage as Christians...[16]

These words can be expanded from one organisation in one state of one nation and applied across the world. They can be a pattern for all who are

---

* When Malaysia became independent in 1957 it consisted of a number of states in a federation. All those in what is now called West Malaysia (the peninsula) were predominantly Muslim and Malay. In 1963, two very different states which comprise East Malaysia (on the island of Borneo) joined the Malaysian federation. The people of these two states, Sabah and Sarawak, were from a non-Malay ethnic group and a large number of them were Christians.

facing the challenge of *dawa*. While putting down a clear marker as to what they will not accept – that is, the destruction of their Christian heritage by political Islam – at the same time these Christians affirm their desire to live in peace and harmony with Muslims who are willing to live in peace and harmony with them. This is not the peace of Islamism, which says that peace cannot come until the whole world is subjugated to Islamic rule with all its injustices. This is the peace of equality, mutual respect and freedom: "peace and harmony", as the Sabahans said.

The Christians of Sabah have also shown that it is possible to live in peace and harmony with Muslims. Their experience can give hope to us all. A similar peace and harmony between Christians and Muslims existed in Indonesia for many generations, where Christians were the minority. Other examples can be found by scanning history and geography. Writing this book would be a pointless exercise if readers were simply to be plunged into despair at a seemingly unstoppable process of global Islamisation. It is not unstoppable. Events in Egypt and Tunisia between 2011 and 2013 showed that Islamisation can be halted and reversed. Sabah and other places show that a stable state of harmonious co-existence can be maintained. There is indeed hope, both for non-Muslims and for moderate Muslims who reject Islamism and its political goals. But urgent action is needed.

— 2 —

THE HISTORY OF *DAWA*

DAWA IN THE QURAN

The term *dawa*, in the sense of a call or an invitation to Islam, is used more than a dozen times in the Quran. The following two verses command the preaching aspect of *dawa*; they tell Muslims that they must invite non-Muslims to Islam.

> Invite [all] to the way of thy Lord with wisdom and beautiful preaching; and argue with them in ways that are best and most gracious: for thy Lord knoweth best who have strayed from His Path and who receive guidance. (Q 16:125)

> Say thou: "This my way: I do invite unto God, - on evidence clear as the seeing with one's eyes, - I and whoever follows me. Glory to God! and never will I join gods with God!" (Q 12:108)

The next verse shows that witnessing for Islam is the primary reason why the original *umma* was created.

> Thus have We made of you an *Ummat* justly balanced, that ye might be witnesses over the nations, and the Apostle a witness over your-selves; (Q 2:143)

A key Quranic verse shows that the scope of *dawa* includes not only to preach but also to establish the rule of Islam and its law, sharia, thus changing the whole of a society:

> Let there arise out of you a band of people inviting to all that is good, enjoining what is right, and forbidding what is wrong; they are the ones to attain felicity. (Q 3:104)

This verse relates to the Islamic principle of *al-amr bi'l m'aruf wa'l nahy 'an al-munkar* (commanding right and forbidding wrong). According to Quranic commentators, "the right" in this verse means Islam.[17] So this verse describes the religious duty of the *umma*, to call all humans to live according to sharia. This can be done, according to Islamic scholars, either in a gentle way by preaching or by force.[18]

DAWA IN THE HADITH

We have already noted how important the example of Muhammad is to Muslims. Muslim scholars in the past put together collections of traditions recording what Muhammad said and did, or as it is usually called in Islam, his *sunna* (way of life). The traditions, called *hadith*, were handed down verbally for generations, each with its own list of the people who had passed the story on from one to another. Eventually they were written down. The *hadith* are often easier to understand than the Quran and they have played a very important part in establishing the rules of how Muslims should live, based on the pattern of Muhammad's actions. But Muslim scholars consider that some *hadith* are more reliable and authentic than others.

The call to conversion is supported by a *hadith* reporting that Muhammad sent one of his followers to Yemen with the instructions to invite its people to Islam:

> Narrated by Ibn Abbas: The Prophet sent Muadh to Yemen and said, "Invite the people to testify that none has the right to be worshipped but Allah and I am Allah's Apostle, and if they obey you to do so, then teach them that Allah has enjoined on them five prayers in every day and night (in twenty-four hours), and if they obey you to do so, then teach them that Allah has made it obligatory for them to pay the Zakat from their property and it is to be taken from the wealthy

among them and given to the poor." (Sahih Al-Bukhari, Vol. 2, Book 23, No 478)

The *hadith* also record that he sent letters to the neighbouring heads of state inviting them to embrace Islam.

The Prophet of Allah (peace be upon him) wrote to Chosroes (King of Persia), Caesar (Emperor of Rome), Negus (King of Abyssinia) and every (other) despot inviting them to Allah, the Exalted. (Sahih Muslim Book 19, No. 4382; also Sahih Al-Bukhari Vol. 1, Book 1, No. 6)

Other *hadiths* speak of the reward to be given to a Muslim who is used by Allah to convert non-Muslims to Islam.

Abu Huraira reported Allah's Messenger (may peace be upon him) as saying: He who called (people) to righteousness, there would be reward (assured) for him like the rewards of those who adhered to it, without their rewards being diminished in any respect (Sahih Muslim, Book 34, no. 6470)

If Allah gives guidance to somebody through you, it is better for you than possessing red camels. (Sahih Al Bukhari, Vol. 4, no. 253)

DAWA UNDER MUHAMMAD

Muhammad saw Islam as the true religion and mission of all earlier prophets. He believed that their call had been limited to their own people but that his was universal. His mission as the final prophet was to repeat to the whole world this call and invitation (*dawa*) to Allah's true religion of Islam. As we have seen, Muhammad wrote to various non-Muslim rulers inviting them to convert. The Byzantine Emperor Heraclius and the Persian Sassanid Emperor Chosroes were said to have refused[19] his invitation, which, from a Muslim point of view, explains why Muslim forces invaded their lands after Muhammad's death.*

When Muhammad began his rule over the first Islamic state, Medina, new converts to Islam were incorporated into the Islamic *umma*. Those who

---

* Ethiopians were treated as a special case because of their king's kind reception of the Muslims who sought refuge with him.

refused to convert were treated in different ways according to their religion. Jews and Christians who submitted to Islamic rule but did not convert to Islam were treated as conquered peoples (*dhimmis*) and allowed to follow their own religions, but under strict and humiliating conditions. Pagans, however, were fought and killed, their wives and children enslaved, and their property taken by the Muslims.[20]

DAWA IN EARLY ISLAMIC HISTORY

The *rashidun* caliphs (the next four Muslim rulers of the Muslim community after Muhammad) followed Muhammad's example and teaching. The Islamic state would issue a call (*dawa*) to its non-Muslim enemies to submit to Islam, either by converting to Islam or (if they were of an eligible religion) by accepting humiliating *dhimmi* status. If they refused both options, war (jihad) was waged against them. Successful jihad then created the conditions in which conversion to Islam could easily take place, supported by newly created, Islamic state institutions and unopposed by enemy forces. This practice was continued under the Umayyad caliphate (661-750) and the Abbasid caliphate (750-1258).

When the Muslims began to divide and splinter into different groups, the concept of *dawa* was also applied to the propaganda of any one of the various Islamic movements, each of which claimed that its version of Islam should be dominant within the *umma*. The Abbasid *dawa* ensured widespread support for the Abbas family in its plan to supplant the Umayyad dynasty in the 8th century and set up the Abbasid caliphate. The Isma'ili *dawa* was crucial in setting up the Fatimid Empire (909-1171) and became institutionalised as the official state *dawa*, with branches all over the Muslim world and beyond. These two models were extremely efficient and successful propaganda machines for advancing their respective causes; today they serve as models for modern Muslim *dawa* organisations.

DAWA IN LATER CENTURIES

Following the great early conquests that had opened up huge areas to Islamic *dawa*, the dissemination of Islam was often carried forward by Muslim traders and Sufis (followers of mystical Islam).

In Central Asia, Sufis were influential in converting Turkic tribes to Islam. At the same time, the conversion of the Mongol conquerors to Islam in the Central Asian steppes (the Golden Horde) served as a catalyst for further conversions, as did the Ottoman conquests of Byzantium and the Balkans. Jihad and *dawa* thus continued hand in hand.

Islam was introduced into south-east Asia mainly by traders and Sufis who engaged in *dawa*. In contrast to other regions, where Muslim states were founded by the invading Muslim military elites, in south-east Asia existing dynasties converted to Islam, gradually converting the vast majority of the population to Islam.

There were two directions of Islamic expansion into sub-Saharan Africa: from North Africa south into the Sahel, and from the East African coastline (Kenya and Tanzania of today) westwards. Islam in sub-Saharan Africa was spread by several methods. In some cases it was by military conquest, for example, from Morocco to West Africa, from Egypt to Sudan, or from Oman to Zanzibar. It was also spread by traders coming from across the Sahara and the Indian Ocean. Berber conquerors and traders moved along the Sahara caravan routes (from Tripoli towards Fezzan in south-west Libya and from the Sous in southern Morocco). Muslim Arab traders and conquerors arrived by sea from southern Arabian regions such as Yemen, Oman and the Hadramaut. There was Muslim migration and settlement, especially in East Africa, as well as purposeful *dawa*, especially by Sufis. Furthermore there were periodic revival movements that included efforts to purify Islam from pagan elements, to establish Islamic states under sharia and expand them by jihad.

In India, successive waves of Muslim invasion and conquest opened the door for conversion of some of the Hindu population to Islam. Turco-Afghan-Mongol slave soldier groups displaced from Central Asia consolidated Muslim rule in North India in intermittent invasions over a long period. The first large-scale invasion was under the Arab Umayyads. The second occurred in the 11th century when Mahmud of Ghazni (997-1030) conducted 17 raids in northern India over the course of his 33-year reign.[21] The Ghaznavids captured Lahore in 1030 and plundered north India. The third invasion was by Muhammad Ghuri (died 1206), who led his first expedition (to Multan and Gujarat) in 1175. The Ghurids began a systematic conquest of India, taking Delhi where they founded the Delhi Sultanate (1206-1526).* The fourth wave of Islamic invasion was by the Turkic-Mongol ruler Timurlane (1336-1405) who crossed the Indus River in 1398 and marched toward

---

* In a symbolic gesture, Pakistan has named its latest ballistic missile, capable of delivering nuclear weapons, the *Ghuri* (or *Ghauri*), a not-so-subtle warning to India to remember the humiliating history of the Muslim invasions.

Delhi, ravaging the country as he went. His capture of towns and villages was usually accompanied by their destruction and the massacre of their inhabitants. The fifth wave of Islamic invasion was led by Babur, founder of the Mughal Empire, and continued under his successors. Some Hindus were forcibly converted to Islam following the main battles, while others gradually converted to Islam through the efforts of the mystical Sufi orders.

DAWA ACCORDING TO MODERN COMMENTATORS

Most modern Muslim commentators, especially those of Salafi, Muslim Brotherhood and related Islamist groups, put a strong emphasis on the political aspects of *dawa*. For them the most important goal of *dawa* is Islamic reform and revival, leading to the eventual establishment of an Islamic state. These commentators focus on Islam as a comprehensive ideological system, regulating not only the private sphere and the relations between a believer and God but also the public sphere and politics.[22]

The *dawa* concepts pioneered by Hasan al-Banna (1906-1949, founder of the Muslim Brotherhood) and by Sayyid Abul A'la Mawdudi (1903-1979, founder of the Jamaat-i-Islami in South Asia) aimed at integrating the religious and the political aspects of Islam into one ideological whole. Both al-Banna and Mawdudi emphasised the importance of reforming the character of Muslim communities so as to reverse the process of Islam's decline from its ancient glory and to prepare the way, by systematically spreading Islamist ideology to an ever-wider audience, for the ultimate establishment of an Islamic state. Several important Muslim organisations, especially Tablighi Jamaat, dedicate themselves solely to the goal of re-Islamising Muslims across the globe.

For some Islamists today, the first priority of *dawa* at present should be establishing Islamic states under sharia in Muslim-majority countries. So they focus their efforts on changing the regimes of most Muslim-majority nations, in order to turn them into Islamic states under sharia, which can then carry *dawa* to the non-Muslim-majority world.[23] Kalim Siddiqui, founder of the Muslim Parliament of Great Britain, explained this process:

> ...the first step in *da'wah* is to establish Islam as a working model of a civilization, of a system, and, therefore, we must use our stay in this country [the UK] not to convert the country to Islam, but to establish Islam in the house of Islam. And once it is established there, then you will be able to establish Islam anywhere. That is *da'wah*. So, if we

mobilize our resources in this country in order to support an Islamic movement overseas, ultimately that is part of *da'wah* in the non-Muslim world... But the message of Allah came as a method. The method was delivered through the Sunnah of the Prophet. The Sunnah of the Prophet was, and shall always be, to establish a working civilization of Islam which will then emerge from wherever it is established, pressing everything else into retreat. It is the base of Islam that we do not have at this moment. We have to build it and once we have built it then *da'wah* will follow as surely as day follows night.[24]

— 3 —

The Agents of *Dawa*

A Communal or Individual Duty?

Muslim scholars over the centuries have argued among themselves about whether *dawa* is a communal duty (*fard kifaya*) or a personal duty (*fard ayn*). Some traditional Quran expositors saw *dawa* as a communal obligation, which either the Islamic state or a selected group of scholarly Muslims undertook to do *dawa* on behalf of all Muslims.

According to Rashid Rida, the command to perform *dawa* implies also a command to establish a special association of Muslims chosen to be professional carriers of the mission. These must be individuals suitable for their calling, possessing special skills and knowledge including knowledge of the Quran and *sunna*, and the culture, history, geography and psychology of the non-Muslim world. In this way, he argued, the early Muslims conquered other nations by using their knowledge of the habits and territory of the non-Muslims. To be effective in *dawa*, Muslims must also know the languages of the people they aim at converting, their political and social affairs, their religion and their legal system.[25]

The late Sheikh Abdul Azeez ibn Abdullah ibn Baaz, former Grand Mufti of Saudi Arabia and head of the Council of Senior Scholars, argued that the obligation of *dawa* is both a collective duty of the Muslim community and a personal duty of each individual Muslim.[26]

Contemporary *dawa* activists generally stress that it is a personal duty incumbent on every Muslim. Mustafa Mashhour, a former leader of the Muslim Brotherhood, declared that:

> It is well known that Islamic Law has made it our responsibility to invite others to Allah, and to permit the good and forbid the wrong. Everyone of us will be questioned by Allah as to whether he actually did invite his family, neighbors, friends and acquaintances to Allah, to adopt the Book of Allah and the *Sunnah* of the Messenger of Allah... As for inviting people to Islam, a Muslim will be rewarded for it, and will be penalized for negligence in this respect.[27]

INSTITUTIONALISATION AND ADOPTION BY MUSLIM-MAJORITY STATES

In the early 1970s many conferences were held and many new organisations created to try to encourage *dawa*. Particularly significant was a conference held in Mecca in 1975 by the Rabitat al-Alam al-Islami, or in English the Muslim World League (MWL). At this conference the League proposed a total reorganisation of international *dawa* activities, with a much greater focus on the role of the mosque in *dawa*.[28]

As this decision was implemented, Islamic missionary efforts grew, and many more institutions and organisations specialising in *dawa* have since been founded. All over the world there is now an extensive network of *dawa* organisations drawn from all streams of Islam, which is seeking to win converts to Islam and change societies and states in the direction of becoming more Islamic. They are especially active in sub-Saharan Africa and the West.

These contemporary, Muslim activist organisations operate as something between a traditional Christian missionary society and a political party, effectively blending *dawa* with politics.[29] Funding generally comes from the oil-rich Arab world and is therefore plentiful. This has in turn resulted in a vigorous programme of founding and funding Islamic institutions and mosques in non-Muslim-majority contexts, with the ultimate goal to create Islamic states in every country of the world. Force and the threat of force are used by some groups.

All Islamist movements see themselves as committed to *dawa* and often set up subsidiaries specifically to promote *dawa*. The Muslim Brotherhood, the Jamaat-i-Islami and the Wahhabi, Salafi and Deobandi movements are all involved in *dawa* activities both in Muslim-majority states and in non-Muslim contexts. *Dawa* organisations join forces to create larger groupings and cooperative alliances, supported by various governments and intergovernmental Islamic bodies.

Especially influential among these Islamist organisations are Saudi-based and Saudi-funded international umbrella groups such the Muslim World League and the Organisation of Islamic Cooperation (OIC, formerly the Organisation of the Islamic Conference). Wahhabi influence is paramount, but the groups work in alliance with the Muslim Brotherhood and with similar groups in the Indian subcontinent.

Some of the Islamist organisations are for training and sending Muslim missionaries, disseminating Islamic literature and building mosques. They have studied the methods of Christian missionaries* and replicated all that seemed effective and productive. They have also added many other methods, as we shall see later in this book.

Other new organisations worked towards the re-shaping of societies across the world so that they would match more closely the wide-ranging requirements of sharia. Notable amongst these was the International Institute for Islamic Thought (IIIT), founded in Virginia by American Muslims in 1981.

The Organisation of Islamic Cooperation (OIC)

The OIC is a coalition of 57 member states, including not only all Muslim-majority states but also some states where Muslims are a minority. It sees itself as "the collective voice of the Muslim world".[30] In its various summit meetings, the OIC has emphasised the need to strengthen and systematise the work of *dawa* in the world. Amongst its recommendations have been the establishment of educational and cultural centres to propagate the Arabic language and Islamic culture, the use of all modern methods of

---

* For example, the Islamic Foundation, based in Leicester, UK, published a number of booklets in the late 1970s and early 1980s with titles including *Mission to Muslims in Germany: A Case Study of the 'Orientdienst' – the Major Mission Organization; Indonesia: How Muslims are made Christians; Christian Mission among Muslims in Bangladesh – A Survey; Christian Mission in Pakistan – A Survey; The Fulani Evangelisation Scheme in West Africa; Christianity and Mission in Mali; Christian Literature Crusade: Case Study of a Mission Organisation; A Select and Annotated Bibliography of Christian Literature for Muslims in Current Usage for Mission among Muslims.*

presenting Islam, appropriately contextualised for the various societies in which Muslims are present, and the creation of institutes to train *da'ees* (Islamic missionaries). A main function of the new educational and cultural centres was to be the propagation of Islam: *dawa*.[31]

At its third Islamic Summit at Mecca in 1981, the OIC pledged to provide the material needs for *dawa* activities:

> Believing in the need to propagate the principles of Islam ... in the world as a whole ... we are determined to cooperate to provide the human and material means to achieve these objectives.[32]

In its sixth Islamic Summit at Dakar, Senegal, in 1991 the OIC declared its intent to:

> Provide the Organization of the Islamic Conference with the required resources in order to support and coordinate Islamic Da'wa efforts and to improve educational curricula and training programmes as well as to disseminate the teachings of Islam throughout the world, within the framework of cooperation among States and in respect of their sovereignty; and also to instill the lofty Islamic values through the implementation of relevant programmes both in the educational institutions and through the media for the purpose of consolidating the moral stature of Muslim peoples and communities.[33]

Similar decisions have been repeated at almost every OIC conference. The 31st Islamic Conference of Foreign Ministers (ICFM) in 2004 approved the development of a joint Islamic *dawa* strategy within the OIC framework.[34]

Gradually over the years, structures have been set up to ensure coordination among the various Islamic institutions working in the field of Islamic *dawa*. These included the Committee for the Coordination of Joint Islamic Action, the Islamic Educational, Scientific and Cultural Organization (ISESCO) based in Rabat, and the International Islamic Council for Dawah and Relief based in Cairo (see Appendices 1, 2 and 3). The OIC has also established the Islamic States Broadcasting Organization (ISBO) with the goal of spreading *dawa* around the world.[35]

National Governments

In the West, Christian missionary efforts are operated only by churches and private voluntary organisations, with governments normally careful not to promote any specific religion. By contrast, the Islamic concept of non-separation between religion and state means that governments of Muslim-majority nations see *dawa* as part of their foreign policy and are willing to create and finance *dawa* organisations and institutions on a large scale, using their considerable resources and influence. These organise and supervise the work of *da'ees* around the world, in Muslim and non-Muslim contexts. *Dawa* is part of the way Muslim-majority states relate to non-Muslim-majority states in their efforts to Islamise the world.

Saudi Arabia has spent tens of billions of dollars on global *dawa*. Its activity is supervised by the powerful Ministry of Islamic Affairs, Endowments, Propagation and Guidance. This ministry oversees the Muslim World League, the International Islamic Relief Organisation (IIRO) and the World Assembly of Muslim Youth (WAMY). It funds Islamic outreach activities all over the world, including conferences and seminars. It has a vast publishing programme in many languages to propagate Islam, and many *da'ees* around the world. It operates the King Fahd Complex for Printing the Quran in Medina, which has printed and distributed millions of copies of the Quran around the world in Arabic and other languages. At a gathering of imams and *da'ees* in London held at the Saudi Embassy in April 2005, Ibrahim Towe, a Nigerian *da'ee*, praised the missionary role of the Saudi Ministry of Islamic Affairs and of the Saudi Embassy in the United Kingdom and Ireland, adding:

> We look at the Embassy as a very important connection. I think, Prince Turki is not only an Ambassador coming from Saudi Arabia, we look at him also as the Ambassador of Dawah.[36]

The ministry also controls some 50 domestic outreach offices in Saudi Arabia, known as Islamic Propagation Offices, Foreigners Guidance Offices, Dawa and Guidance Centres and Cooperative Offices for Call and Guidance; these offices work to convert non-Muslim residents in Saudi Arabia (mainly expatriate workers). They manage "Care Centres for New Muslims" and "Communities Sections", where lectures in various languages are offered. In 2005 these were employing around 500 Saudi staff and 40 Filipino converts to Islam.[37]

Qatar, now hosting the Muslim Brotherhood, has become another major player in promoting radical Islam worldwide.

Libya founded the World Islamic Call Society (WICS) in 1972 to further its version of Islam around the world.[38]

Dawa Education and Training

We have already seen that Muhammad Abduh and Rashid Rida taught that, in order to fulfil the command of *dawa* most efficiently, the Muslim community must study all branches of knowledge that can help it understand the non-Muslim nations, including their languages, psychology, history, geography and religions. The goal of such study is to devise better ways of persuading non-Muslims to convert to Islam.[39] The same goal lies behind the IIIT's careful study of Western thought, which forms a part of the contemporary drive to Islamise all branches of human knowledge (see pages 73-80). Interestingly, Yusuf Al-Qaradawi's mighty work on the way in which Muslims should fight a violent jihad contains a very similar instruction to learn everything about the enemy – their beliefs, likes, dislikes, strengths, weaknesses and vulnerabilities – with a view to creating fear and despair amongst them by psychological warfare.[40] At what might seem the opposite pole to violent jihad, namely interreligious dialogue, the same theme re-surfaces; according to Islamists, it is essential for Muslims engaging in dialogue with non-Muslims to be familiar not only with the Quran and Islamic doctrine but also "with the intellectual and spiritual background of Christianity".[41]

Today, *dawa* training has become very formalised. *Dawa* is now an academic subject, and many academic *dawa* institutions have been founded.[42] In addition to formal and institutional training, many self-help handbooks for the training of *da'ees* have been published. These usually stress the moral characteristics necessary for the missionary, and then provide instruction on the skills needed for reaching out to non-Muslims. One such manual, published in Malaysia in 2003, recommends a psychological approach. The "Islamic preacher" must understand the various types of people to whom he is reaching out. He should be flexible in modifying his approach to suit the level of the specific person he is dealing with so as to awaken that person's interest in Islam.[43] An eight-step approach is suggested:[44]

1. Court the individual by showing great concern for his welfare. Build up a friendly relationship without pushing Islam.

2. Awaken the individual from his apathy by drawing his attention to the wonders of God's creation and its purpose while sharing neutral activities such as conversations, outings and meals.
3. Start the process of indoctrination with Islamic doctrine and practice, providing books of guidance on Islamic faith and ritual and encouraging him to seek the company of Muslims and avoid sinful practices.
4. Move on to detailed instruction on Islamic worship and practice, emphasising that Islam demands that everything be done to gain God's pleasure.
5. Explain that Islam is more than a religion: it is a social and political system, a civilisation and a complete way of life. Explain that individual faith is not enough and that one must be part of an Islamic community obedient to the whole of Islamic law (sharia).
6. Convince the new convert of the necessity of establishing a "full fledged Islamic state" with the coercive power to enforce full compliance to Islamic law, following the example of Muhammad at Medina.
7. Move on from the Islamic state to the necessity of continual jihad to ensure the survival of Islam.
8. Mould the convert into a "walking Quran" who can witness to Islam in every place and situation.

— 4 —

DAWA THROUGH INDIVIDUAL CONVERSION

Muslim missionaries around the world are active in *dawa* amongst non-Muslims, seeking to gain individual converts. There is no necessity for the converts to be genuinely convinced of the truth of Islam; it is enough that they choose – for whatever reason – to repeat the Islamic creed and call themselves Muslims. Because of the Islamic apostasy law and its death sentence for those who leave Islam, conversion to Islam is effectively a one-way street. Those who become disillusioned rarely dare to re-convert away from Islam (except perhaps secretly in their hearts). Another advantage for Muslim mission is the Islamic teaching that all the children of a Muslim are automatically deemed to be Muslims too, so in a mixed marriage the non-Muslim parent should have no say in the religious upbringing of the children.

A vast *dawa* project of publications, translations and radio, TV and internet has been initiated. Other methods include lectures and study circles for those interested in Islam, and *dawa* stalls in universities and other venues. Intellectual persuasion is used with the assistance of well-produced material across the whole gamut of modern technology including a multitude of websites. Muslims are encouraged to give up their holidays in order to go on *dawa* missions and to use personal visitation and tourism to promote Islam.[45]

The United Kingdom Islamic Mission (UKIM) cautions *da'ees* to be mindful of the sensitivities of the people being addressed, have an understanding of their background, beliefs and ideas and employ the most appropriate and effective methods and channels of communication for the context in which they are working. It offers these principles:[46]

1. The Islamic message should be made relevant to the particular society in which one is working, just as it was made relevant by all the Prophets to their own people.
2. The Islamic message should be presented using a language and terminology that is understood by the people being addressed, in a logical, reasonable, convincing and friendly way.
3. The Islamic message should not be forced on people; rather a dialogue and social interaction at a deeper level should be established.

A wide variety of *dawa* methods is used not only by UKIM but by all engaged in *dawa*, varying according to context. In Africa, with its traditional pagan religions as a backdrop, where many Christians are very poor and have little understanding of their faith, material inducements can play an important part in persuading them to leave one monotheistic religion for another. On offer could be money, a car, a flat, or a job. Or it could be something much smaller. A church leader in a Muslim-majority area of Uganda reported the "buying of Christians especially the younger ones by giving them sweets, clothes, scholastic materials and many other basic needs with the aim of converting them in to Islam".[47]

In Cambodia, converts to Islam are reported[48] to be paid US$1,000 to convert, part of which is to enable them to buy a Quran and other items they need to follow their new religion. They are also paid a monthly sum of US$30 to $50 for some while after conversion.

In Sabah state, Malaysia, Christians are often given houses, monthly allowances and other privileges if they will become Muslims. According to the Perpaduan Anak Negeri organisation, a government-backed *dawa* movement is using "intimidation, threat, deception and inducements" to win Muslim converts in Sabah.[49] One incident that created an outcry occurred in a particularly poor district of Sabah, called Pitas, where there is no running water or electricity in most villages. A group of 64 illiterate Christians, including children, from three villages were tricked into converting to Islam. According to the villagers, they were told that the federal government was going to give them each 800 ringgits (£160, US$240), which they had to collect from Pitas district council office. When they arrived in Pitas on 1 January 2014, they were surprised to find that they were not taken to the town hall but to a nearby mosque. There each was given 100 ringgits (£20, US$30) and asked to put their thumb print on a document. Then they were told to stand in a line and recite some "foreign words". They did not realise they had been converted to Islam until they got back to their villages and showed the document to their church leaders.[50]

The offer of education in an Islamic school is a great draw for families too poor to afford any other kind of education for their children and is much used in Africa. Sometimes the family must attend the mosque, or at least attend prayers at the mosque, before their child is eligible to attend the school. But in other cases, the education is offered without strings attached. In East Malaysia, many free Islamic schools are being set up to serve the Christians living in long-houses in the jungle; it is reported that some actually pay the children "pocket money" to attend. Fee-paying Christian schools cannot compete. Not surprisingly many youngsters attending Islamic schools are influenced by what their Muslim teachers say. In East Malaysia, little girls from Christian families have gone home after school and asked their mothers to buy them Islamic headscarves and rebuked their parents for praying the wrong way.

Another method is to arrange for the student simply to live amongst Muslims. Africa has many orphans, and some of them are given free places at Islamic boarding schools. Top students may be given scholarships to attend universities in countries such as Pakistan or Saudi Arabia; many have become radical Muslims by the time they complete their degrees.

Free health care is another way in which converts to Islam are won in Africa, where HIV/AIDS, tuberculosis, malaria and a host of other diseases are common, and infant mortality is high. In many parts of the continent, health care is expensive or poor quality, but Islamic clinics offering excellent care are being set up, especially in non-Muslim rural areas, sometimes with mosques attached to them. However, often the patient will not be treated unless he or she converts to Islam. In Burundi, Muslim clinics offer free maternity care if the mother promises to bring up her baby as a Muslim. The newborns are often registered with Islamic names by the hospital.

In cases of natural or human disaster, when people have lost everything or have been displaced, Islamic charities and humanitarian organisations often favour Muslims when distributing aid. After the 2004 Indian Ocean tsunami, Indonesian Christians in the strongly Islamic province of Aceh were refused aid unless they converted to Islam. In the African Great Lakes region of Rwanda, Burundi and the Democratic Republic of the Congo, refugees returning home who have lost everything through war or famine are often given houses, land and businesses by Muslim groups if they convert to Islam. Even when there is not an outright disaster, some parts of Africa are more or less permanently in a situation of food insecurity, giving scope for the continued use of such methods In Malawi, some people have had to receive and put on Islamic clothes before they are allowed food aid.

An effective argument that gains many converts in Africa is the claim that Christianity is the "white man's religion", whereas Islam is the proper religion for black people. The same argument is used in the Caribbean, amongst African Americans, and even amongst the Aboriginal people of Australia.

Marriage is used in a variety of ways to gain converts to Islam. It is assumed in Islam that the religion of a couple will be decided by the husband. Muslim men, who can have up to four wives simultaneously, are therefore able to make converts by the simple and attractive method of marrying non-Muslim women. In many places, it seems that Christian young women will quite readily marry a Muslim man who charms and woos them. Churches in Sabah, East Malaysia, estimate that around 15-20% of their young people marry Muslims. Not only the Christian girls but even some of the Christian boys are marrying Muslims and converting to Islam. The churches also believe there is a deliberate strategy by the Malaysian government to post newly qualified teachers, one Muslim man and one Christian woman, to serve together in remote and isolated schools in jungle areas, in the hope that they will fall in love and marry. In south India, young Muslim men are reported to be deliberately luring women from other religions into marriage and forcing them to convert to Islam.[51]

It is reported from many African countries that Muslims are paid a sum of money for each Christian woman they marry or at least impregnate; if they manage to marry a pastor's daughter, their financial reward can be greater. In one three-month period at Iganga High School in Uganda, twelve Christian girls, three of them the daughters of pastors, were made pregnant by Muslim boys; the boys were reported to have been paid £30 ($50) for each Christian girl they impregnated.[52] The customary bride price required from husbands-to-be in many parts of Africa, often cripplingly high, can greatly delay or even prevent marriages amongst Christians, so this must make it easier for well-financed Muslim men to marry Christians.

Pakistan and Egypt both have large minorities of very poor Christians and a culture in which it is extremely shameful for a girl not to marry young. But if the impoverished Christian families cannot afford the small sum needed for a simple wedding celebration and a few items to set up home together, the girls remain single. When a wealthier Muslim family then offers their son in marriage, some Christian families see this as the way to save their daughter from the dishonour of staying unmarried.

There are also many appalling cases, in both Pakistan and Egypt, of Christian and other non-Muslim girls being raped, kidnapped, and forcibly married to Muslim men; often they are tricked or forced to convert to Islam. Although these practices are illegal both in sharia and in the national laws of the two countries, the authorities generally turn a blind eye to them and do little or nothing to intervene. A report by the Asian Human Rights Commission in 2012 estimated 1,000 such cases a year in Pakistan, involving 700 Christian and 300 Hindu girls.[53] The number of cases in Egypt increased following the 2011 "Arab Spring", and it was reported that over 500 Christian girls had been abducted in little more than two years since January 2011.[54] The attacks are often carefully planned and may involve drugging the girl or arranging to have a third person get to know and befriend her before the attack. A 2011 report from Egypt reveals an organised operation based at a mosque in Alexandria to compromise young Coptic girls who then flee their homes and convert to Islam to escape their shame. This is described as a systematic "religious call" plan, i.e. *dawa*.

> The investigation by Egypt4Christ, carried out under secrecy, exposed a highly organized Muslim ring centered in the Fatah Mosque in Alexandria. The investigation also uncovered a systematic "religious call" plan, where young Muslim males in high school and university are urged to approach Coptic girls in the 9-15 age group and manipulate them through sexual exploitation and blackmail. The plan, called "operation soaking lupin beans" (small dried beans, soaked until they grow in size and are then eaten raw), aims at sexually compromising Christian girls, defiling them and humiliating them in front of their parents, thereby forcing them to flee their homes, and use conversion to Islam as a "solution" for their problems.[55]

Willing marriage is one of the most successful ways in which white Western women (both young and old) are converted to Islam, typically having been courted by a handsome young Arab or African. The wife and children are considered Muslims for ever.[56]

Many people also convert to Islam because they are attracted by its teachings and traditions. These can be presented in one-to-one discussions, public debates and literature and on the internet. Islam can be seen as easier to follow than its usual rival, Christianity, in that there is more emphasis on external rules and less on the challenging question of what is going on in the believer's heart. It does not have hard-to-imagine doctrines such as the Trinity or the incarnation. Many Westerners are drawn to the mystical Islam known as Sufism.

Islam can be appealing to men because of Islamic gender roles, particularly to some African American men who have lived in a culture of matriarchal dominance and are wrestling with pain, rage and the desire to rediscover and reclaim the lost essence of manhood. For such individuals, Islam offers dignity, identity, significance and the renewal of masculine identity.[57] It can be particularly appealing to angry and frustrated young men, especially those in prison in Western countries, who gladly embrace a religion that gives them permission to be violent and to seek to destroy the hated authorities who took away their liberty. In Africa, where traditional pagan religions allow polygamy, the sharia rule that permits a man to have four wives can be an important factor in converting men to Islam. In the country of Georgia, a predominantly Orthodox Christian nation, Muslim missionaries are winning converts, who are mainly men, with the message that Islam is the religion for strong people and Christianity the religion for weak people.[58]

Islam can be appealing to women if they are told only how important the family is in Muslim culture and not how vulnerable they would be under sharia law. African American women in particular are often attracted to Islam by the image of the Muslim man as protector and provider, keeping the women and children safe from violence and poverty.[59]

— 5 —

DAWA THROUGH ISLAMISATION

One aspect of Islam that makes it different from any other religion is the way in which it seeks to address the structures and institutions of society through political power. This goal is derived from two important doctrines of Islam: the one-ness of Allah (*tawhid*) and the sovereignty of Allah (*hakimiyya*). Therefore, say Islamic scholars, there can be only one law for the world, which is Islamic law, sharia, and Muslims must impose it, by force if necessary. This has been an essential part of Islam since its origins in 7th century Arabia, when Muhammad was the law-giver and judge of the first Islamic state, in Medina. Islam's ability to put into practice this part of its doctrine has varied over the centuries in different times and places, but the basic principle has never been removed from Islamic teaching.

Nowadays Muslims who place a major emphasis on the political aspects of Islam are often referred to as Islamists and their ideology as Islamism. Other Muslims (traditional Muslims and liberal Muslims) are largely content to keep their religion, Islam, in the private sphere, like the adherents of other religions. This latter type of Islam, whose followers focus on personal morality and devotion, was its familiar face two generations ago, whether in Muslim-majority countries or amongst Muslim immigrants who had settled in the West.

But since then, there has been a great revival and resurgence of Islam. Seeds of Islamism, which had been putting down inconspicuous roots since they were planted in the 1920s, 1930s and 1940s, burst at last into luxuriant growth. Islam became again a major player on the world stage, including the world political stage, with a power and prestige it had not enjoyed for many centuries.

What triggered this dramatic change in Islam's profile? One of its most prominent scholars, Dr Mona Abul-Fadl (1945-2008), wrote that the IIIT, "as one of the many robust young institutions which the first decade of the fifteenth century *hijrī** has spawned, has consecrated itself to the cultural imperative".[60] The IIIT's website describes its desired impact not in terms of culture but in terms of civilisation, saying that the organisation is

> dedicated to the revival and reform of Islamic thought and its methodology in order to enable the Ummah to deal effectively with present challenges, and contribute to the progress of human civilization in ways that will give it a meaning and a direction derived from divine guidance. The realization of such a position will help the Ummah regain its intellectual and cultural identity and re-affirm its presence as a dynamic civilization.[61]

In order to understand the significance of this public statement, it is important to realise that most Muslims would consider that "the present challenges" to their worldwide community or nation, the *umma*, include everything that hinders the advance of Islam towards its rightful, Allah-ordained position in control of every human institution in the world. Near the top of a list of such hindrances would be Western cultural and political dominance. These are what the IIIT seeks to "deal effectively with". The idea of giving human civilisation "a meaning and a direction derived from divine guidance" can be seen as referring to Allah's guidance and is therefore a coded way of describing the Islamisation of all civilisation. Enabling the *umma* to "regain its intellectual and cultural identity and re-affirm its presence as a dynamic civilisation" would mean restoring Islam to the glory of its Golden Age. This Golden Age is generally considered by Muslims to run from the 7th to the 13th centuries, a period beginning with the founding of Islam by

---

* i.e. the fifteenth Islamic century, dated from the *hijra* or flight of Muhammad from Mecca to Medina in AD 622. Islamic years are lunar and only 356 days long, so the fifteenth Islamic century began on 21 November 1979. Islamists saw great significance in the dawning of the new Islamic century.

Muhammad and ending with the period of Abbasid rule from 750 to 1258, during which arts and sciences flourished within the Islamic empire.

Abul-Fadl, in one of the IIIT's publications, describes the challenge as the West's control of politics and therefore of civilisation. This, she says, is unsatisfactory not only because it is unfair, but also because of "the inadequacy of the cultural underpinnings which lend it its qualitative dimension".[62] Exploring in more detail the inadequacies and generally poor quality of contemporary Western culture and civilisation, she remarks that, by the late 20th century,

> the exuberant optimism which had [in the Western world] marked the onset of the century had to all intents and purposes become extinguished. There was an impoverishment in philosophy, the cornerstone of the Western intellectual tradition, and theology, periodically resuscitated from recurrent bouts of exhaustion, could hardly shoulder the burdens of a new transitional epoch unfolding in the guise of a "postmodernity". Confusion and scepticism became pervasive.[63]

Abul-Fadl's description of the problem has much to commend it. The Christian theology of the West, which traditionally has underpinned its culture and civilisation, is indeed so sapped and weakened that it has been unable to cope with postmodernism. The result is confusion and scepticism, relativism and utilitarianism.[64] But the answer she offers is: "An Islamic reading of the West can contribute to the sanctification of the culture of the West".[65] Or, in the famous slogan of the first Islamist organisation, the Muslim Brotherhood, applied to any and every context, "Islam is the solution." The process that Abul-Fadl and the Brotherhood advocate is called Islamisation.

THE NATURE OF ISLAMISATION

Islamisation is a form of *dawa* that aims to convert whole societies and their structures. It can be defined as a process by which not only individuals but also groups, societies and cultures become more and more Islamic. It is like what happened when Islam began in Arabia, which until then had been in a state of *jahiliyya* (ignorance of Allah's teachings). From the Muslim point of view, Islamisation, in whatever century it occurs, is:

> the transformation of an entire worldview from a crooked or 'Jahiliyya' basis to an Islamic one.[66]

The ultimate aim is to establish Islam's power, honour and rule (three qualities included in a single Arabic word), in accordance with what the Quran says:

But honour belongs to God and His Apostle, and to the Believers. (Q 63:8)

Islam requires people's full surrender to Allah and his will as revealed in Quran and *sunna*. Because all power and territory are viewed as belonging to Allah, Islamists deduce that they have a duty to Islamise the world. They feel obliged to call (*dawa*) all humanity to submit and acknowledge the total rule of Allah. If non-Muslims do not respond to this approach, then Islamists will implement Allah's rule by subverting and transforming non-Muslim societies and some by threatening or even using violent jihad.

From its beginning, Islam created a fusion of politics and religion which were inextricably linked: religious truth sanctified political power, and political power confirmed and sustained religion.[67] For modern Islamist activists, Islam's doctrine of *tawhid* – the unity of God – is not just a theory, but a political, social, economic (and even scientific) framework for a revolutionary re-making of society everywhere, according to God's will as revealed in Quran and *sunna*. *Tawhid* opposes and destroys all *jahili* powers and sets up a totally different way of life.[68] In the hands of such activists, Islam becomes an ideology: Islamism. It shifts from a passive mode of mere religion in the Western sense, as practised in the colonial era, to an active revolutionary mode, becoming a political tool for transforming society and state in all spheres of human activity. In this sense political Islam resembles secular totalitarian systems such as Fascism, Nazism and Marxism.

Much of this new Islamisation discourse is based on reclaiming Islam's sacred sources and early Muslim history. We have already seen that originally Islam was not satisfied with individuals' personal choices to embrace the religion; rather it sought political domination of the new territories and peoples and the total transformation of all their societal structures by imposing sharia and subjugating the non-Muslim population to Islamic rule. This was achieved through a combination of direct military aggression and missionary efforts. After countries and populations had been conquered, they were Islamised and their former non-Muslim identity erased. Over many centuries of subjugation, minority communities who managed to retain their original non-Muslim faith were taught to feel grateful to the Muslim majority for tolerating their existence and not destroying them altogether.

But before that stage had been reached, there was a period when the first generation of Muslims were a minority in the world they had conquered. This status made them fearful that they would be overwhelmed by the conquered communities. Accordingly, Islamic law excluded non-Muslims from any position of power in the Islamic state. These fears have persisted until today; in spite of centuries of Muslim dominance, the original Muslim mistrust of non-Muslims has continued through the generations. Most Muslims accept it as natural that non-Muslims should face restrictions on their right to practise their religion in public. They see it as perfectly normal to feel contempt for non-Muslims and to discriminate against them. They expect non-Muslims to show publicly that they submit to Islam. They feel that it would damage the honour of a Muslim if a Muslim had to submit to a non-Muslim, whether in marriage, employment or politics. Just as Muslims submit to God, so, by logical extension, must non-Muslims submit to Muslims.

THE *UMMA* CONCEPT AND MUSLIM VICTIMHOOD

The *umma* concept is currently experiencing a dramatic revival owing to the rise of Islamism, the development of a large Muslim presence in the West, and the effects of globalisation. It has become a significant driver of Islamisation.

The idea of the global Muslim nation, the *umma,* as a community of shared values has always had deep political implications, particularly because of Islam's broad reach, which embraces legal, social, territorial, economic and other aspects of life.[69] The *umma* concept expresses the group-consciousness of all Muslims and their essential felt unity based on their shared religion. This unity transcends all cultural, ethnic and national differences.[70] All Muslims in the world are united into a supranational body by their submission to the one god Allah and to his revelation through Muhammad in the Quran and *sunna.*[71] The *umma* is both the community of Allah and the community of Muhammad, the community that accepts Allah's unity (*tawhid*) and Muhammad's prophethood (*risala*) as part of its self-definition. It implies both Muslim unity and Muslim power.[72] Ziauddin Sardar sums up: "God is one, the Prophet is one, the *ummah* – the international Muslim community – is one".[73] Hence the virtually universal belief amongst Muslims that they must support each other against non-Muslims, no matter how much they may differ amongst themselves. The individual's needs and desires are to be subordinate to those of the *umma.*

The *umma* is the religious, social and political embodiment of *tawhid* in human society. There is therefore a stress on the uniformity of Islamic views. Any divergence is seen as a sign of unbelief, of lack of dedication to *tawhid*.[74] Multiple opinions lead to discord, so simple monolithic unity is seen as the solution to the *umma's* weakness.[75]

While there is much variety in Islam, there seems to be a majority consensus that the *umma* deserves the primary loyalty of all Muslims. This religious identity is often masked by secondary identities of nation-state, ethnic and tribal background and social groupings. However, in times of crisis the deeper primary identity and loyalty to the Islamic *umma* takes over. For many Muslims, loyalty to the *umma* overrides loyalty to any nation state.[76] Most Muslims, even liberal and secular ones, feel a sense of belonging to the *umma,* even if they are not happy with various parts of it. Liberal and secular Muslims see the *umma* as a mosaic of identities, interpretations, histories and cultural, regional and ethnic variations, of which they are an integral part.[77]

Some Islamists build on the *umma* concept to develop the idea of Muslims everywhere as global victims. They encourage Muslims to see themselves as a vulnerable and besieged community, as they were under Muhammad's leadership in Mecca. We have seen also how the memory of their vulnerability as a minority amidst their conquered subjects in the early days of the Islamic expansion still shapes the Muslim mind. This creates a defiant and aggressive response to non-Muslims and strengthens bonds with the universal *umma*. Having developed a sense of victimhood, they can then present Islamist violence as a "liberation struggle" to strengthen Muslim group identity.[78] (See page 127.)

The link created between local Muslim frustrations and global *umma* causes has become a powerful motivating force. Local struggles against perceived Islamophobia and discrimination are transformed into part of the global struggle of the *umma* against non-Muslim domination. Even Osama bin Laden began by focusing on a local issue: the presence of American troops in his homeland, Saudi Arabia.[79] Caught between a sense of communal powerlessness and a utopian hope for the restoration of global Islamic rule, the sense of global Muslim identity can unite widely divergent movements and can lead to a focus on jihad.[80]

SECULARISATION AND RE-ISLAMISATION

In modern times, under the impact of Western colonial rule, sharia was gradually phased out in most Muslim countries. If any part of the Islamic legal system was retained within their more secular legal systems, it was usually family law. At the end of the colonial period, the rise of secular and socialist forms of nationalism brought a temporary suspension of traditional Muslim hostility to non-Muslims. There were great hopes of creating new national identities across religious and ethnic divides. Turkey under Atatürk's leadership had already set itself on a strongly secular course since the Ottoman Empire came to an end in 1923.

Over the next few decades, however, this secularisation process went into reverse. The advances in secularisation have now disappeared in a growing tide of Islamism. It was as a reaction against the growth of socialism and nationalism in Egypt, a leading Arab state where great efforts were being made to suppress the Muslim Brotherhood, that the influential Muslim World League was founded in 1962 in Saudi Arabia, with a strongly Islamist and Wahhabi agenda. Muslims have renewed their hatred for the "Christian" West and their mistrust of non-Muslims in Muslim-majority countries, seeing them as spies for the West and traitors to their own nations. Conspiracy theories emerged, with indigenous non-Muslims always the scapegoats. These attitudes resulted in the erosion of the hard-won freedoms from the colonial and independence era.

Discrimination, persecution and attacks by armed jihadi militias on indigenous non-Muslims (Christians, Hindus, etc.) are now on the increase in many Muslim-majority states. An Islamist government took power in Turkey in 1995. The "Arab Spring" of 2011 has exemplified, in a speeded-up, miniature version, the swing to and fro between secularists, who initiated the uprisings in Tunisia, Egypt and Syria, and Islamists, who soon took over in what could be called an "Islamist Summer". However in Egypt and Tunisia the Islamists soon lost political power again, and at the time of writing, three years on, it remains to be seen what the long-term result will be.

Islamic law has been reintroduced in many Muslim states in varying degrees. The official introduction of the Islamic penal code (with punishments such as amputation and stoning) has a deep symbolism for the population, even though this may or may not be fully implemented, depending on power relations within the state and various interpretations of the legal issues.

ISLAMISATION TODAY

The resurgence of Islam since the 1970s and the growing power of Islamism have strongly impacted Muslim communities everywhere. By fusing together politics and religion, and by using the twin concepts of *dawa* and jihad, Islamists are increasing the influence of Islam right across the globe. The rapid Islamisation of the West is evidence of the significant shift in power from the West to other global players, among them the bloc of Muslim-majority states funded by oil wealth. This is accompanied by a growing Islamisation of the Muslim-majority states themselves and a drive to destabilise non-Muslim-majority states with Muslim minorities and then to Islamise them.

The main contemporary Islamist movements, such as the Muslim Brotherhood, are dedicated to *dawa* as part of what some of them have termed a "civilisational jihad" that will establish Islam firmly as the dominant religion in non-Muslim-majority states. This view of *dawa* prioritises the Islamisation of the non-Muslim society in order to create an environment conducive to Islam. Thus organisational, institutional, legal, economic, educational, cultural, social and welfare endeavours are not just small separate steps to meet the needs of Muslim individuals and the local Muslim community but are considered to be part of an overall strategic plan to change the character of the host state and society and establish the dominion of Islam.[81]

Many Muslims today hold this Islamist view of a civilisational conflict between the *umma* and the West. It was taught by Islamist leaders and thinkers such as Sayyid Qutb (1906-1966) and Sayyid Abul A'la Mawdudi, long before Samuel Huntington made famous the phrase "clash of civilisations" by his 1996 book of that title.[82] Islamists believe that this confrontation started with the spread of Western colonialism to Muslim-majority states, by which the West corrupted and humiliated the Muslim world and destroyed its will-power. The West is blamed for all problems faced by modern-day Muslims, including their "backwardness" and their inability to unite and regain their former glory. In this view, the *umma* remains under constant attack by an aggressive West. This, however, they consider to be only a temporary setback, as the *umma* has previously experienced many cycles of crisis and recovery in its long history. It is argued that Muslims must respond by resisting Western cultural influences, by judging everything according to authentic Islamic norms, by casting off their defeatist attitudes and adopting instead the belligerence of Muhammad in Medina. Muslims must regain their self-confidence, affirming that they are different from the rest of the world, so that the *umma* can be strong and united once more.[83] Thus Islam can regain its ancient power and glory.[84] In response to this perceived need, many Muslim conferences were held in the 1980s (often with Saudi funding) to discuss the weakness of the Muslim *umma*. At these conferences the idea of Islamisation was introduced as the solution. In the words of Ziauddin Sardar, a leading British Muslim and journalist, "The *ummah* was the focus and Islamisation the programme."[85] These conferences remained largely unnoticed by Western observers.

Modern Islamisation could be considered the brainchild of Ismail Raji al-Faruqi (1921-1986), a Palestinian Islamic scholar based in American universities.[86] It is aimed both at Muslims, who need to be revived by a return to authentic, original Islam, and at non-Muslims, who need to be enfolded in an Islamic embrace. Islamists believe that Islamisation will bring an end to all confrontation and conflict, as true peace is possible only under an Islamic political and cultural system, i.e. an Islamic state governed according to sharia.

As mentioned above, Saudi Arabia and its vast wealth are playing an important part in the contemporary Islamisation process. Wahhabi Islam, the state religion of Saudi Arabia, is one of the strictest and most radical of Islamist movements. This austere version of Islam is linked to Salafi Islam, for both base Islam only on the Quran and *sunna* and the first three generations of Muslims, ignoring later developments such as sharia. Wahhabism is strongly allied to other reform movements that call for a return to the original sources – movements such as the Ahl-i Hadith, the Deobandi movement and the Jamaat-i Islami of the Indian subcontinent – as well as to the Muslim Brotherhood.

Saudi oil money has been used to spread Saudi Wahhabi Islam across the world, and it has gained tremendous power in most Muslim societies, promoting a shift to a more puritan and inflexible type of Islam. It has also contributed generously to the funding of mosques, charities, and various Islamic institutions as well as most radical and violent Islamic movements around the world.

— 6 —

ISLAMISATION METHODS USED WORLDWIDE

MIGRATION, TRANSMIGRATION AND DEMOGRAPHICS

Some Islamist leaders strongly discourage Muslims from living in non-Muslim-majority contexts unless it is absolutely unavoidable.[87] By contrast, other Islamist leaders consider that the mass Muslim migration to non-Muslim countries in recent years can have only one reason: participation in *dawa* to convert non-Muslims to Islam and establish Islam in the West and in other non-Muslim regions. They see it as an opportunity to be used to help the revival of Islam and its power.[88] As early as 1952, the American umbrella organisation, the Federation of Islamic Associations, stated in the preamble to its constitution that it sought to "participate in the modern renaissance of Islam".[89] No matter for what personal reasons individual Muslims migrate from their home countries, these leaders see a divine cause behind it all[90] and a new opportunity to be of service to Islam.[91] Such is certainly the opinion of one of the most significant Islamists today, Dr Yusuf al-Qaradawi, based in Qatar, who is a main spiritual guide to the Muslim Brotherhood, chief special advisor to Aljazeera television, dean of the Faculty of Sharia at the University of Qatar, chairman of the European Council for Fatwa and Research, involved in many academic institutions in the West and adviser to many banks:

Thanks to Allah, Islamic presence in West existed through divine predestinations and natural causes that facilitated its existence, through no planning or arrangement on part of us as Muslims.[92]

For such Islamists, Muhammad's migration from Mecca to Medina in 622 (the *hijra*) is a model to be followed by Muslims throughout history. They see this as an example of fleeing from a region of persecution to a safe haven that is to be infiltrated and won for Islam, so it can then become a launch pad for the further expansion of Islam. The original Muslim community developed in clearly defined stages which, say the Islamists, must be copied today. First came the stage of weakness, in which the message of Islam was proclaimed (*dawa*) to an unbelieving society in Mecca. Second the stage of migration (*hijra*) to a safe place, Medina, where Muslim strength could be built up. The third and final stage was the sacred fight (jihad) to reconquer lost territory, extend Muslim political dominion and create Allah's ideal state on earth. Migration is thus viewed by Islamists as a stage in the quest to establish the ideal Islamic state modelled on Muhammad's example. It forms an important part of the Islamist strategy for *dawa* and Islamisation.

Muslims in their new host states must, say such leaders, seize this unique opportunity to communicate their religion and expand its sphere of influence, radically changing the culture of the countries they have moved to and re-shaping it in the mould of Islam.[93] It is the duty of all individual Muslims to witness to Islam, seek to establish the Muslim *umma* in their adopted states and implement sharia as the law of the land.[94]

Al-Qaradawi lists four specific *dawa* and related activities that Muslim minorities in Europe, the Americas and Australia should engage in:

- Inviting non-Muslims to Islam through preaching, dialogue and good example
- Caring for new converts to Islam and teaching them more about how to live as Muslims
- Caring for newly arrived Muslim immigrants and showing them how they can continue to practise Islam in their new context.
- Defending the causes of the umma and defending "Islamic lands in the face of hostile and misleading powers and trends"

Al-Qaradawi urges Muslims to engage actively with non-Muslims in order to achieve these aims, even though he also advises that they should live in a "Muslim ghetto" and have their own religious, educational, cultural, social and entertainment institutions so that they do not get assimilated into the majority.[95]

The population explosion in Muslim-majority countries, coupled to the growth in the number of Muslims migrating to non-Muslim-majority states and the biological growth of these Muslim minorities, is seen by many Muslims as being in Allah's providence to tilt the demographic balance decisively in favour of Islam, through a new *hijra* that will restore Islam's glory and its power in world affairs.

In a talk to the UK Islamic Mission, Ismail al-Faruqi stated that:

> We are here to stay, we are here to plant Islam in this part of the world and we must utilize everything in our power to make the word of Allah supreme... In the process of living here, we can become ambassadors of Islam... Allah ... has carved out a vocation for you, a new mission, and this mission is to save the West, to save the humanity of the West by converting that humanity to Islam... we want to live henceforth as if we were *muhajjirs*, Companions of Muhammad from Makka to Madina... And so let us invest our *Hijra* with this new meaning, let us appoint ourselves as ambassadors of Islam in this country and let us begin a programme, a programme of real action.[96]

An important aspect of this is the higher birth rate amongst the Muslim minorities than amongst the majority in their European host nations. Even if immigration were to cease, a continued difference in birth rate would mean that the Muslim minorities would in time become majorities. Britain's Office of National Statistics analysed the 2011 census figures and found that the percentage of Muslims among the under-fives in England and Wales was almost twice as high as in the general population. However, according to Oxford University demographics professor David Coleman, the high birth rate amongst British Muslims was declining.[97]

Numerical growth in the West will give Muslims a more effective political lobby that could bring with it legal changes in favour of Muslim causes such as the introduction of blasphemy laws to protect Islam from criticism, increased Islamic education, the introduction of sharia family laws as binding in the personal affairs of Muslims, and the state recognition of a Muslim community. The final goal is the full Islamisation of the host countries and the establishment of Islamic states under sharia.

Most Muslim countries regard their large populations as a political weapon and are glad to send their citizens to settle in Europe, America, Canada, Australia, Latin America, Japan, South Korea and other non-Muslim contexts. They know that that the larger the Muslim diaspora, the greater the political influence it will exert, and the more concessions the Islamic world will be able to gain from the non-Muslim-majority states.[98]

A wide variety of Muslim leaders have expressed their vision of an Islamic Europe in the foreseeable future, in which demographic changes play a key part.[99] The famous charismatic Egyptian Muslim preacher, Amr Khalid, stated in 2008 his belief that Muslims would form a majority in Europe by 2028:

> The Muslims keep having children, while the Europeans do not – this means that within 20 years the Muslims will be the majority.[100]

Bernard Lewis, the distinguished scholar of Islam, predicted in 2006 that Muslims would form a majority in Europe by the end of the 21st century.[101] The following year, he warned again of the dramatic shift that Europe is experiencing as it stands on the point of being taken over by Muslims. The Islamisation process, he said, is being helped along by immigration and misapplied democratic freedoms. Europeans have surrendered to this process in an atmosphere of political correctness and multiculturalism.[102] These processes can also be seen in other non-Muslim-majority states in Africa, Asia and Latin America. However these predictions need to be viewed with considerable caution as many factors could change. There is no inevitability about current trends continuing indefinitely. Muslim birth rates in the West might decline. Muslim migration to the West might decrease. Many Muslims might choose to reject the Islamist vision and instead embrace a more secular outlook and be assimilated into the majority society as most other immigrant groups have done in the past.

Some Muslim governments have deliberately increased the Muslim proportion of certain areas of their countries by the simple method of arranging for Muslims from elsewhere to move in and live there. This trans-migration policy is generally applied to places where indigenous non-Muslim minorities predominate. The policy is often supported by Islamist groups who are keen to transform non-Muslim-majority localities into Muslim-majority ones. Muslims from densely populated areas are encouraged and subsidised to resettle in areas where non-Muslims predominate. Rather than cleansing an area by removing its non-Muslim population, the non-Muslims are left *in situ* but swamped with incoming Muslim settlers. Not only does this alter the whole cultural environment, but also the new Muslim inhabitants are able to cast their votes in elections. A significant tipping point is reached once the Muslims become a majority and the path is set for them to vote in their co-religionists to all available posts and positions. The issue of the Muslim vote helped to trigger the Second Ivorian Civil War in Ivory Coast in 2011.

Indonesia

Indonesia's 1984-1989 Five Year Plan called for the movement of five million people from highly concentrated Muslim regions, such as Java and Madura, to places with local Christian majorities, such as Kalimantan, Sulawesi, the Malukus, East Timor, and Papua.[103]

In the Malukus and in Central Sulawesi, religious cleansing of Christian communities by jihadi groups such as Laskar Jihad in the late 1990s and early 2000s reinforced the government policy of transmigration. In order to consolidate Muslim-majority control of the region, jihadi organisations initiated a violent programme of attacks on Christian communities. More than 6,000 Christians were killed and 750,000 forced to flee their homes. The Malukus, which previously had a majority Christian population, is now 60% Muslim.[104]

Malaysia

A Royal Commission of Inquiry in Malaysia revealed in 2013 how the electorates of the East Malaysian state of Sabah had been manipulated by the highest authorities to increase the Muslim vote. Beginning in the 1980s, Muslim illegal immigrants to Sabah from the Philippines and Indonesia had been given identity cards and put on the electoral roll so that they could vote for the ruling Barisan National party and keep it in power. The plan, as reported by witnesses to the Royal Commission of Inquiry, was to add up to 150,000 Muslim names to the Sabah electoral roll, deploying them to particular constituencies where the Muslim vote was most needed. Muslim citizens of West Malaysia were also added to the Sabah electoral roll to help this effort.[105]

Another issue in Sabah is the allegedly deliberate misclassifiying of some Christians as Muslims, by altering their identity cards. In 2010, the Sidang Injil Borneo sent a list of 162 such cases to the national Registration Department to be rectified; the reply was that all 162 files had been lost, so nothing could be done.[106]

43

The Muslim population of Sabah had reached 65.4% by 2010, at least according to the census. Over a third of the Muslims were not Malaysian citizens, so that nearly a quarter of the total population (23.5%) were Muslims who were not Malaysian citizens.[107]

Sudan

Throughout the Sudanese civil war of 1983-2005, it was the policy of the Arab, Islamic government in Khartoum to implement ethnic cleansing of non-Muslims along the border areas with the South, especially the Abyei area, Southern Kordofan (the Nuba Mountains) and borderline Dinka and Nuer regions.[108] Muslim tribes were encouraged to settle in these areas.[109]

THE PROLIFERATION OF ISLAMIST ORGANISATIONS

Organisation is seen as a religious obligation by many Muslims. Mawdudi explained the reason:

These aims cannot be realized so long as power and leadership in society are in the hands of disbelieving rulers and so long as the followers of Islam confine themselves to worship rites… Only when power in society is in the hands of the Believers and the righteous, can the objectives of Islam be realized. It is therefore the primary duty of all those who aspire to please God to launch an organized struggle, sparing neither life nor property, for this purpose. The importance of securing power for the righteous is so fundamental that, neglecting this struggle, one has no means left to please God.[110]

The Moroccan-born engineer, Professor M. Ali Kettani, who has extensively studied Muslim minorities, believes that organisation is the key to their survival:

The secret of the Muslim communities which have been able to survive across the centuries and generations lies in one word: organisation. Islam cannot survive if individual Muslims believe it is a personal affair… When a group of Muslims is formed the first thing they should do in order to keep Islam among themselves is to organise themselves on an Islamic basis. To keep Islam alive from one generation to another, they should establish two basic Islamic institutions: the mosque and the school.[111]

Muslim communities tend to be highly organised, establishing a wide variety of institutions in which their beliefs and values can be articulated and developed (see pages 16–20, 71–72). These institutions can be used to represent various Muslim views to the general public and to the authorities and to lobby for Muslim causes. In non-Muslim-majority states, many of these organisations have now been taken over by Islamists, yet are presented as independent, moderate and not linked to any ideological movement. They compete with secular Muslim organisations for influence and power within Muslim communities and to speak on behalf of Muslims to governments and the public. The OIC is especially influential at the United Nations.

THE DEMOCRATIC PROCESS

Where possible, Islamist movements set up Islamist political parties and join the democratic process, seeking to Islamise the population and the legislative system and to achieve power in the state through the electoral system. They are willing to practise patience (*sabr*) to achieve this, as the leader of the Jamaat-e-Islami party in Bangladesh, Motiur Rahman Nizami, stated when his party joined the ruling coalition in 2001:

> But we are not in a hurry. We don't expect anything to happen overnight but pursue a slow but steady policy towards total Islamisation of the country.[112]

(In the case of Nizami's own party, the progress is definitely slow but not necessarily very steady, as the Jamaat-e-Islami was declared illegal in 2009 and barred from contesting future polls.)[113]

For a survey of contemporary Islamist politics in ten Muslim-majority countries of the Middle East, North Africa and Asia, see Appendix 4.

There is disagreement amongst Islamists as to whether or not it is permitted for Muslims to form political parties in Western countries and stand for election. Some forbid such activities, partly at least because of the dilemma a Muslim would face if elected and then had to take an oath of office to uphold a constitution that they might feel would conflict with their Islamic beliefs.

Others, however, view politics and political parties as an essential tool to assist in promoting Islam in the West. Yusuf Al-Qaradawi sees them as a logical extension of what Muslim minorities are seeking to do to influence other spheres of life, arguing that:

if Islamic presence in the West is maintained, in terms of religious, cultural and social – and sometimes economic – presence, then it is natural and logical that Muslims seeks (*sic*) to corroborate such presence through maintaining political presence. For, politics has now interfered in everything, and if we abandon politics, politics would still have an impact on us.[114]

THE SPREAD OF SHARIA

The detailed body of legislation that is sharia was gradually evolved by Islamic scholars in the 8th and 9th centuries. They used the Quran and *hadith* as their main sources and employed a logical reasoning process called *ijtihad*. *Ijtihad* provided them with a "toolbox" of methods, such as abrogation, analogy and scholarly consensus. Despite the emphasis on consensus, the various scholars did not totally agree with each other. The result was a range of schools of sharia, each developed by a different scholar. Five of these remain important today, varying in detail from each other. For example, they differ in the punishment laid down for a woman who leaves Islam, although they all agree that a male apostate should be killed. By the 10th century it was felt by most Muslims that all the necessary scholarship had been done and no more changes should ever be made to sharia. This is still the opinion of the majority of Muslims today.

Most Muslims see sharia as the divine law code that defines their faith, their ultimate point of reference,[115] a crucial part of living in accordance with God's will.[116] Despite the fact that five alternate versions are in use today, it is seen as uniting the diverse parts of the Islamic community, even though Muslims may disagree with each other on how to interpret it and implement the medieval legal formulations in today's world.

Islam defines itself in terms of submission rather than freedom, and of duties rather than rights.[117] Both traditional Islam and Islamism promote authoritarian systems of governance based on sharia, in which the individual is subordinated to the community, non-Muslim communities are subordinated to the Islamic community and women are subordinated to men. The concept of individual rights is subordinated to the concept of duty within the sharia framework; so human rights, religious freedom, pluralism and multiculturalism are all seen through this prism.

In Islam there is no separation between state and religion. Sharia is therefore intended to govern every aspect of life from personal prayer to home and family life, from politics and economics to crime and punishment, from slavery to warfare. The problems come because of sharia's inbuilt discrimination against women, its inbuilt discrimination against non-Muslims and the high priority it gives to protecting the reputation of Islam. Even non-orthodox Muslims can be discriminated against if they are classified as apostates, heretics or infidels.[118] In a 2003 case, the European Court of Human Rights stated that sharia law is incompatible with the fundamental principles of democracy as set forth in the Convention for the Protection of Human Rights and Fundamental Freedoms (European Convention on Human Rights).[119]

There are some specific differences between sharia and the principles of human rights laid down in the Universal Declaration of Human Rights (UDHR). The UDHR specifies that all humans are equal before the law.

Article 7

All are equal before the law and are entitled without any discrimination to equal protection of the law. All are entitled to equal protection against any discrimination in violation of this Declaration and against any incitement to such discrimination.

By contrast, sharia says that when compensation is payable for an injury, a woman receives less than a man does for the same injury. Her testimony in a court of law is worth only half that of a man. Non-Muslims are discriminated against in a similar way.

Article 18 of the UDHR guarantees freedom of conscience, including the freedom to change religion. In sharia this right to change religion is restricted; non-Muslims can convert to Islam, but Muslims cannot change to follow another religion.

Article 19 guarantees the freedom to express and impart information and ideas. But sharia is designed to safeguard Islam, Muhammad and the Quran from any criticism, a principle that becomes so important in Islamism that it effectively stifles freedom of speech.

It is important to realise that what the United Nations described in 1948 as "universal" rights are not necessarily seen as such by large portions of the world's population. Though they may have been declared by the UN to be universal, they are not universally held. During the drafting of the UDHR, the crucial phrase in Article 18 about the freedom to change one's religion was bitterly disputed by many Muslim-majority countries. The principle that all humans are of equal worth irrespective of gender or religion is by no means universally accepted. This is one of many attitudes in which

Westerners are so strongly but subconsciously conditioned by their Judeo-Christian heritage that they feel all the planet must agree with them; they assume such attitudes are in the DNA of human beings. Yet to huge sections of the world, it seems perfectly right and proper for women and non-Muslims to be treated as second-class; indeed it would seem an offence against Allah's plan for creation to raise them up as equal to Muslim men. This is why Islamist initiatives to embed sharia across the world must be viewed with extreme caution.

The Cairo Declaration on Human Rights in Islam[120] was adopted by the OIC on 5 August 1990 at a meeting of the foreign ministers of its member states. The first 23 Articles abound in liberal-sounding statements that seem to resonate well with a Western worldview. But they are all meaningless in the face of the final two Articles, which read:

Article 24
All the rights and freedoms stipulated in this Declaration are subject to the Islamic Shari'ah.

Article 25
The Islamic Shari'ah is the only source of reference for the explanation or clarification of any of the articles in this Declaration.

In effect, these two Articles are saying that anything in the first 23 that contradicts sharia is to be discounted. So the whole document is nothing but a reaffirmation of sharia principles.

Led by Islamists, Muslim communities around the world constantly demand legal changes to protect Islam and give it a privileged position in state and society. Their ultimate aim is to live under sharia. Many Muslim-majority countries have two parallel law systems: an Islamic one based on sharia and a secular one. Some Muslims in the West are requesting a similar arrangement,[121] starting with sharia family law.*

A survey carried out in Britain in 1989 revealed that 66% of Muslim respondents said that in cases of conflict between sharia and British law, they would follow sharia.[122] A poll of British Muslims in 2004 found that 61%

---

* Sharia family law regulates matters such as marriage, divorce and inheritance. According to sharia it is easy for a man to divorce his wife and hard for a woman to divorce her husband. A man may have up to four wives but a woman can only have one husband. A daughter can only inherit half as much as her brothers inherit.

would prefer sharia courts to the secular court system. An ICM survey in February 2006 found that 40% of British Muslims supported the introduction of sharia in predominantly Muslim areas of the UK.[123] Another poll six months later found that 28% hoped that the UK would one day become a fundamentalist Islamic state under sharia.[124]

The plan for a gradual implementation of sharia in non-Muslim-majority states is expressed in Muslim requests for changed rules and laws in areas such as food, marriage, divorce, politics, policing, hospitals, prisons and banking. There are insistent demands for *halal* food in prisons, schools and hospitals, for time off for Muslim employees to attend Friday midday prayers, for Muslim check-out staff in supermarkets to be protected from having to handle alcohol, for schoolgirls to wear the *hijab* and gender segregation during sport and swimming, for special concessions to help Muslim schoolchildren during the fasting month of Ramadan and for Islamic banking, pensions and mortgages (see pages 51–53). Good-natured agreement to adapt to these Muslim requests is resulting in the gradual establishing of many aspects of sharia in Western nations. Most of these concessions are being granted in areas where Muslims are concentrated demographically.

Informal, voluntary sharia courts are operating in many Muslim-minority communities in the West, offering mediation, reconciliation and adjudication services on the basis of sharia. There is a consistent drive to have these courts classed under the category of arbitration courts and for the secular legal system to accept and enforce their verdicts. This is the current position in the UK, where sharia tribunals are allowed to give verdicts in certain civil cases, which can then be enforced by the ordinary civil courts. This in itself does not give Islam a privileged position, for when two parties agree to have their dispute settled by arbitration rather than through the ordinary courts they can choose to have the arbitration conducted under any legal system they like. However, it appears that the Muslim Arbitration Tribunal may have been going beyond its authority by using arbitration for criminal cases, domestic violence, divorce and child custody, and in other areas where British law does not allow arbitration.[125] There have also been complaints about sharia courts or councils falsely claiming or implying that they have legal jurisdiction over family or criminal law.[126]

In March 2014 the Law Society in the UK issued guidelines to solicitors for drawing up sharia-compliant wills that could be enforced by British courts. This seems to be a step further along the way to include sharia law in the British legal system. The guidelines were distributed to lawyers in

England and Wales to "assist solicitors who have been instructed to prepare a valid will, which follows Sharia succession rules" while remaining valid under British law. According to the Law Society, the guidelines would be recognised by Britain's courts in order to promote good practice in applying Islamic principles in the British legal system. Some have been disturbed by this move fearing that, if followed through, these guidelines would undermine equality before the law and discriminate against several categories of people. According to sharia, male heirs receive double the amount inherited by a female heir; non-Muslims may not inherit at all, and only Muslim marriages are recognised for inheritance purposes thus excluding partners married in a civil or non-Muslim ceremony. Furthermore, according to sharia, neither adopted children nor illegitimate children may inherit at all.[127]

Also in 2014, Britain's Chief Inspector of Constabulary expressed concern about the fact that "some communities born under other skies … from other cultures" prefer to police themselves. He said that chief constables had told him that the calls they receive from some urban areas in the Midlands were "close to zero". So the police had no idea what injustices or crimes were being committed in those areas. The police "never hear of any trouble because the community deals with that all on its own".[128] He refused to name the communities he had in mind, but it is hard to think he could have meant anything except the densely concentrated Muslim communities with their sharia courts.

The demands for sharia raise important questions about the vulnerability of Muslim women under sharia. They face severe discrimination especially in matters of divorce, custody of children, polygamy and inheritance. Furthermore, according to sharia (a system in which the number of witnesses on each side of the case is an important factor in deciding the verdict), the testimony of a woman carries only half as much weight as the testimony of a man. The very existence of sharia tribunals or courts makes Muslim women vulnerable. It is easy to imagine how a British Muslim woman (very likely not well educated and not fluent in English) could be pressurised by male relatives to let her case be heard by a sharia court instead of an ordinary court. She might be told that other legal options were non-existent or that it would be sinful for Muslims to use them.

In a number of non-Muslim-majority secular countries, judges are beginning to take sharia principles into consideration when deciding cases and Muslims are offered special arrangements in court.[129]

In northern Nigeria, sharia principles had been applied to certain issues of civil law, such as marriage, divorce and adultery, since colonial times (and of course before). In recent decades Muslims have been pressing for the extension of sharia to cover all civil and criminal matters. This is part of the campaign to challenge the secular nature of the state, which Islamists refuse to accept. The modern controversy started in the 1970s when the Constitutional Assembly rejected Muslim demands for a new federal sharia court of appeal. Christians saw the demand as an attempt to impose Islam on Nigerian society, which has similar numbers of Muslims and Christians, though the Muslims are concentrated in the north and the Christians in the south.

Calls for sharia in Nigeria experienced a revival in the 1980s. Muslims, especially students and intellectuals in Kano and Zaria, inspired by the 1979 Iranian Revolution, organised pro-sharia demonstrations. The problem resurfaced in 1999 when Governor Ahmed Sani of Zamfara state announced that Zamfara would adopt Islamic law in January 2000. The Zamfara news came at a time when Muslims were aggrieved over their loss of power following the fall of the military regime in 1999 and the rise to power of a Christian president. They feared a drift to a pro-southern and pro-Christian bias. In Zamfara, it was said, sharia would cover all criminal cases and was to include *hudud* punishments (stoning, amputation, flogging and the death penalty), contrary to Nigeria's federal constitution, which barred cruel and unusual punishments. Governor Sani said that sharia was necessary to re-create a clean living and honest society. His announcement reopened Nigeria's religious rift and constitutional crisis. Other northern states, including Niger, Kano, Borno and Sokoto, soon followed Zamfara's lead. Sharia was an immensely popular theme with ordinary Muslim people, who saw it as the solution to all their problems. It became an identity marker and a deeply emotional slogan. By 2001, twelve northern states had adopted sharia, and there were attempts to expand it to states in the Middle Belt where Christians and Muslims are roughly equal in number.

The Spread of Islamic Finance

In the last two decades there has been spectacular growth in Islamic finance and banking. Islamic financial products were worth nearly a trillion US dollars by 2010. The significance for *dawa* is that Islamic finance helps to strengthen the Islamic identity of Muslims. It creates a dividing line between Muslims and non-Muslims and is a factor in the growing separation and isolation of Muslim minority communities from the majority amongst whom they live. If, on the other hand, non-Muslims start to use Islamic financial products, this too is good for *dawa*, as anything that makes non-Muslims live like Muslims is a step forward in the Islamisation process.

The concept of Islamic finance is a new phenomenon, initiated by Mawdudi and promoted by 20th century Islamist movements who claim that Western financial products are inconsistent with sharia. They have invented a range of alternative "sharia-compliant" products and are pressurising Muslims (and encouraging non-Muslims) to use them. Malaysia and several Gulf states are competing to become global centres for Islamic finance.

Significantly, there is no consensus amongst Muslims about what Islam actually teaches on finance. All agree that the Quran bans *riba*. But there is disagreement about the meaning of the term *riba*. Contemporary Islamists claim that it means any kind of interest, but the traditional Muslim interpretation – still held by many Muslims today – is that it means very high and exploitative interest. The Islamists are rapidly winning this argument and using sharia finance as a tool to help bring about the Islamisation of all aspects of society. This is seen as complying with Muhammad's *dawa* command recorded in the *hadith*:

Narrated by Anas ibn Malik :

The Prophet (pbuh) said: use your property, your persons and your tongues in striving against the polytheists. (Abu Dawud, Vol. 14, No. 2498)

Mawdudi argued that Islamic economics was to be a vehicle to help establish Islamic rule and law in society and state.[130] This idea was further developed by his disciple Khurshid Ahmad, a main leader of the Jamaat-i-Islami and a prominent intellectual, politician and economist, who helped transform Islamic economics into a contemporary academic discipline. Ahmad also argued that Muslims must use Islamic economics to build up the power of Islam:

It is a direct demand of *ummah*'s position as *khalifah* that its dependence upon the non-Muslim world in all essentials must be changed to a state of economic independence, self-respect and gradual building-up of strength and power.[131]

The media in many Western countries have made very positive comments about Islamic financial products and have backed demands for the establishment of Islamic banks and financial institutions in non-Muslim-majority countries.[132] Islamic finance is increasingly being placed in the category of "ethical investments". Western governments often support the introduction of Islamic finance, hoping to attract investment from the huge pool of money in the Middle East. The British government, for example, has plans for London to become a global centre for Islamic finance.[133]

In a 2005 survey, several Islamic companies indicated that the UK had the most sharia-friendly environment (in terms of human capital and expertise, institutional and legal framework and political environment) of all Western countries. The UK was also the most favoured European location for sharia investors.[134] According to some experts, by 2007, London had become the main Western centre for Islamic finance.[135]

Sharia finance is growing in the United States as well. More Islamic and conventional banks are offering sharia-compliant mortgages and other products. The Dow Jones Islamic Market Index includes 69 country indexes and thousands of broad-market, blue-chip, fixed-income and strategy and thematic indexes that have passed rules-based screens for sharia-compliance. The list of companies on the Dow Jones Islamic Index is growing as more businesses become involved and the US government acts to approve and expedite the implementation of sharia finance.

By accepting the Islamist interpretation of sharia economic principles as if all Muslims held this viewpoint, Western media and governments have empowered Islamists, while weakening Muslim moderates and progressives. The latest developments have also placed individual Muslims under increasing communal pressure to use so-called sharia-compliant financial products.[136]

The *Halal* Industry

Closely allied with Islamic finance is the *halal* industry. In 2011, the Malaysia-based World Halal Forum (WHF) stated its intention to press for the convergence of these "two Shariah-based industries" to form an "integrated Halal Economy". It expressed the hope that the shared values of the two sectors would "play an increasingly strategic role in shaping global markets in the coming decade". The shared values that the WHF hopes will shape global markets are, of course, Islamist values, so the vision is for an Islamisation of global markets.[137]

The director of the WHF at that time, Abdalhamid Evans, had been even more forthright two years earlier about the role of *halal* in the Islamisation project. He spoke of the potential political influence of *halal* and how it could be used by American Muslims to shape the future of their country.

Halal consumer power is a real, yet almost-unnoticed, force that is capable of significant commercial and political influence. To what extent can the Muslim American community use this force to shape the future of our communities and our country?[138]

Halal food laws in Islam are just one part of the much wider set of sharia regulations about what is permitted (*halal*) and what is forbidden (*haram*). The *halal/haram* regulations cover goods and services, entertainments, finance and commerce, tourism and lifestyles as well as food. (Sharia finance could equally well be called *halal* finance.) In the Muslim view, these laws are based on Allah's direct revelation in the Quran and *sunna*; they show his sovereign will and cannot be changed by humans.

Things that are impure include blood, pus, vomit, urine, pigs, dogs, alcohol, carrion, corpses, water and uneaten food left by an unclean animal. A Muslim who comes into contact with something impure must try to wash it off his body or clothing and perform the ritual ablutions to become pure again.[139] For meat to be *halal*, it must not only be from an animal considered pure; it must also have been slaughtered in the correct Islamic way, with the blood drained out of the living (and normally conscious) animal, while an Islamic prayer is spoken over it. The prayer is either the *bismillah* (in the name of Allah) or the *shahada*.

Several criteria must be met before any food product can be certified as *halal*.[140] Manufactured products should be free of contamination and must not come into contact with *haram* substances during their preparation, production and storage. *Halal* ingredients must not be mixed with *haram* ingredients like enzymes and emulsifiers that have been derived from pigs or other non-*halal* animals.[141] *Halal* rules are also applied to clothes, vaccines and other injections, pharmaceuticals, antiseptic wipes, cosmetics and anything which enters or touches the body.

Contemporary Muslim scholars argue that, in Islam, eating is regarded as a form of worship, like prayer and other religious activities. That is why Muslims must ensure that the food they consume is pure and prepared in the correct manner, avoiding all items that are prohibited in Islamic dietary laws.[142]

The concept of *halal* and *haram* was traditionally seen by Muslims as the way in which Allah marks the boundary between his *umma* and the infidels. *Halal/haram* rules of purity form a system that defines the Muslims as a community, separate and different from non-Muslim communities. Traditional and Islamist leaders, scholars and institutions stress the *halal/haram* complex of laws as protective insulation for the Muslim community to keep it safe from the polluting influences of secular non-Muslim society.[143]

However, many Muslim scholars now assert that *halal* and *haram* rules are not just for Muslims, but for all human beings.[144] This means that it is the duty of Muslims to spread sharia's *halal/haram* rules to non-Muslim-majority societies and states, both to implement God's will and for the good of the non-Muslims. *Halal* food thus becomes part of the Islamisation agenda to increase Islam's sphere of influence amongst non-Muslims. In Europe, this often begins with demands for *halal* food in prisons, schools and hospitals. A leading European Muslim cleric, Dr Mustafa Ceric, the Grand Mufti of Bosnia-Herzegovina, Sanjak, Croatia and Slovenia, has urged the international Muslim community to use the *halal* movement to take control of the global economy.[145]

Halal food (like sharia finance) is sometimes presented as the ethical alternative for all people, non-Muslims and Muslims alike. Dr Ceric has also claimed that *halal* means "pure and hygienic" and that *halal* food and other services meet the basic needs of every human being. He said that the non-Muslim world has no hesitation in accepting it.[146] Likewise in Africa there is a growing perception, even amongst Christians, that *halal* food is safer to eat than non-*halal* food; in fact, *halal* slaughter in Africa is often very unhygienic.

Prime Minister Abdullah Badawi of Malaysia, at a WHF meeting in May 2006, said that *halal* food products and services offered an opportunity for non-Muslims too.[147] His country is positioning itself to become a world hub of the global *halal* industry, just as it has become a main hub in the global Islamic finance industry. The state has effectively certified, standardised and bureaucratised Malaysian *halal* production, trade and consumption. Even bottled water in Malaysia can now be bought with a *halal* certification stamp on the label. Now, the vision is to export this model using appropriate networks around the world.[148]

Large Western food manufacturers, distributors and caterers are waking up to the size of the *halal* food market, estimated at $685 billion.[149] Many have started to introduce *halal* products into their ranges. Large multinationals like McDonald's, Nestlé and Tesco are now targeting *halal* as a major global market.[150] Some have gone over to marketing only *halal* products to simplify their processes and cut costs. Major *halal* meat producers are found in Argentina, Australia, Canada, China, India, the UK, the USA, and New Zealand.[151] Not all the *halal* meat goes to Muslim-majority countries, but many producers find it is more convenient and cost-effective to treat all their meat the same way and therefore it is all *halal*. In Africa some countries with a tiny Muslim minority, such as Botswana and Zimbabwe, nevertheless have a meat trade that is almost 100% *halal*. In other African countries, for example Tanzania, the *halal* meat issue is so hotly contested that there has been much violence against Christian butcheries.

The role of *halal* food in the Islamisation of the non-Muslim-majority world is potentially a very significant one. In some countries, including non-Muslim-majority ones such as Australia (where the Muslim population is only 2.2%, according to the 2011 census), food products are increasingly being labelled with a mark or stamp to indicate that they are *halal*. This stamp is applied to products such as yoghurt, some types of which would be *haram* because they contain pork gelatine. But it is also applied to others such as honey, which could not possibly be *haram*. We have already seen that in Malaysia even water is labelled *halal*. The only reason for such "unnecessary" *halal* labelling must be to raise the visibility of Islam in everyday life, so that every shopper and consumer is subtly reminded of the Islamic presence.

In certain other non-Muslim-majority countries, such as the UK, a different but related issue arises, because much of the meat on sale is *halal* but *not* labelled as such. So non-Muslims may be eating *halal* meat unawares, whether at home or in a restaurant. For many this is not a problem, but Sikhs are forbidden by their religion from eating *halal* meat, and some Christians want to avoid consuming food that has had an Islamic prayer offered over it. Others are concerned about the cruelty of Islamic slaughter if the animal is not stunned beforehand. Furthermore, even unlabelled *halal* meat will have been certified as *halal* by an appropriate Islamic organisation, and this certification must be paid for by the manufacturer, exporter or retailer. Of course, the cost is eventually passed on to the customer, meaning that shoppers are unknowingly funding Islamic organisations. In at least some cases the same organisations are active in propagating Islam worldwide. For example, the Federation of Islamic Associations of New Zealand claims to certify as *halal* over 90% of the meat exports from the country, and it has been at the forefront of financing the construction of mosques and Islamic centres across New Zealand. It has plans for Islamic schools, Islamic libraries and a resource and research centre in the future,[152] as well as "consistently supporting the needs of the Muslim community for Dawah activities through a regular contribution of annual Dawah grants to its affiliated Regional Associations".[153] Thus non-Muslims are funding Islamic *dawa*.

USE OF THE LAW

Muslim minorities persistently complain about "Islamophobia" and demand laws to protect Islam from criticism. The result is a speedy move towards silencing any negative comments about Islam or Muslims, no matter how factual the remarks may be. This accelerates the pace of Islamisation in all spheres, as non-Muslims dare not oppose it.

Laws protecting religions from incitement to hatred and violence have been passed in many non-Muslim-majority nations. While phrased in general terms as protecting all religions, the real driving force behind most of these laws are Muslim-minority communities, aided by Muslim states and Muslim international organisations (such as the OIC) that are seeking to give Islam a privileged and protected place in all societies, a position not granted to other religions. Islam, its source texts (for example, the Quran), sharia and Muhammad must all be protected from any criticism. This verges on the introduction of a "thought-crime" mentality into non-Muslim societies.

In 2001, the Australian state of Victoria passed into law a Racial and Religious Tolerance Act. This law prohibited citizens from engaging "in conduct that incites hatred against, serious contempt for, or revulsion or severe ridicule of" another person or group on the ground of their religious belief or activity. An exception written into the Act was conduct "engaged in reasonably and in good faith – in the course of any statement, publication, discussion or debate – for any genuine religious purpose". Nevertheless, in 2005 two Christian pastors were convicted under this law for making critical statements about Islam in a church seminar. Although the Supreme Court of Victoria subsequently allowed their appeal,[154] many Australian Christians fear the introduction of similar laws nationally, believing that Muslims will try to use them to stifle all criticism of Islam.

The OIC and its member states are putting pressure on the United Nations and its various bodies to pass resolutions along these lines, usually in the form of "religious defamation". These in effect tend to protect, strengthen and support Islamist terrorism and its sources of finance. Banning speech critical of radical Islam and Islamist terrorism is a step towards legitimising violence committed in the name of Islam.[155] The process began in 1999,[156] when the OIC asked Pakistan to bring before the UN Commission on Human Rights (now the UN Human Rights Council) a resolution called "Defamation of Religions".[157] It was an attempt to counter the view that "Islam is frequently and wrongly associated with human rights violations and with terrorism".[158] In the following years, many similar resolutions[159] were passed within the UN, all ostensibly concerned with the defamation of religions in general but specifically mentioning Islam (and only Islam).

However, in 2011 a significant change occurred in the wording. Instead of being concerned about the defamation of religions, the focus shifted to "derogatory stereotyping, negative profiling and stigmatization of persons based on their religion or belief".[160] In other words, it was no longer religions but people who were to be protected. Also, the 2011 resolution did not specifically mention Islam. These changes seem to indicate that other nations had begun to realise the agenda behind the OIC's concern with "religious defamation" and were keen to protect free speech. Indeed, the UN Human Rights Committee's General Comment No. 34 (paragraph 48) about freedoms of opinion and expression, issued 12 September 2011, not only banned the banning of religious defamation but also banned the favouring of one religion and/or its adherents over another.

> Prohibitions of displays of lack of respect for a religion or other belief system, including blasphemy laws, are incompatible with the Covenant [the International Covenant on Civil and Political Rights] except in the specific circumstances envisaged in article 20, paragraph 2, of the Covenant. Such prohibitions must also comply with the strict requirements of article 19, paragraph 3, as well as such articles as 2, 5, 17, 18 and 26. Thus, for instance, it would be impermissible for any such laws to discriminate in favour of or against one or certain religions or belief systems, or their adherents over another, or religious believers over non-believers. Nor would it be permissible for such prohibitions to be used to prevent or punish criticism of religious leaders or commentary on religious doctrine and tenets of faith.[161]

Since then, the defamation resolution has never been passed again.

Following the violent demonstrations against the West in many Muslim countries in September 2012, allegedly as a response to a video about Muhammad produced in the US, Islamic scholars insisted that the UN should draft an international convention criminalising insults against religion. The Grand Sheikh of Al-Azhar University, Egypt, Ahmed Al-Tayeb, also demanded that those involved in the production of the film should be "penalised for committing these heinous acts of abuse against the Prophet Mohamed (PBUH)".[162]

In non-Muslim-majority states, Islamic organisations pursue what could be called a "litigation jihad" against any person or organisation perceived to be critical in any way of Muslims or of Islam. One of the most active is the Council on American-Islamic Relations (CAIR), based in Washington DC.[163] Religious hate legislation is a bonus to such organisations, helping them intimidate those who write critically on subjects touching Islam, and thus stifling free speech. They are also skilfully manoeuvring within the court systems to use libel laws and human rights and equality legislation in order to silence any criticism of Islam. Large sums are set aside for hiring expert lawyers to sue critics in the courts and silence them.

The widespread use of this strategy is beginning to restrict public discussion of Islam, including the threat posed by Islamist terrorism. A shift has been taking place in many Western governments regarding the vocabulary and terminology used to describe the terrorist threat they face. Officials are advised to abandon the use of terms such as "Islamic terrorism" and "Islamist terrorism". The idea is that this vocabulary will anger and alienate Muslims, preventing them from happily integrating into Western societies, and will increase tensions with the wider Muslim world.[164]

A gradual process of self-censorship can be seen in American counterterrorism. The 9/11 Commission Report, issued in July 2004, used the word "Islam" 322 times, "Muslim" 145 times, "jihad" 126 times and "jihadist" 32 times. Five years later, however, the National Intelligence Strategy of the United States, issued in August 2009, used none of these terms. Similarly, the FBI Counterterrorism Analytical Lexicon published in 2008, the purpose of which is "to standardize the terms used in FBI analytical products dealing with counterterrorism", does not contain the words "Islam", "Muslim" or "jihad". In 2012, US General Martin Dempsey, Chairman of the Joint Chiefs of Staff, issued a memorandum to the Chiefs of the military services, the Commanders of the Combatant Commands and the Chief of the National Guard Bureau, requesting a second review of counter-terrorism (countering violent extremism) training materials and lecturers used by the Department of Defence. The memorandum expressed concern that nothing should be "disrespectful of the Islamic religion" and that there should be no particular focus on Islamic radicalism.[165] This was a response to complaints by Islamists that the training provided had an anti-Islam bias.[166] Effectively, it banned US Department of Defence lecturers from mentioning the concept of Islamic ideology. Clearly such a refusal even to discuss the causes of a large proportion of contemporary terrorism presents a real challenge to national security in non-Muslim-majority states.

Dr Taha Jabir al-Alwani, an Iraqi who emigrated to the US in 1985, has been described as "the father of the Islamic minority legal institutions". A founding member and President of the International Institute of Islamic Thought in Virginia, al-Alwani created the doctrine of Muslim Minority Jurisprudence (*Fiqh al-Aqaliyyat al-Muslimah*) and simultaneously emphasised that it was important for Muslim minorities to establish and run their own "identity institutions", such as mosques, schools and places to learn the Arabic language. He made clear how vital he thought a minority jurisprudence was, not only for the cause of *dawa*, but also to prevent Muslim minorities in the West from being assimilated by the majority:

> May what we mentioned help the brethren, who are presenting their message, in persuading for the settling-down of the religious call [*tawtin al-da'wa*] as a worldwide service to Islam, and the finality of the appearance of The Religion, and to protect the Islamic presence from deviating. The building of "Minority Jurisprudence" shall answer an urgent necessity and an immediate need. It is not a luxury of thought...[167]

One of the greatest triumphs of al-Alwani's doctrine of Muslim Minority Jurisprudence came in 2001, when he managed quietly to introduce the idea that the US government could not assume that Muslim soldiers in its army would automatically serve in a theatre of war where they would be fighting fellow-Muslims; such soldiers might have to get permission from foreign Muslim scholars before obeying American military orders. It is interesting to note that at one point he supervised the progamme for training US Army Muslim chaplains.[168]

By working to prevent Muslim minorities from being assimilated by the non-Muslim majority, al-Alwani was engaging in internal *dawa*. But when his doctrine affected the non-Muslim majority itself, for example by inducing them to allow American Muslim troops to disobey certain orders, he was engaged in external *dawa*.

MEDIA

We have already noted the effective use that *da'ees* and *dawa* organisations make of literature, radio, TV, satellite channels and the internet in trying to persuade individuals to convert to Islam. Indeed, as one *dawa* agency explains,

> The term 'Islamic media' is a modern term for Islamic *dawa* because it disseminates information . . . The purpose of Islamic media is to guide mankind to the Unity of Allah, the Qur'an, Sunnah, Hadith and Islamic history.[169]

Muslim scholars in Malaysia have argued that the communication system for *dawa* necessarily differs from one place to another according to differences in culture. In the contemporary world, the mass media offer the best means of *dawa,* as a sophisticated communication network already exists. The work of *dawa* should take full advantage of these new technologies and use them to disseminate the message of Islam.[170]

On the opposite side of the world, a Nigerian Muslim writer urged all Muslims working in media in his country to unite and organise and create a strategy for the most effective utilisation of the mass media for the propagation of Islam. Newspaper editors as well as radio and TV producers should use Islamic preachers who call people to Islam. Skilled Islamic scholars and professionals should advise on the best products for *dawa,* and these should be made available in Hausa, Yoruba and Igbo languages to reach many.[171]

In the Middle East, Sheikh Abdul Azeez ibn Abdullaah ibn Baaz argued that the most successful contemporary means for *dawa* is the modern mass media. Modern media such as radio, press, television and the internet should be used for *dawa* to present Islam to non-Muslims around the globe so they can comprehend its virtues and "realize that it is the only way to success in this life and the Hereafter". Muslim rulers are duty bound to support and participate in this effort so it can reach the whole world in all spoken languages, and for ordinary Muslims engagement in *dawa* is a personal duty.[172]

Following ibn Baaz, even the strictest Wahhabi scholars have legitimised the internet and launched personal websites. They have grasped the enormous potential of the internet in the fight for the minds of the younger generation and for spreading Islam. Jaafar Sheikh Idris, a Sudanese professor of theology, wrote in 1999 that new media technologies should be used by

Muslims to spread *dawa* more easily and are, indeed, proof that Islam is the true religion, as only God could have known 14 centuries ago that the day would come when the world would turn into one global village, needing one global prophet: Muhammad.[173]

But the media are also being used very effectively for furthering the Islamist cause in general. With massive oil-money funding, Islamists have come to dominate the main Arabic media channels: Aljazeera TV, funded by the Qatar royal family, and al-Arabiyya TV, funded by the Saudi royal family. While seemingly offering professional journalism, in their Arabic programmes especially they are airing Islamist viewpoints and supporting Islamist causes in Iraq, Egypt, Tunisia and Syria. Analysts supportive of the Muslim Brotherhood are often invited to comment, while other points of view are ignored. Their rhetoric and emphasis differ greatly depending on the language used; English-medium broadcasts may carry a very different message from Arabic-medium broadcasts.

Numerous programmes on other channels present a rosy and uncritical view of Islam for non-Muslim viewers, as do many films. Secular, Western media channels are also being used, perhaps unwittingly, for Islamic *dawa* efforts. Thus on 9 July 2013, which was the first day of Ramadan, the UK's Channel 4 television channel marked the beginning of the Muslim fasting month with a live broadcast of the Islamic call to prayer in the morning and then provided 20-second reminders before each of the other four set prayer times during the day so that viewers could go to the Channel 4 website and hear the call to prayer. On every subsequent day of Ramadan, the morning call to prayer was broadcast live. The aim, said Channel 4, was not only to remind Muslims to worship but also to make non-Muslim viewers "notice that this event is taking place".[174] Channel 4 does not give similar respectful and serious prominence to the festivals of other religions, so this is a clear example of the use of the mainstream media for Islamisation.

Prince Alwaleed Bin Talal of Saudi Arabia is building a news and entertainment media empire based in Bahrain. He holds major stakes in Twitter and News Corporation and has teamed up with Bloomberg on a 24-hour television news initiative for the Arab world.[175]

Many Muslims have embraced the internet as a medium in the service of Islam. Websites run by Muslim scholars and organisations now play an important role in promoting Islam. Some of these sites reserve significant space for reports on Christians who have converted to Islam. There is a huge diversity of narratives, with enough variation to allow many readers the opportunity to identify with one of the narratives. To the non-Muslim audience, these serve as a celebration of different aspects of Islam's superiority over Christianity, while explaining that any difficulties faced during the process of conversion are easily overcome. Another role the narratives play is to reassure Muslims that Islam is the true religion and educate them in tactics of persuasion for converting non-Muslims to Islam.[176] The internet appears to be more effective than print media or DVDs in promoting conversions. There are websites offering basic introductions to Islam, information for non-Muslims who wish to convert, news celebrating Islam as the world's fastest growing religion and guides instructing Muslims in the West on how to bring others to Islam. Such guidelines are at times detailed and have the ring of marketing expertise.[177]

The MWL has given great attention to modern media and how to use them in propagating Islam. To that end, it is striving to develop networking among the media institutions and authorities around the Muslim world. It has also set up the International Islamic Organisation for Media, which aims at developing media modules directed towards Muslims and non-Muslims, modernising the discourse of Islamic media with the aim of "rectifying the image of Islam in the minds of non-Muslims".[178]

At its Second International Conference on Islamic Media, held in Jakarta, Indonesia, in December 2011, the MWL discussed the development of communications for *dawa* strategies. It decided to establish a permanent Secretariat-General for Islamic Media based in Mecca, with a duty to cooperate and liaise between Muslim media people throughout the world. The Secretariat would arrange conferences and meetings aimed at upgrading Islamic media. It also decided to create the International Muslim Media Supreme Council, with the mission of implementing overall Islamic media policies around the world and discussing the idea of creating an Islamic Media Fund.[179]

Organisations and charities using media for *dawa* have sprung up all over the West. Islam Channel, for example, is a television channel based in London that seeks to offer a quality media alternative for Muslim, to present Islamic perspectives and values to a non-Muslim audience and, amongst other goals, "to remove the misconceptions people have about Islam".[180]

Another London-based charity, "The Dawah Project" aims to "utilise Media: the most powerful tool in the 21st Century to spread the message of Islam on an International scale". Founded in 2007, it specialises in radio broadcasts to Africa.[181]

In the USA, the Islamic Media Foundation (IMF) and its broadcasting arm, Islamic Broadcasting Network (IBN), was set up in Sterling, Virginia, as a national non-profit *dawa* organisation. Its main mission is to "share the guidance of Allah with mankind, through broadcast media and the Internet, to enjoin what is right and condemn what is wrong, and to provide the North American Muslim community with Islamic programming that will cater to their needs". IBN programming aims to promote and clarify Islam for all people in North America and the West and covers religious and contemporary issues including youth issues, family matters, legal advice, health tips, community affairs, world news and national news. It offers Islamic perspectives on political matters and current affairs as well as information on the Quran.[182]

IMF urges its Muslim supporters to utilise the open door offered by media for *dawa* in America:

> Let's all take advantage of the unique opportunity we have in America, using the broadcast media and the Internet to fulfil our duty of inviting others, to better understand Islam and spread righteousness. First and foremost, we need your du'aa, or supplication, that Allah bless this effort and give it success. Give from your wealth, knowing that Allah will multiply it for you. And give from your time and advice to make this work fruitful.[183]

LANGUAGE

Languages usually spread as the political influence of their speakers expands. One of the main reasons why English is so widely spoken today is the world-embracing spread of the British Empire as well as of British colonists. The rise of Arabic to the status of a major world language in the Middle Ages was linked to the rise of Islam as a major world religion and its spread across many regions. Within a hundred years of the death of Muhammad in 632, Arabic had become the official language of a world empire, the boundaries of which stretched from Spain and North Africa in the West to India and the Chinese borders of Central Asia in the East.[184] The success of this early Islamisation strategy is evident today in the widespread use of Arabic as the primary language in the Middle East and North Africa. The political and cultural domination of a people by another culture and religion is also revealed in the infiltration of their language by that of the people who dominate them. Over the centuries a great number of Arabic loan words have entered Persian, Turkish and other languages of nations that were Islamised in the early centuries of Islam.

The increased use of Arabic/Islamic words and phrases in contemporary English is an indication of the rising influence of Islamic religion and culture in the English-speaking West. Furthermore, the OIC is actively seeking to impact Western languages in its ongoing efforts to prevent criticism of Islam. After the United Nations thwarted the OIC in 2011 by passing a resolution protecting people rather than religions

the OIC had some very creative interpretations of the language embodied in the new resolution. By its manipulation of words such as intolerance and incitement, giving new meanings to what many thought was plain English, the OIC made it clear that it had not dropped its ultimate goal of protecting Islam from "defamation."[185]

Muslim-Majority Contexts

The Turks were mainly Islamised as they migrated from Central Asia through Persian-speaking regions before finally settling in Anatolia (also known as Asia Minor, the territory of modern Turkey) from the 11th century onwards. During this process, the Turkish language gained both Persian and Arabic loan words. Ottoman Turkish used in the 19th century included a very large number of borrowed Arabic and Persian words and was written in the Arabic script.[186]

In the 20th century, secular reformers and especially Kemal Atatürk launched a project aimed at purifying Turkish from Arabic-Islamic domination. Atatürk ordered that modern Turkish should be written in the Latin script and that a very large number of Arabic and Persian words should be purged from it (1928-1934). Some 7,000 Arabic and Persian words were duly banned and replaced.[187] By exchanging the Arabic alphabet for the Latin alphabet, he cut a major link with Turkey's Islamic heritage and culture and consciously moved Turkey towards the West.[188]

However, the emergence of a popular Islamist political movement in the 1990s has resulted in the reintroduction of many Islamic terms into spoken Turkish. It will be interesting to see whether the Islamist party now in power in Turkey (the AKP) will take the opportunity to re-Islamise the Turkish language in a deliberate way.

Persian (Farsi) likewise was "colonised" by Arabic/Islamic vocabulary following the Muslim conquest of Sassanid Persia (633-651). In his effort to purify Persian in the 1930s, Reza Shah retained the Arabic script but purged Farsi of many Arabic loan words. The 1979 Islamic Revolution in Iran has reversed many of these reforms and reimposed the Islamic/Arabic vocabulary on Farsi.

The Kurdish national movement has been involved in a similar purification effort. It is estimated that Sorani (one of the two main Kurdish dialects) had some 46% loan words in the 1920s-1930s (mainly from Arabic and Persian), of which only some 4.4% had survived by the 1960s.[189]

The Contemporary English-speaking West

While it is natural that English-speaking Muslim populations will bring many Islamic/Arabic terms into their English usage, it is more difficult to understand why such words are increasingly being used in English in the Western media and in Western academic and political discourse. The most likely reason is a well-intentioned desire to be multiculturally sensitive and respectful to Islam, but terms are often used without fully understanding their meanings and implications.

English-speakers now know words such as "sharia", "jihad", "*hijab*", "*halal*" and "*madrasa*" almost as well as "Quran". For Islamists, it is very encouraging that Islamic religious terms are becoming part of the daily vocabulary of Westerners, as this will make it easier for the Westerners to convert to Islam. It is part of their *dawa* strategy to get non-Muslims to think in Muslim categories. Westerners are even beginning to use Muslim Arabic versions of Biblical names such as Ibrahim for Abraham, Mariam for Mary and Daoud for David. Many English-speakers are going out of their way to pronounce Arabic words such as "Allah" in what they think is the authentic Arabic/Muslim way, with the emphasis on the second syllable. All this is equivalent to pronouncing "Paris" as "Paree" in an English sentence so as not to hurt the feelings of the French.

It has become common for journalists and others to refer to the founder of Islam as "Prophet Muhammad", rather than simply "Muhammad". Sometimes the prayer "Peace be upon him" is added, in the normal Muslim way. Referring to Muhammad in this way implies that the writer or speaker accepts the status of Muhammad as a genuine prophet; some would argue that anyone who accepts Muhammad as a true prophet is a Muslim.

The Quilliam Foundation Report

A 2010 report by the Muslim-led Quilliam Foundation in Britain high-lighted the deleterious effect of using Muslim vocabulary in English, on the grounds that it inadvertently strengthens the narratives and arguments of Islamism.[190] The Quilliam report serves to illustrate the importance of language when discussing matters relating to Islam and to Muslims. It highlights the importance of avoiding inaccurate terms that endorse and strengthen extremist Muslim narratives.

It offers five examples and provides alternative terms that better convey the intended meaning. One of the examples concerns the phrases "Islamic world" and "Muslim world", which, the report says, reinforce the unhelpful and inaccurate suggestion that Muslims form a homogenous bloc united by a single political and religious outlook. The problem is that such phrases "can be manipulated by Islamists to support their belief that 'the Muslim world' constitutes a monolithic religious bloc with a shared political agenda – and that it should consequently be united into a single supra-national state." Alternative phrases that are recommended are "Muslim communities world-wide", "Muslim-majority countries" or "Muslims around the world".

The Church, Islam and Language

Many church leaders and missionaries are now using extreme contextualised approaches to Islam and Muslims. Part of this contextualisation involves using Islamic vocabulary for Christian entities, for example, calling a church of converts from Islam a *jamaat* (the Arabic word for a group or assembly, used in the names of many Islamic organisations) instead of a *kanisa* (the normal Arabic word for a Christian church).

The prominent American evangelical pastor and author Rick Warren, when praying at President Obama's inauguration in January 2009, used the Islamic term "Isa" for Jesus. No doubt he meant to be politely inclusive for the benefit of his multi-religious audience. But by using this term he failed to express the Christian belief that Jesus is Saviour. (The Biblical name Jesus means "Saviour" and was given to him specifically because "he will save his people from their sins", as recorded in Matthew 1:21.) The Quranic name Isa has no known meaning and refers to a person who resembles the Biblical Jesus in some ways but crucially did not die on the cross or rise again and is not God.[191]

— 7 —

Islamisation in Muslim-Minority Contexts

In the Islamic cultural tradition, the protection of Islam and its honour is the supreme guiding principle, and therefore respect for individual rights and the right to critique other people's beliefs are not accepted as the norm in the way that they are in liberal, secular states. Societies based on tolerant values are therefore vulnerable to attack from Islamic organisations that use a society's very tolerance to promote Islamist intolerance.

For many non-Muslim-majority states, contemporary Islam poses a challenge unlike any other seen for many centuries. Indigenous or long-established Muslim minorities and new immigrant Muslim communities alike are being radicalised and taught to demand self-governing autonomy under sharia or even outright separatism. In the West and in several other non-Muslim-majority contexts, massive Muslim immigration in recent decades is creating a range of challenges over the way in which the Muslim communities may develop in the future and how state institutions appear to be yielding to the process of Islamisation.

Politically correct multiculturalism now threatens to dissolve the glue that has been binding society together in Western states. Such multiculturalism tends to belittle the majority's traditions and norms, especially those based on Christianity. At the same time it respects all other cultures and relativises their values, so that none can be criticised. "Islamophobia" is now presented as the great sin of non-Muslim-majority societies; this ties the hands of those who may wish to critique and limit certain negative aspects of Islam. This development has some very practical implications. Western welfare agencies and police fear being labelled Islamophobic if they interfere to help women who are suffering violence or other forms of abuse within a Muslim family or community. According to a 2008 report by the Centre for Social Cohesion in Britain, there exist informal networks that seek to protect what they perceive as the honour of the Muslim community by tracking down and punishing women who are seen as having brought shame on their family and community. The report cites cases in which women who were fleeing domestic violence or forced marriages have been betrayed and forcibly returned to their families by Muslim police officers, Muslim councillors and Muslim civil servants.[192]

Zaki Badawi, a significant leader of British Islam,* was generally considered a moderate, yet he stated that Islam finds it difficult to function as a minority, and that it has an inherent drive for expansion that is not limited to spiritual matters but includes politics, society and law:

> A proselytising religion cannot stand still. It can either expand or contract. Islam endeavours to expand in Britain… Islam is a universal religion. It aims at bringing its message to all corners of the earth. It hopes that one day the whole of humanity will be one Muslim community, the 'Umma. As we know the history of Islam as a faith is also the history of a state and a community of believers living by Divine law. The Muslims, jurists and theologians, have always expounded Islam as both Government and a faith. This reflects the historical fact that Muslims, from the start, lived under their own law. Muslim theologians naturally produced a theology with this in view – it is a theology of the majority. Being a minority was not seriously considered or even contemplated… Muslim theology offers, up the present, no systematic formulation of the status of being in a minority.[193]

These are the theological reasons why Muslims tend to struggle if they need to take on minority status in a majority non-Muslim society. More than other minority communities, they constantly, whether consciously or

---

* Dr Zaki Badawi (1922-2006) was accepted by many as the unofficial leader, representative and advocate of Britain's mainline Muslims. He was an Islamic scholar, Islamic theologian and expert in Islamic law, a teacher and a community activist. He was president of the Muslim College in London and was awarded an OBE in recognition of his contribution to race relations.

subconsciously, strive to redress the balance and assume an expanding and dominant position in their host countries.

Islamisers have a programme for infiltrating non-Muslim societies and their power centres. They were quick to recognise the potential usefulness of the Muslim migrants who were settling in the West. As early as 1973-74 the MWL surveyed Muslim minority populations in Europe and the Americas "in order to identify the type of missionary activities it ought to support".[194] Professor M. Ali Kettani (Ali ibn al-Muntasir al-Kattani) was commissioned to produce a report for the MWL.[195]

The contemporary Islamisation strategy calls on Muslims in non-Muslim-majority states to organise themselves with the aim of establishing viable Muslim communities that will engage in a process of step-by-step Islamisation of their non-Muslim societies. Muslim-minority communities are urged to develop a separate Muslim identity, linked to the global *umma*, presenting a unified front to the outside world and gradually establishing autonomous spheres while Islamising the majority community.[196] Every Muslim enclave becomes a potential base for further expansion of Muslim rule in the struggle to unite all Muslim enclaves everywhere.[197]

At all costs, argue the Islamisers, Muslims must avoid being assimilated by the majority. In order to resist assimilation, they must group themselves geographically, forming areas of high Muslim concentration within the population as a whole. Yet they must also interact with non-Muslims so as to share the message of Islam with them. The ultimate goal of this strategy is that the Muslims should become a majority and the entire nation be governed according to Islam. Complete success will have been achieved when Muslim minorities are transformed from weak minority communities to become the majority community that dominates the entire host society in all spheres.[198]

The preferred approach for the Islamisation of non-Muslim-majority states is the introduction of Islamic concepts and practices gradually and subtly into the spheres of politics, economics, law or culture, through an unending stream of small demands for more rights, special privileges and exceptions.[199] Islamisers are never content with what has been achieved but use every opportunity to ask for more. In Britain, the then Bishop of Rochester, Michael Nazir-Ali, complained that in dealing with some Muslims "there can never be sufficient appeasement and new demands will continue to be made".[200]

Islamisers teach that it is the duty of every individual Muslim living within a non-Islamic political entity to be involved in the Islamisation effort; it is not allowed for anyone simply to live as a "good Muslim" without assisting the overall Islamisation strategy. The Muslim minority community must establish its autonomous institutions, including mosques, community centres and Islamic schools (with or without help from Muslim-majority states) and lobby the host state to grant the Muslims recognition as a separate religious community under sharia, a status that the Islamisers see as a step towards gaining political rights and finally political domination. This practical template for the step-by-step Islamisation of non-Muslim societies was set out at a seminar about Muslim communities in non-Muslim-majority states held in London in 1978, organised by the Islamic Council of Europe and sponsored by the OIC.[201]

> Once the community is well organized, its leaders should strive to seek recognition of Muslims as a religious community having its own characteristics by the authorities. Once recognized the community should continue to request the same rights the other religious communities enjoy in the country. Eventually, the community may seek to gain political rights as a constituent community of the nation. Once these rights are obtained then the community should seek to generalize its characteristics to the entire nation.[202]

The diagrams opposite illustrate the staged Islamisation process advocated by the London seminar.

The transformation of non-Muslim societies follows a clear strategy that, as a first step, emphasises the importance of the creation of an Islamic consciousness in the population. Like communists, Islamisers stress the importance of a total shift in the consciousness of the masses and of all of society. For example, wearing the *hijab* is one way in which the presence of Islam can be made very visible. This is followed by the establishment of numerous Islamic institutions that can engage with the political and social structures of the state, influence them and change them. When sufficient power has been accumulated, the threat of violence (jihad) and its actual use will be applied if necessary to gain full control of society and state, resulting in a new Islamic state under sharia.

As a result of these efforts, several non-Muslim-majority states are gradually being transformed into societies in which Islam takes its place, not just as an equal alongside the many other faith communities, but often as the dominant player. This is not primarily a matter of numbers, but is more a matter of control of the structures of society. As Tarik Ramadan, the Swiss

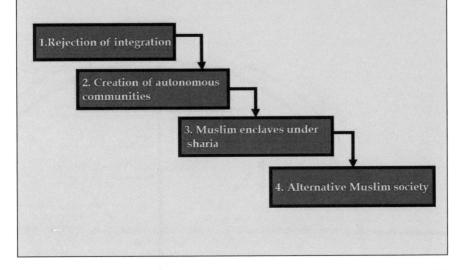

Strategy for creating a parallel Muslim society in a Muslim-minority context

1. Rejection of integration

2. Creation of autonomous communities

3. Muslim enclaves under sharia

4. Alternative Muslim society

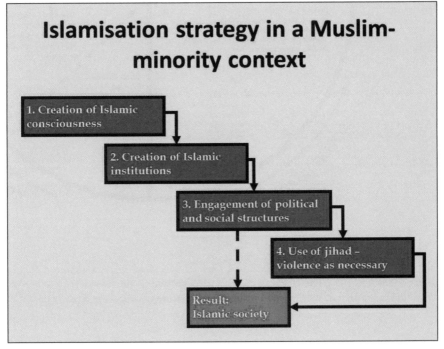

Islamisation strategy in a Muslim-minority context

1. Creation of Islamic consciousness

2. Creation of Islamic institutions

3. Engagement of political and social structures

4. Use of jihad – violence as necessary

Result: Islamic society

Eight types of threat from radical Islam

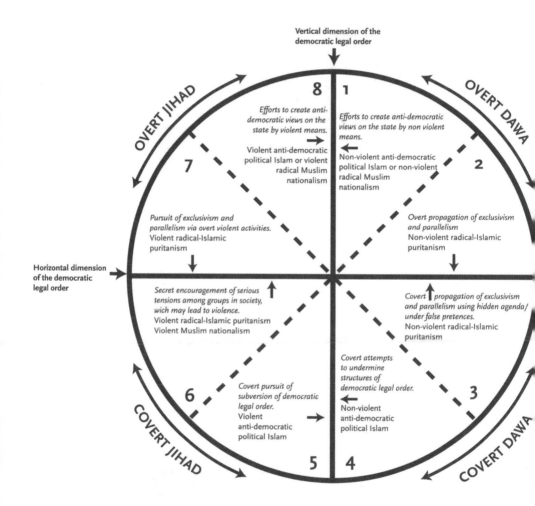

Ministry of the Interior and Kingdom Relations, *From dawa to jihad: The various threats from radical Islam to the democratic legal order*, The Hague: General Intelligence and Security Service, December 2004, p.36. Used by kind permission of the General Intelligence and Security Service, the Netherlands.

Islamist academic, has said, "Even though the Muslim Diaspora is a genuine minority in number, it is a majority by the principles for which it calls."[203]

THE ISLAMISATION OF KNOWLEDGE

The idea of the Islamisation of knowledge was proposed in the late 1970s and early 1980s by a number of Islamist scholars, including Ismail Raji al-Faruqi. It involves the transformation of every academic discipline in the light of Islam, and the integration of all human knowledge into one Islamic system based on the Quran, *sunna* and Islamic civilisation.

The scholars held that the conflict between Islam and the West was not merely historical and political but also metaphysical and spiritual. They argued that in the West, all branches of knowledge are controlled and directed by ideas and concepts that are opposed to the spirit of Islam. Western knowledge is based on secular presuppositions such as human reason, anthropocentrism, materialism, doubt, and disregard of God's existence and revelation. Therefore Western knowledge is in deep crisis. For example, Western natural sciences – bound as they are to secular Western culture – are opposed to nature, twisted and tortured in the name of progress. Islam, however, does not encourage confrontation between humankind and nature; rather, it teaches humans to be natural and work in harmony with nature. Similarly, Western social sciences demand that humans should not believe in any predetermined code or permanent moral values for society, but accept the principle that human nature and society are continually changing. Islam, however, teaches that moral values do not change.[204]

The proponents of the Islamisation of knowledge project also argued that the postmodern, secular, Western intellectual enterprise has run aground because of moral relativism and permissiveness and excessive individualism. As Mona Abul-Fadl explains:

> Having renounced God, Western man rendered himself impotent in the face of the problems of knowledge and power. The "death of God" theology brought with it, together with the inevitable darkness of the human soul, an imminent blankness in the human mind resulting in a sense of loss of meaning and direction.[205]

The West is thus ripe for an Islamic transformation and Islam is the "vital civilizing agent and a force of renewal and regeneration" that the West needs.[206]

In contrast to the Western, secularist, human-centred worldview (seen by Islamists as polytheistic), Islamisers offer a theocratic universe, centred on Allah's sovereign rule and his perfect divine revelation in Quran and *sunna*, with humans in a position of submission to him. Islamisers of knowledge believe that Allah's revelation in the Islamic sacred scriptures is the only basis of all truth, knowledge and morality.

Part of the necessary total submission (Islam) to Allah's rule, not just in personal life but in all political and social areas, they say, is the Islamisation of all human knowledge to bring it back under the unitary rule of Allah. In the universe and in nature, as in human society and human religion, there can be only one law. Thus all systems of knowledge must be based on Allah's revelation.

So, for example, it is possible to create an Islamic science, which would be subordinated to the claims of Islamic tradition and morality and would help to strengthen and revive Islam. Islam is an all-encompassing ideology, and therefore it must formulate its own ideas about an Islamic science in the light of early Islamic history, which is seen as sacred and normative.

Tawhid (divine unity) – the core doctrine of Islam – is seen as the central principle of the universe and of human society and knowledge. It is *tawhid*, say the supporters of the Islamisation of knowledge project, that will integrate and unite the diverse and fragmented branches of human knowledge and restore their harmony within the overarching unity of Islam.[207] The basic principle is: One God, One Faith, One Law, One Knowledge.

Tawhid allows no dichotomies and no fragmentation. Despite what reality may seem like to the modern secular observer, *tawhid* states that the universe is a unified, harmonious whole, in which Allah's rule is imposed on nature, knowledge and society. Humankind's responsibility is to recognise and accept this model of reality and to move with its flow.[208] A culture, state and society based on *tawhid* will mirror the divine unity and harmony. According to the Islamists, the fragmentation seen in Western secular knowledge is the result of rejecting the *tawhidic* model. This rejection is in turn due to a polytheistic and idolatrous worldview that sees creation as full of many equal but opposed forces.[209] But the core values of Islamic culture give it the capacity to accommodate the diversity of the fragmented world within an overarching unity based on *tawhid* and the divine revelation in the Quran and *sunna*.[210]

In 1981 Ismail al-Faruqi, Anwar Ibrahim and others co-founded the IIIT as an Islamic think-tank. It was established with an endowment of 25 million dollars provided by a number of Saudi businessmen and has developed a global following. Located in Herndon, Virginia, USA, it hosts scholars from throughout the Islamic world to make the proposed "Islamisation of knowledge" a reality. Economics, sociology, anthropology, psychology, political science: all must be recast within the Islamic framework, based on *tawhid*, Quran and *hadith*. The specific relevance of Islam to each subject of modern knowledge must be established. This project soon caught the attention of whole Muslim world. Pakistani President Zia ul-Haq placed the newly established Islamic University in Islamabad at al-Faruqi's disposal. The IIIT opened branches in a number of cities across the globe and recruited young Muslim scholars to work on the project. [211]

In 1982 al-Faruqi published his analysis, *Islamization of Knowledge: General Principles and Workplan,* which remains the primary source for the project. In this work, al-Faruqi claimed that Muslims were victims of injustice and aggression in the modern world. They had been massacred, robbed, tricked, exploited and forcibly converted. They had been colonised, secularised, Westernised and de-Islamised by internal and external agents of the West. They were stereotyped as violent, lawless, fanatical terrorists. [212] To remedy this situation al-Faruqi suggested twelve steps towards the Islamisation of knowledge. These included mastery of modern academic disciplines by Muslim scholars, mastery of the Islamic legacy, critical assessment of modern disciplines in the light of the Islamic legacy, and a creative synthesis that would establish Islam as world leader in every sphere of human life.[213]

Ten years later, Mona Abul-Fadl, who wrote several books about the Islamisation of knowledge project,[214] argued very similarly that a programme to achieve the goal of Islamic cultural dominance should involve a two-fold process: first, a reassessment of the Islamic cultural and intellectual heritage, to learn how Islamic societies in the past responded to the challenges of their times, and, second, a critical reassessment of Western culture, to discern its strengths and weaknesses and create methods of transforming it within an Islamic framework.[215] Thus the "Western Thought Project" was developed as a part of the Islamisation of knowledge project.[216]

The Islamisation of knowledge project includes the funding of academic chairs and the encouraging and funding of Muslim academics to take up lecturing posts in universities of non-Muslim-majority states so as influence students and the teaching of academic subjects using Islamist concepts. It also includes a massive publication programme and the establishment of Islamic universities, research institutions and think-tanks, particularly in the

West, which are used to disseminate Islamic views on the integration of all human knowledge into an Islamic system. For example, the Islamic University In Uganda was established "to ensure that Islamic culture is promoted in all courses taught in the university".[217] Some of these institutions are linked to Islamist movements while presenting a moderate face to the public. They develop links to Western academia and liberal Christian institutions that tend to cooperate with them because of their academic credentials, ignoring their hidden agendas.

Those engaged in the Islamisation of knowledge are also trying to influence school and university curricula and to have input into the process of rewriting textbooks used for religious education, history and other branches of academic study. Students, scholars and intellectuals are introduced to the great "Islamic legacy" and supposedly scientific Islamic knowledge and sciences. A version of Islam is presented that ignores its more violent aspects and the historical atrocities committed in its name. The guidelines offered are also silent about the inferior position of women and non-Muslims in Islamic societies as required by sharia. Saudi funding of Western universities, particularly in America, has had an adverse effect on the teaching of Middle Eastern studies, as the integrity of departments has been compromised and their willingness to portray a truthful picture of Islam undermined. (See pages 83–85.)

Dr Abul-Fadl held that the fate of civilisation lies in the balance of culture, not power. She believed that transforming culture should be the goal of Islamisation, for it is culture that in the long run determines the power relations between societies and states. In other words, it is necessary to take steps to transform the prevailing Western culture in order to enable Islam to take the West's dominant position in the world. The Muslim world, she said, has a cultural identity and heritage that qualify it for world leadership, but it needs to work actively to "revive its culture, recover its *tawhidi* ontology, and rediscover and activate its episteme".[218] Islam must critique the Western intellectual culture, recover its own cultural autonomy and aim at rebalancing the cultural relations between the Muslim world and the West. A revolution in the self-consciousness and identity of Muslims will revitalise Islam and help Islam to transform Western culture and knowledge into its own image.[219]

What is the contribution Muslims can bring to this critique, and what are the grounds for assuming both the nature of this contribution and its inevitability? The fact that Muslims are heirs to a Civilization of the Book as well as repositories of Divine Scripture provides the cornerstone to this assumption. Historically, Islamic Civilization was inspired by the kind of knowledge that grew out of the Book to foster its matrix of humanist learning and scientific inquiry.[220]

She saw the project of Islamising Western culture and civilisation as part of the great overall project of Islamising knowledge. Rather than make a direct bid for political power, Muslims must first Islamise knowledge in what she calls "the new *da'wah*", a process that gives priority to cultural reconstruction in Islamic terms. She saw knowledge as opening the way not only to power but also to "virtue and wisdom". [221] She was encouraged by a new openness that she saw in the modern/postmodern West as it re-thinks its heritage and considers what other cultures and traditions have to offer.[222]

Abul-Fadl's diagrams in her 1992 book *Where East Meets West: Appropriating the Islamic Encounter for a Spiritual-Cultural Revival* explain some of the principles of the project and its implementation (see pages 78–80). The first diagram expresses the initial Islamisation of knowledge drive and the graded steps that were proposed. The second diagram is a revised, critical version of it, stressing the complexity of the process. The third diagram places the Islamisation project in the context of an Islamic intellectual revival and shows the impact of the project on the renewal of the Islamic *umma* and the reform of its social and cultural institutions. The fourth diagram focuses on the Islamisation project's more immediate objectives and goals.[223]

POLITICAL CORRECTNESS AND SANITISING ISLAM

Any religion seeking to win converts and extend its influence on society naturally wishes to present itself in an attractive light. But in their efforts to present Islam to the non-Muslim-majority world, contemporary Islamists have developed a large-scale project of sanitising and rewriting texts dealing with Islam, especially texts that are likely to be read by non-Muslims. Much of Islamic history has already been sanitised in the newer Western textbooks, so that unpleasant features, such as violence, are ignored. Critics are discredited as Islamophobes and Orientalists. It appears that older books that provide a less attractive view of Islam are being sought out and removed from public access. An example is the disappearance from second-hand bookshops of literature on the Armenian genocide of the late 19th and early 20th

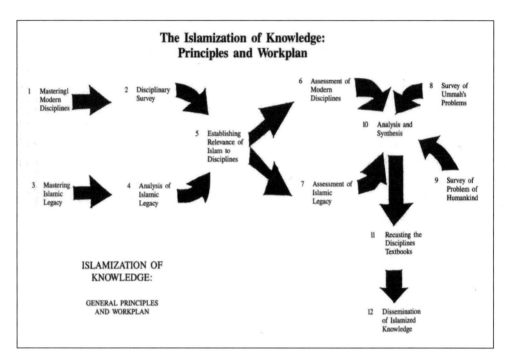

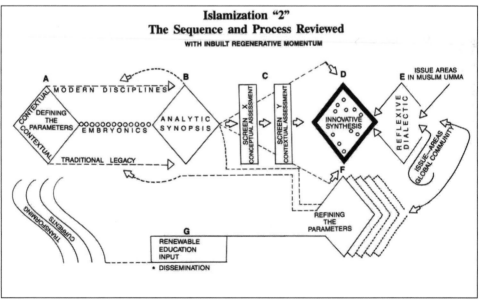

Source: Mona Abul-Fadl, *Where East Meets West*, pp. 54, 58.

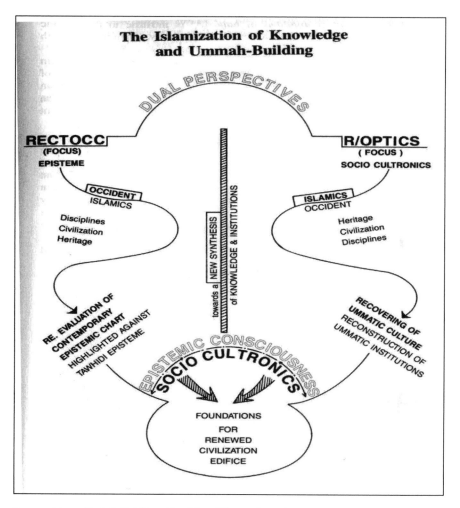

Source: Mona Abul-Fadl, *Where East Meets West*, p. 61.

Reviewing the Cultural Topography of the Occident: Aims and Objectives

While figure 3 sought to place the Western Thought Project in the wider context of an Islamic intellectual revival, figure 4 below closes in on its more immediate objectives and aims.

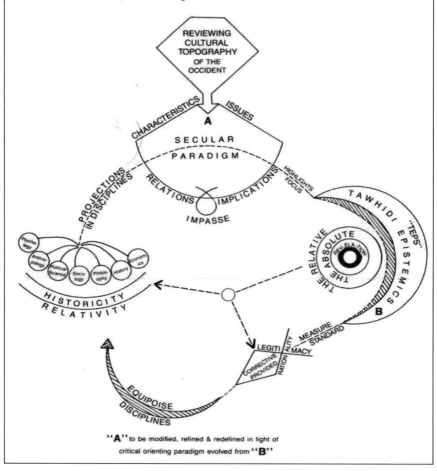

"**A**" to be modified, refined & redefined in light of
critical orienting paradigm evolved from "**B**"

Source: Mona Abul-Fadl, *Where East Meets West*, p. 66.

century.* The academic world is being seriously affected. At the simplest level, some academic libraries in the UK have discovered that relevant pages (i.e. those critical of Islam) have been torn out of books. At the other end of the scale, some Islamists aspire to control the choice of books on Islam kept in British schools and public libraries.[224] A 2003 report on American textbooks for schools and universities cites jihad as an example of a concept that is "defanged or oversimplified" in the texts, while Islam is presented as a timeless religion of peace, and its incessant wars of expansion over many centuries are simply ignored. Alternatively, violent episodes in Islamic history are attributed to a few marginalised, heretical groups and presented as nothing to do with true Islam.[225]

Education authorities often dare not refuse to use such books for fear of being accused of prejudice and Islamophobia. Likewise, Western academics and education authorities, not to mention Western media and politicians, have largely been intimidated by this discourse. Because so many fear to be labelled as prejudiced, illiberal, reactionary or Islamophobic and are perhaps also burdened with post-colonial guilt, there are few who care to point out what is happening.

EDUCATIONAL SYSTEMS

Islamists aim to control educational systems and institutions at all levels, from primary to tertiary. For example, the Muslim Council of Britain (MCB) requested the following in state-run primary schools in the UK:[226]

- Major changes to school uniform policies to accommodate Islamic clothing requirements such as *hijab*[227] and *jilbab*[228]
- Prayer rooms laid out according to strict specifications and permission for children to leave school premises for extended periods of time to perform Friday midday prayers
- Alternatives to certain sports activities, such as mixed-gender contact sports, and exemption of Muslim pupils from dance, drama and other expressive arts, with provision of alternative activities
- Islamic worship in schools where there are Muslim pupils, and the right for Muslim pupils not to attend non-Islamic religious worship

---

* The Muslim Ottomans were responsible for the deaths of around 1.5 million Armenian and Assyrian Christians.

- Major changes to provision of Sex and Relationship Education (SRE) according to Islamic beliefs, or exemption of Muslim pupils from attendance in the event of non-compliance

These guidelines seek to create the impression of a unified Muslim stand on issues such as the *hijab*, uniform, gender segregation and attitudes to sports and to the arts. In fact, there is a wide diversity of opinion within the British Muslim community on these issues, and some were critical of the MCB document. The British Muslims for Secular Democracy (BMSD) organisation stressed that it should not be seen as representing the majority of Muslims.[229]

Similar demands are now widespread in various other non-Muslim-majority states, and many of them have been accepted by authorities. In some other places, individual educational institutions have been captured by the mobilising of local Muslims.

One particular high school in South Africa had about 1,000 students, most of them Christian. Students met before assembly for Christian prayer and worship. A banner flew over the school entrance, dealaring that the school and the students followed Christ. The governing body was made up of parents and local people, and its Christian chairperson had been in place for more than a decade. At the annual election for the post of chairperson, most parents expected that this individual would be voted in again as usual, and so very few parents attended the meeting. But a few minutes before the vote, over 60 Muslims arrived at the meeting. Because they outnumbered the Christian parents, they were able to vote in a Muslim chairperson. A week later, all Christian prayer and worship was banned. All Christian banners, notices and literature were removed. Within the first month, the Christian head teacher had been replaced by a Muslim, and by the end of the first year, almost all the Christian teachers had been replaced. Within two years of the election of the Muslim chairperson, the majority of students were Muslims. Local Muslim groups had attempted the same at more than 15 other schools in the area, most of which were Christian schools.[230]

In the UK, claims began to surface in 2013-14 of the growing influence of radical Islam in supposedly secular state-funded schools. The allegations include the takeover of governing bodies by Islamists, harassment of non-Muslim heads, bullying of female staff and the segregation of boys and girls in lessons. The first case highlighted was in Derby, but other claims related to Birmingham, Bradford and Manchester, with an alleged Islamist action plan for the latter three set out in a document entitled "Operation Trojan Horse", which came to light in March 2014. In response, a special programme of inspection was instituted by the government in order to identify schools where "religious conservatism [was] getting in the way of learning and a balanced curriculum and enabling children to make their way in a multi-cultural society".[231]

Radical Muslims at Universities[232]

While Western universities used to be hotbeds of Marxist and anarchist radicalism in the 1950s and 1960s, in recent decades they have become centres of Islamist radicalism. In Britain, for example, a number of Islamist terrorists have had links to British universities.[233] A 2005 report by the Social Affairs Unit highlighted the scope of radical Islamist activities on university campuses, revealing that many young Muslims within the British higher education system have imbibed terrorist ideas and some have gone on to perform terrorist acts in the UK and abroad. Two of the 7 July 2005 London bombers had studied at British universities and colleges of higher education. Mohammed Siddique Khan, who detonated the Edgware Road bomb, and Shehzad Tanweer, the Aldgate bomber, had studied at Dewsbury College and then at Leeds Metropolitan University.[234]

Islamic student societies in colleges and universities in many non-Muslim-majority countries tend to be dominated by Islamists. Their activities radicalise Muslim students, encourage separation and isolation from the secular staff and the non-Muslim students and encourage female Muslim students to wear the *hijab,* the *jilbab* and even the *niqab.*[235] Many of the students join Salafi groups and start Salafi mosques.[236] Others join established Islamist movements linked to the Muslim Brotherhood or the Jamaat-i-Islami. A few join the more radical groups such as Hizb ut-Tahrir, and some end up in the violent jihadi groups.

Academic Centres of Islamic and Middle Eastern Studies

A growing proportion of senior staff positions in Western academic departments of Islamic and Middle Eastern studies are now being filled by lecturers from Muslim-majority countries, while much of the funding of such departments now comes from Arab countries with oil wealth. Increasingly, attitudes and curricula are shaped by the perceived wishes of the main funders rather than by purely academic factors.

In 1992 the noted Muslim academic Professor Akbar Ahmed warned of this process at the universities of Oxford and Cambridge and elsewhere, claiming that these institutions were representing the views of their respective financial backers, and thus "assume a surrogate position for the larger political confrontation in the Muslim world".[237] In a 2002 report on the state of British academic Middle Eastern studies, Professor Anoush Ehteshami, Director of Durham University's Institute for Middle Eastern and Islamic Studies, stated that funding from Muslim sources always has strings attached.[238]

In April 2009, the Centre for Social Cohesion published a study on foreign funding of strategically important subjects in British universities. The report found that the largest amount of foreign funding to British universities came from Arab and Islamic sources. Between 1995 and 2008, eight universities, including Oxford and Cambridge, had accepted a combined sum of more than £233.5 million from Muslim rulers or those closely connected to them. By 2011, such sources of external funding were not just the largest, but the largest "by quite a long way". The study found evidence that this funding has led to unofficial censorship of aspects of Islam in UK universities, as university staff sometimes appear reluctant to criticise donors publicly and strive instead to conform to the donor's opinions. There is clear evidence that, at some universities, the choice of teaching materials, the subject areas, the degrees offered, the recruitment of staff, the composition of advisory boards and even the selection of students are now subject to influence from financial donors.[239]

These processes are replicated in Europe, the US and many other countries. According to figures from the US Department of Education for the period 1996-2012, Middle Eastern countries accounted for 23.4% of all foreign gifts and contracts to American universities, having given $1.26 billion. The top four recipients were Georgetown University ($294 million), Carnegie Mellon University, Harvard University and California Institute of Technology. The top four donors were Qatar ($603 million), Saudi Arabia, the United Arab Emirates and Kuwait.[240]

However, it is likely that the figure given for Saudi Arabia ($340 million) is a considerable underestimate and that many universities have not reported, for example, contracts with the King Abdullah University of Science and Technology,[241] which alone contributed more than $200 million between 2009 and February 2013.[242] Bearing in mind that Campus Watch estimated at least $322 million in gifts and contracts from the Gulf between 1995 and

May 2008,[243] a figure of over $500 million therefore seems more realistic for Saudi Arabia. Figures for the other Middle Eastern countries can possibly be extrapolated in the same way, because donations or contracts made directly to or with professors or researchers need not be reported and neither need any individual donation of less than $250,000.

A notable individual Saudi donor is Prince Alwaleed Bin Talal, who gave Harvard and Georgetown Universities $20 million each in 2005 to be spent on centres for Islamic Studies.[244] He also endowed similar centres at the American University in Cairo, the American University in Beirut, the University of Cambridge and the University of Edinburgh.[245]

INDIVIDUALS IN POSITIONS OF POWER AND INFLUENCE

In many non-Muslim-majority states, Islamists are gradually gaining influential positions of authority in various spheres of society. This process could increase exponentially in contexts where it is easy for those in power to appoint their fellow-Muslims to high positions. Once they are in a position to make things happen, the Islamists can accelerate the process of Islamisation.

In the West, a number of Islamists have been appointed as special advisors on Islam to senior politicians and thus can potentially exert great influence on the course of events. In certain sub-Saharan African countries, Islamists have been very successful in gaining political office themselves, by mobilising the Muslim community to vote them into any post from mayor to president. Many African countries also have disproportionately high numbers of Muslims in senior positions in the judiciary, education and other spheres as well as in politics.

In Kenya, which is around 15-20% Muslim, General Mohamed Mohamood was appointed Chief of the General Staff because he was credited with saving President Moi by quelling an attempted military coup in 1982. Once he had become head of the army, he built mosques in every military institution in the country from barracks to army camps and promoted many Muslims to high rank. In other spheres, many Kenyan Muslims have been appointed to key positions because they are seen as neutral in the conflicts between the major (Christian) tribes. For example, a Muslim was appointed to chair the Independent Electoral and Boundary Commission.

In Uganda (85% Christian) there are a disproportionate number of Muslim Members of Parliament, many of whom serve on strategic committees.

The Muslim MPs form an organised bloc, which they call the Uganda Muslim Parliamentary Caucus, and use their combined voice to protest if the government does not appoint plenty of Muslims to senior posts; they also organise the Muslim community to protest. For example, when in 2014 President Museveni named six new judges, none of whom was a Muslim, the Muslim community submitted a petition to the Parliamentary Appointments Committee seeking to block their appointment on the basis that all of the new judges were Christians.[246] The Uganda Muslim Supreme Council is active on such issues, and typically the Mufti of Uganda will appeal to the president, who will generally yield. Two key Ugandan positions held by Muslims in January 2014 were the Chairman of the Electoral Commission and the Chairman of the Uganda National Examination Board of the Ministry of Education and Sport. The latter has made Christian Religious Education a hard subject to pass, but Islamic Religious Education very easy, so many Christian school-children are opting to study Islam instead of their own faith.

Tanzania

Detailed research[247] was conducted in 2013 on Tanzania, a country that is approximately 60% Christian and 36% Muslim overall.[248] But it includes the archipelago of Zanzibar, which is about 98% Muslim, with a strongly Islamic history and culture.

In 2013 the President of Tanzania (who was also Commander-in-Chief of the armed forces), the Vice-President of Tanzania and the President of Zanzibar were all Muslims, although the Prime Minister was a Christian.

A list of all the judges showed that the majority were Christians, but, significantly, the Chief Justice of the Court of Appeal was a Muslim, as was the next judge below him in rank, who was "responsible to direct all the judges on their case rulings". The Principal Judge of the High Court, described as being responsible for day-to-day running of affairs and daily decisions, was also a Muslim.

The government-funded University of Dodoma (on the mainland), which is supposed to cater for the whole population, had a Muslim majority amongst its students and Muslims in the top four administrative positions.

There was also a phenomenon known as "the Islamisation of the army". This had begun in response to requests from Zanzibar that its people should have an equal opportunity to serve in the army. Zanzibar has about 3% of the total population of Tanzania,[249] but in response to the complaints a policy was put in place that 50% of all future recruits to the army should come from Zanzibar and 50% from the mainland. As Zanzibar is almost completely Muslim, almost all its army recruits would be Muslim. But about a third of those recruited from the mainland would probably be Muslim too, in proportion to the Muslim population of the mainland. Clearly, if this policy is maintained year on year, the army will soon become predominantly Muslim. (The Defence Minister at the time of establishing this policy was a Muslim from Zanzibar.)

Another area of great concern to non-Muslims in Tanzania in 2013 was the Constitutional Review Commission, which had been appointed to gauge public opinion on the content of a proposed new constitution. The Commission comprised twelve Christians and 22 Muslims, and 34% of its suggestions related to the implementation of sharia.

Ivory Coast

After gaining power in 2011 through a turbulent electoral process during which thousands of people were killed, President Alassane Ouattara undertook a programme of "ethnic affirmation". This turned out to mean the placing of Northerners in key positions in the civil service, judiciary and army. Northerners in Ivory Coast are 99% Muslim, and many of them are immigrants from other West African nations such as Mali and Burkina Faso. They represent about 40% of the entire population. Christianity is the dominant religion amongst indigenous Ivorians.[250] The Christians who previously occupied these key posts were dismissed or demoted.

After the implementation of this programme, the army Chief of Staff and his deputy are Muslims, and most military units are commanded by Muslims, including special forces; the navy, police and customs are headed by Muslims; the Chief Justice of the Supreme Court is a Muslim, as are most of the judges presiding in most of the courts across the country. The Electoral Commission is headed by a Muslim Southerner.

ECONOMIC POWER

In relatively impoverished non-Muslim-majority countries, such as many in sub-Saharan Africa, Islamic investment is taking place on a massive scale. Muslim businessmen are buying property, land, shops and other businesses, while Muslim-majority countries and Islamic groups are buying vast amounts of crop-growing land across Africa, apparently in preparation for a global food crisis. They are also developing trade routes in Africa, so that many railways, waterways and ports are now in Muslim hands.

Research conducted in 14 regions of Tanzania in 2013 found at least 1,768 Muslim-owned roadside petrol stations, each with its own mosque and employing only Muslims. At the Muslim prayer times, all the staff were required to stop work and go to pray. The 4,325 workers included 457 converts from Christianity. Christians were either converting or changing their names to Muslim names in order to get jobs.[251]

Islamisation through economic power can also take the form of economic aid from government to government. A Ugandan academic explains that

> the economic aid Uganda receives from Islamic countries like Libya and Saudi Arabia is regarded by these donor countries as the most valuable form of jihad, and its purpose is largely to further the frontiers of Islam.[252]

Many of the smaller and poorer Caribbean nations are reluctantly accepting economic aid from Muslim-majority nations, as Western countries are not supporting them sufficiently. It is in the hope of economic advantages that some small non-Muslim-majority countries have joined the OIC, effectively self-defining themselves as Islamic.

One example is Suriname in South America, a country that was only 14% Muslim when it joined the OIC in 1996. Two years later, its neighbour Guyana also joined, although the Guyanese population was only 8% Muslim at the time.[253] The governments of these countries saw membership of the OIC as a golden opportunity for economic development and did not appear to understand the OIC's strategic agenda or why the OIC was so keen for them to join that it even waived the normal membership fees. Since joining, both countries have been required to make many changes, all of which benefit the Muslim minority only. Suriname has granted Muslims many special privileges in the workplace in terms of time off for Friday midday prayers and Muslim holy days and special privileges during the Islamic fasting month, Ramadan, such as a lighter workload and more time off. Guyana has changed its marriage laws so that Muslim couples must have their wedding ceremony performed by a Muslim. A judge in Guyana has controversially allowed a female Muslim witness to give evidence in court with her face covered,[254] setting a precedent for others. The governments must promote a greater understanding of Islam, for example through inter-religious dialogue (now an annual fixture in the Guyanese government's calendar), and must support Islamic schools, Islamic banks and other Islamic organisations and institutions. Any OIC financial support seems to be directed only at Muslim organisations and efforts to promote sharia.

MOSQUE BUILDING

The pivotal 1975 conference of the MWL highlighted the importance of mosques as the focal point of *dawa*.[255] In compliance with a resolution of this "Message of the Mosque" conference, the World Supreme Council of Mosques was set up.[256]

In some non-Muslim-majority countries, early Muslim immigrants started with simple prayer rooms, often in private houses and makeshift buildings that served as "safe havens" for the worshippers and a place to express their communal identity.[257] Later, many mosques were established in factories and warehouses. There was then a shift in the function and significance of mosques; from being simple prayer rooms, they became fully fledged mosques, centres of networks of migrant organisations and communities, and many were beautiful, purpose-built constructions.[258]

Some observers estimate that the UK, Germany and France now have at least 2,000 mosques each.[259] Hundreds more are in the building or planning stages. This change is replicated across the world in many non-Muslim states, with new mosques often situated on airport roads or in other very conspicuous locations. The proposed "mega-mosque" in Newham, London, would – if allowed to be built – have been seen by the many thousands of visitors arriving from all over the world for the 2012 London Olympics, effectively communicating to them the dominance of Islam in London.[260] In sub-Saharan Africa, mosques are being built at intervals of a few kilometres along the main roads and railways. In a purely Christian area of Burundi, there are dozens of new mosques built within sight of each other along one particular stretch of road. A traveller in Malawi (20% Muslim) drove 480 km and passed 145 mosques on the way, averaging one mosque every 3.3 km. There appears to be a plan to build mosques at 5 km intervals along a railway from Zambia through to Mozambique. African Christians also notice that mosques are often built next to churches, Christian schools and Christian businesses. The proliferation of mosque-building in non-Muslim-majority states is one sign of the growing confidence of Muslim communities. It also symbolises the permanence of Islam in these countries. Their large size and impressive architecture add weight to this message.[261]

Muslims often claim that the new mosques are needed to accommodate the ever-growing number of Muslims living in non-Muslim-majority countries, especially the West.[262] Where this claim is patently untrue, they may make the more revealing comment: "Build a hive, and the bees will come." In other words, build a mosque and the people will come. This remark has been heard in Kenya and Burundi, for example, and clearly indicates the important part that mosque-building plays in *dawa* and Islamisation. It has been a very successful *dawa* method in Tanzania, where many roadside mosques were built, starting from around 1990, in areas where there was no Muslim community, for example, on the road from Morogoro to Dodoma and the road from Morogoro to Iringa. By 2013, many of these empty mosques had developed large congregations of local people who had left Christian denominations and converted to Islam.[263]

In some parts of Africa, where impoverished Christian communities may worship in very small and shabby church buildings, the sheer size and beauty of a mosque building can be an incentive to follow Islam rather than Christianity. A Ugandan Christian, living in an area of the country which he estimated as 85% Muslim and 15% Christian, wrote in 2009:

> It is quite often noted that the Moslems tend to Challenge the Christians and look down on their faith, dilapidated church structures and some other basic aspects of Christians… Mosques have been planted close to one another in every village in Yumbe District as the Moslems are well aided by their development partners in Middle East.[264]

A spate of plans and requests to build grandiose mosques across the non-Muslim-majority world is generating controversy and inter-communal tensions. From the non-Muslim perspective, the problem is not with modest, normal-sized mosques that meet the needs of local Muslim congregations, but with the disproportionately large structures that seem primarily aimed at making a public statement. A very controversial proposed mosque in Cologne, Germany, would have a minaret 55 metres high, according to the plans.[265]

The need for Muslim places of worship could be met by smaller, less eye-catching buildings that do not aim at dominating the local cityscapes. Often dwarfing nearby Christian cathedrals and churches, the magnificent and imposing design of many such mosques hints at a plan to dominate visible public space and attest to the superiority of Islam. This is in line with sharia, which specifies that non-Muslim places of worship must never be higher than nearby mosques (something which causes problems today for Christians in Egypt and Malaysia, for example).

Mosques also play a very practical role in the process of *dawa* and Islamisation in that they provide facilities and resources for all kinds of activities, going way beyond the religious to include the political and more. Some have even been used to store weapons.[266]

Islam teaches that there is a special blessing in living within sound of the five times daily call to prayer from the minaret of a mosque. Even if the call to prayer is not actually allowed to take place in a particular country, Muslims still feel it is good to live close to a mosque. Thus areas of almost 100% Muslim residents develop in Western cities, and these can develop into no-go areas for non-Muslims.[267]

INTERRELIGIOUS DIALOGUE WITH CHRISTIANS

Islamists often engage in interreligious dialogue as a way to promote Islam.[268] Hasan al-Turabi, the noted Sudanese Islamist politician, formerly leader of the National Islamic Front, has said specifically that interreligious dialogue belongs to the duties of the Islamic *dawa*.[269] Ahmed Deedat (1918-2005), the South African Muslim famed for his participation in many Christian-Muslim debates, justified dialogue only as a part of *dawa*.[270] The Islamist aim in dialogue is to weaken and divide Christian churches[271] and hinder Christian mission to Muslims.

By contrast, Church leaders generally engage in Christian-Muslim dialogue with the aim of promoting harmonious relations between the two religions. Both sides, for their different reasons, tend to avoid any areas that could be uncomfortable for the Muslim participants, for example, the persecution of Christian minorities in Muslim-majority contexts. So the result is generally the compromise of Christian truths and acceptance of Islamic claims.

One of the most significant of these dialogues was the 2007 Muslim "Common Word" statement and the Christian "Yale statement" issued in response.

In November 2007 some evangelical Christian theologians at Yale University's Center for Faith and Culture published a letter, signed by over 300 evangelical and other Christian leaders, which has come to be known as "The Yale Statement".[272] Written in response to an October 2007 Muslim open letter called "A Common Word Between Us and You", the Christian "Yale Statement" uses language in a manner that comes close to accepting Islam as a legitimate way to God, Muhammad as a prophet of God and the Quran as a revelation from God. None of the writers or signatories of the Yale Statement would actually agree with these three beliefs, but they have inadvertently given the impression that they do.

The Muslim scholars in their open letter respectfully call Muhammad "the Prophet Muhammad", adding the compulsory PBUH (Peace be upon him) after every mention of his name, and placing him immediately after God in the opening invocation. The Christian scholars on the other hand, marginalise the person of Jesus. Rather than calling him, for example, "our Lord and Saviour Jesus Christ", they merely refer to him as "Jesus Christ" as the Muslim scholars had done, as though he were a mere human being with no special status for Christians. "Christ" is a title given to Jesus in the Quran as well as in the Bible, so the Christian scholars chose to add no distinctively Christian affirmations when they mentioned Jesus. They did not refer to his deity and lordship; they did not exalt his person and rank. They thus unwittingly confirmed the Muslim and Quranic view of the superiority of Muhammad over Jesus.

A similar problem arose when the Muslim and Christian scholars referred to their respective scriptures. The Muslim scholars respectfully wrote of "the Holy Qur'an". The Christian scholars, on the other hand, simply referred to "the New Testament" rather than to "the Holy Bible".

The Yale Statement also uses the term "Prophet" to designate Muhammad. As we have already seen, this signifies some measure of acceptance that he was a true prophet of God, despite that fact that he denied all the key elements of Christian doctrine. A better term would have been "Muhammad the prophet of Islam" or "Muhammad the founder of Islam" or something similar.

Many more such dialogues take place at the denominational level, the local level and amongst Christian NGOs such as the Institute for Global Engagement (IGE), and the International Center for Religion and Diplomacy (ICRD). Of equal concern are those taking shape in Christian seminaries such as Hartford and Fuller and amongst mission agencies.

Well-funded Christian-Muslim dialogues are happening at the very highest political levels, some of them financed by Western government institutions. British Foreign Office funding has gone into conferences, consultations and Christian organisations with the aim of promoting peaceful coexistence between Islam and Christianity. Stand for Peace, a Jewish-Muslim counter-extremism organisation, has warned of the way in which taxpayer-funded interreligious dialogue initiatives in the UK have been infiltrated and exploited by extreme Islamist groups and are in effect providing them with a platform.[273]

In 2009 the US Department of State appointed its first ever Special Representative to Muslim Communities, whose task was "engagement with Muslims around the world on a people-to-people and organizational level".[274] The White House Office of Faith-Based and Neighborhood Initiatives, started by President Bush and expanded under President Obama, now fosters "inter-faith dialogue" around the world. A special Task Force dealing with "the role of faith-based and community organizations in interreligious dialogue and cooperation" was also instituted.[275] Determined attempts have been made to engage with Muslims in order to improve America's image in the Muslim world.[276] This process was to be based on defining common interests and initiating a new partnership based on mutual respect and mutual interest.[277]

In 2004 the World Economic Forum established the "West-Islamic World Dialogue (C100)".

CREATION OF *DHIMMI* CONSCIOUSNESS

According to sharia, a person's status and legal rights depend on which religion s/he follows. There are three categories: Muslims, People of the Book (primarily Jews and Christians), and others. Only free, male Muslims of mature age are seen as persons with full legal capacity, full citizens enjoying all rights and liberties offered by the Islamic state. People of the Book are despised but tolerated, i.e. allowed to live in the Islamic state and follow their non-Muslim faiths. Those who are neither Muslims nor People of the Book can, according to classical Islam, be killed.

People of the Book were considered to have made an agreement with the Islamic state in which they submitted to Muslim rule, acknowledged their lowly status, paid the *jizya* poll tax and received protection (*dhimma*) in return. The protected Jews and Christians were known as *dhimmi*.

Dhimmi status is based on two important concepts. The first is that Muslims are far superior to any other religious group:

Ye are the best of peoples, evolved for mankind enjoining what is right, forbidding what is wrong, and believing in God. (Q 3:110)

The second is that Christians and Jews who had not accepted Islam should be conquered, humiliated and subjected to the payment of *jizya*, (which was not payable by Muslims):

> Fight those who believe not in God … (even if they are) of the People of the Book, until they pay the *Jizya* with willing submission, and feel themselves subdued. (Q 9:29)

Numerous petty laws restricted and humiliated the early *dhimmi* in their daily lives, all reinforcing the fact that they were inferior to Muslims. For example, they were not allowed to ride horses (as Muslims did) but only mules and donkeys.[278]

> An infidel subject of our Sovereign may not ride a horse; but a donkey or a mule is permitted him, … He must go to the side of the road to let a Moslem pass. He must not be treated as a person of importance, nor given the first place at a gathering.[279]

Dhimmi were excluded from public office and were not equal with Muslims before the law. When the various schools of sharia were created in the 8th and 9th centuries, these rules were included. The *dhimma* condition became the formal expression of legalised discrimination and oppression against Jewish and Christian minorities living under Islam.

However, the "agreement" between the *dhimmi* and the Islamic state held only as long as the *dhimmi* kept all the rules, behaved meekly, treated Muslims with respect and did not bear arms. If they failed in any of these areas, they were no longer protected, and a jihad could be launched against them. "If non-Muslim subjects of the Islamic state refuse to conform to the rules of Islam, or to pay the non-Muslim poll tax, then their agreement with the state has been violated."[280] Anything that their Muslim rulers thought was a sign of arrogance and any requests to improve their status could be interpreted as breaking the *dhimmi* agremeent, and thus making them liable to violent jihad.

With the rise of secular nationalism in the 19th century, it seemed that the traditional distinctions between Muslims and non-Muslims would fade away as the concept of the equality of all citizens gained ground. Although personal status laws based on sharia persisted, discrimination did lessen in the early to middle 20th century. Following independence from colonial rule, some Muslim-majority states introduced modern, Western, secular constitutions that gave equality to all citizens regardless of religion. These however enraged traditional and radical Muslims who saw them as breaking the sharia rules about *dhimmi*. With the waning influence of secular nationalism since the 1970s, and the growing dominance of Islamism as a political ideology, the condition of non-Muslim minorities has deteriorated. The Islamic resurgence is dedicated to restoring the original dominant-subordinate relationship between Muslims and non-Muslims.[281] There have been calls for the reinstatement of sharia regulations about *dhimmis*.

Yusuf al-Qaradawi, for example, argues that non-Muslim minorities in a Muslim-majority state must accept the Allah-given right of the Muslim majority to be ruled by sharia, including the application of the *dhimmi* legislation to non-Muslims. If the non-Muslim minority insists on equal rights and freedoms, says Al-Qaradawi, it is actually imposing a dictatorship of the minority on the majority, which is totally unacceptable.[282]

Non-Muslim efforts to resist such demands for *dhimmi* rules are interpreted by some Islamists as a declaration of war against Islam. Violent jihad can then logically be applied, say the Islamists, to subjugate these minorities who do not know their Allah-appointed place under the Islamic umbrella and will not willingly submit to Islamic domination.

There have been many reports from the more rural areas of Egypt that Christians are being unofficially forced to pay *jizya*. In Dalga village, Minya province, where the Muslim Brotherhood had taken control after the ousting of President Morsi in July 2013, a church leader reported that all the Christians were being charged *jizya* at a daily rate varying from 200 Egyptian pounds (£20, US$30) per day to 500 Egyptian pounds (£45, US$70) per day. This was said to safeguard them from violence or vandalism against their homes and shops. For many of the Christian villagers, the sums demanded were unaffordable. In some cases those who could not pay were attacked and their wives and children beaten or kidnapped. In the village of Sahel Selim, Assuit province, two Christian men were shot dead on 12 September 2013 after refusing to pay *jizya* of 10,000 Egyptian pounds (£900, US$1,400). Knowing the danger they were in, they had asked for police protection, but it was refused.[283] This sequence of events follows exactly the classical Islamic teaching that a *dhimmi* who refuses to pay *jizya* is no longer protected by the Islamic state.

The Psychology of *Dhimmis*

Living for many centuries in a dominant Muslim society, *dhimmi* communities could not help but be affected by the Muslim majority's attitudes and way of life. In the Middle East, most non-Muslims became Arab in language and culture and Islamised in their social life and popular ethics.[284] Some even became so assimilated that they were able to play a role in the social, administrative, literary and other realms of Islamic civilisation.[285]

However, one result of generations of degradation and humiliation, repeatedly reinforced in the minutiae of ordinary life, has been a particular *dhimmi* mentality, the main points of which are vulnerability, gratitude and self-abasement. The vulnerability arises in particular from the ban on weapons and the ban on testifying against a Muslim in a sharia court. Even self-defence is forbidden, and *dhimmis* can only beg for mercy or offer money to their attackers to leave them alone. This vulnerability reinforces the Islamic message that *dhimmis* are fortunate to have any protection at all and creates a pathetic gratitude towards their Muslim oppressors for such small rights and freedoms as they do have. The constant degradation of a *dhimmi's* daily life generates a response on their part of humiliation, fear and servility towards Muslims, which has often shocked Western travellers to Muslim-majority countries. *Dhimmis* came to view themselves as Muslims view them, i.e. as contemptible and weak.

The *dhimmi* mentality tends to result in apathy and an acceptance of the *status quo*. Most *dhimmis* are unwilling even to consider attempting to improve their situation. They just want to keep a low profile and stay out of trouble. It is typical of *dhimmis* not to protest if a Christian cross is burned by an angry crowd, nor even to feel that anything outrageous has occurred. *Dhimmis* often express anger if Muslims are criticised and strive to prove that they are loyal citizens of the Muslim-majority state, and they sometimes even embrace the most radical forms of Muslim causes. The historian Bat Ye'or has popularised the term *dhimmitude* to describe this type of behaviour.[286]

Dhimmi Psychology in the West

In the West, the majority society strives to affirm Muslims and to avoid giving any accidental offence. This kind of reaction by non-Muslims, even though they are the majority, can be seen as the typical behaviour of *dhimmi*, who, in order to survive the long centuries of persecution, learned to be submissive and to consider the dominance of Muslims as normal. While some in the West behave like this because they believe in multiculturalism and a postmodern political correctness, many others appear simply afraid of provoking Muslim rage and violence.[287] This fear expresses a clear *dhimmi* attitude that blames the victims for provoking the attacks and yields to the traditional Muslim threat of violence in return for any perceived insult to Islam or hindrance to its dominant place in society.

Example of Dhimmi Psychology: Kazenga P. Tibenderana in Uganda[288]

Uganda is a Christian-majority state with a growing Muslim population now estimated at 15%. Tibenderana is a prominent Ugandan academic described as being from a Christian background.[289] In his book *Islamic Fundamentalism: The Quest for the Rights of Muslims in Uganda*,[290] he seeks to justify Muslim claims for special treatment, saying that they have been victimised and oppressed by the Ugandan government and the Christian majority. He describes Islam in Islamist terms and suggests a long list of Muslim rights.

Tibenderana recommends that the secular Ugandan authorities should refer drafts of proposed legislation to the Uganda Muslim Supreme Council (UMSC) for scrutiny to check whether these are compatible with sharia. He also recommends that the government should not enact laws that contravene sharia and that the Ministry of Justice and Constitutional Affairs should establish a Department of Sharia Affairs to advise the government on the compatibility of national laws with sharia.[291] He argues that "sharia will always remain valid, whether or not it is recognized by the state. Hence a law which openly contravenes the sharia is not likely to command legitimacy among the Muslim population. And, as such, it will be openly flouted by those who regard it as illegitimate." Tibenderana seems to be ignorant of traditional sharia concepts such as *darura* (necessity) and *maslaha* (public good), which were developed to enable Muslims to live in lands governed by non-Muslims.

Tibenderana acknowledges the fact that countries such as Iran, Sudan and Saudi Arabia are helping to radicalise Ugandan Muslims, but he sees this process as justified and inevitable. His solution for the rising extremism among Muslims is to give in to many of their demands, such as for the rights to have Muslim political parties, to implement family sharia for Muslims and to grant Muslims prominent positions in government.

He recommends that: Ugandan government educational institutions should not schedule lessons on Friday between noon and 2.00 pm so as to enable Muslim students to attend Friday prayers; the government should grant Muslim employees an extended lunch break on Friday for the same purpose; the government should actively encourage employers and educational institutes to provide places of worship for Muslims on their premises; the government should actively and financially support the teaching of Arabic and Islamic studies in secondary schools and universities and these should be made compulsory for Muslim students. He calls for more resources to be put into Islamic universities and for new Islamic institutions to be created. Finally, he recommends that the government should enable the introduction of Islamic banks and finance in Uganda to ensure that *zakat* funds (the compulsory alms that Muslims must give for Islamic causes) "are not subjected to non-Islamic financial rules and obligations".

This wholesale yielding to Islamist claims of rights and superiority is typical of the *dhimmi* mentality. The main goal is to avoid trouble with Muslims, and any price to be paid in terms of national sovereignty and human rights and equality is considered worth it.

— 8 —

Islamisation in Muslim-Majority Contexts

The full Islamisation of Muslim-majority states, including the destabilising of secular regimes and their replacement with an Islamic state based on sharia, is the goal of all involved in the contemporary Islamic resurgence. Some seek to further this goal by legitimate use of democratic means, while others engage in violence to hurry the process along. Iran, Sudan, Algeria and Egypt are but a few examples of countries in which democracy and/or violence have been used.

While most modern Muslim states have ratified international agreements on human rights, they often change the whole meaning of what they have signed up to by adding that the agreements must be subject to the authority of sharia. (This practice resembles the way in which the Cairo Declaration on Human Rights in Islam has two final Articles that put sharia in a position to overrule any or all of the other Articles; see page 48.) Human rights and equality of all before the law are thus interpreted in the light of sharia, which inherently discriminates on the basis of both religion and gender. Many Muslims defend this stance by claiming that Western human rights notions are based on a radically secular worldview and that human rights must be applied in culture-specific ways, respecting the deep religiosity of the Muslim world.[292]

In societies dominated by Islam, sharia plays a large part in determining personal identity and social status according to religious criteria. Sharia is deeply embedded in the consciousness of most Muslims, regardless of its legal status in the constitution of the country where they live.

Many Muslim-majority states had secular constitutions when they became independent in the mid-20th century but have engaged in a gradual process of Islamisation since. Most have declared Islam to be their state religion, and many have declared sharia to be the primary source of their legislative system. There is usually a dichotomy between the two totally different legal systems – the Western, secular one and Islamic sharia – and most states have a mixture of the two with different weightings given to each element in different states. While most states with a mixed legal system and a written constitution guarantee freedom of religion and equality of treatment to all citizens, including those belonging to religious minorities, in practice the authorities often give Muslims more rights than non-Muslims[293] and males more rights than females. Similarly, a Muslim who leaves Islam is severely punished (on some pretext if the law does not actually forbid apostasy from Islam), but a non-Muslim who converts to Islam faces no difficulties. The Civil Codes of several states, including Algeria, Syria and Kuwait, allow the use of religious *fatwa*s based on sharia.[294]

Islamists are careful and deliberate strategists and know how to benefit from the major social changes affecting many Muslim-majority societies.[295] They and their sympathisers have developed programmes for Islamising the world in stages in order to create an environment where Islam can flourish. They have a well-planned and well-funded programme of infiltrating Muslim-majority communities and states and replacing those of their leaders whom they consider have not fully implemented sharia.

Islamists also try to purify Islam from any hint of syncretism, attempting to replace local "contaminated" versions of Islam with an authentic universal Islam based on the source texts. A good example is seen in Indonesia, where Islamist movements are promoting a strict, Arab Islam instead of the flexible and tolerant, traditional Indonesian Islam.[296] The fruit of the Islamists' work in Indonesia can be seen in deteriorating community relations, growing intolerance and disharmony and escalating anti-Christian violence.

In contemporary Muslim-majority states Islamists are becoming increasingly dominant in public discourse and in the awareness of the general population. They are allying themselves with traditionalists and setting severe limits to any attempts at liberal reform. Islamisers present sharia as a perfect solution to all problems faced by Muslim societies. As a political movement, Islamism has adapted well to changing political and social contexts in

Muslim-majority states, adopting a multitude of strategies, ranging from infiltration and agitation to violent action. Islamisers have challenged the state by dictating Islamic norms to the public and presenting their radical concepts as the only authentic Islamic position. To protect its legitimacy in the eyes of the general public, the non-Islamist government must then prove it is more Islamic than the Islamists, a competition it cannot win. But in the process of trying to do so, many small changes are made by the government, moving the country in the direction of following Islam more closely.[297]

Gradualist Islamisers realise that their goal is not to be achieved through an immediate, forcible takeover of the state but through social activism and engagement. In many countries, for example, Egypt, they have rivalled the state in providing social services, mobilising local resources and responding to vital needs and emergencies in the name of Islam. They have been simultaneously active in monitoring gender relations in public, enforcing Islamic dress codes or other restrictive sharia rules.[298]

As a result of Islamising activism, most Muslim nations have seen an increased Islamisation of their constitutions in recent years. Where, some decades ago, Saudi Arabia was the only Muslim state implementing sharia in a substantial way, today Sudan and Pakistan have implemented sharia to varying degrees along with twelve states in Northern Nigeria. In Malaysia, two states have declared sharia as their law. Aceh, in the far west of Indonesia, began enforcing a series of local laws based on sharia from 2001 onwards.

In many other countries around the world radical Islamists are engaged in violent struggles to establish Islamic states with traditional sharia as their constitution. Following the "Arab Spring" of 2011, Islamist parties gained power temporarily in both Egypt and Tunisia, and made efforts (more actively in Egypt than in Tunisia) to Islamise the constitutions and legal systems of these countries.

In the early centuries of Islam, many non-Muslims, driven by the daily frustrations and humiliation of life as *dhimmi*, converted to Islam. However, although conversion to Islam was made temptingly easy, others clung to their Jewish or Christian faiths, enduring second-rate *dhimmi* status. As a result, there are today historic, indigenous, non-Muslim minorities in many Muslim-majority countries. There are also Christian minorities who are the descendants of Western missionary efforts, especially in the 19th century. Recent decades have also seen new converts from Islam to Christianity in every Muslim-majority state, but in especially large numbers in Iran and Algeria. Pakistan and Bangladesh have substantial, historic, Hindu minorities. Saudi Arabia, some of the Gulf states, Libya and other countries also have large populations of expatriate Christians, particularly from Africa and Asia, who live and work in the Arab states for many years.

These non-Muslim minorities are currently being increasingly discriminated against, marginalised and often brutalised. In many Muslim-majority states, Christianity, Judaism, Hinduism and other religions are constantly mocked, criticised and defamed in mosques and in the media. Yet any criticism by non-Muslims of discriminatory legislation based on sharia is classified as an attack on Islam and leads to loud protests, threats and, all too often, violence against non-Muslims.

Some are yielding to the relentless pressure and converting to Islam. Others are trying to blend in and pass as Muslims. For example, in Zanzibar, where schools are strongly Islamic and girls who do not wear the *hijab* are caned, it is reported that "sometimes Christians pretend to be Muslims and with Muslim names to avoid embarrassment and being failed in their final exams!"[299]

At this time, it looks as if sharia will be increasingly implemented in Muslim-majority states, with devastating effects on relations with non-Muslims as well as negative effects on Muslims, who will find it even harder to adapt to the realities of the modern world.

ISLAMISATION FROM BELOW

Many Islamists realise that they cannot capture the state by force, and therefore they attempt to subvert it by infiltration. In Muslim-majority states this subversion involves active attempts by Islamists to change the conscious-ness of the masses by direct involvement at all levels of society. Societal and cultural transformation are seen as paving the way for political change. Islamists establish themselves in government, professional and civil society institutions at all levels while also creating their own organisations. A grass-roots movement is developed that includes the poorest as well as the middle classes. The aim is to change the society of the country from the bottom up. This strategy often allows Islamists to gain a considerable amount of power without the need for any violence. The capture of civil society is a powerful agent of Islamisation and can be the prelude to the capture of the state itself, as was vividly seen in the 2011 "Arab Spring" in Egypt and Tunisia.

Islamist movements seek to enhance their popularity by building alterna-tive welfare systems that include health and educational facilities, often relying on Saudi or Gulf Arab funding. These facilities offer help that is usually much better than anything the government can offer and are more effective at meeting the needs of the local populations. They are also less corrupt, a key to their rising popularity.[300]

Egypt

Egypt serves as a classic example of the process of Islamisation from below. Under Nasser's presidency (1956-1970) it was a secular, Arab-socialist republic committed to limiting the power of Islam in the state and controlling it. The Muslim Brotherhood was severely suppressed. Sadat (president 1970-1981), however, manipulated Islam to gain legitimacy for himself as president in the eyes of the people. He unshackled the Muslim Brotherhood and accepted sharia as the main source of the legal system. Under Mubarak, the Islamists were blocked from full political participation but given freedom of action in civil society. Unable to achieve their revolutionary goals directly by conquering the state, Islamists set about Islamising Egypt from below, in the process gradually re-making Egyptian society and culture.

Islamist success was based on the Muslim Brotherhood's infiltration of civil society, which enabled the transformation of everyday life in Egypt. The Islamist movement used its network of civil society organisations to create an alternative society that propagated the movement's ideas. Islamic values and norms have permeated all sectors of society, including gender roles, consumption habits, entertainment and education.[301] While the Egyptian government focused its attention on Islamist terror groups, a far greater number of Islamists gradually took control of Egypt's social institutions, such as schools, universities, the media, courtrooms, hospitals and clinics, and trade unions.[302] By combining their message with social action, Islamists strengthened their appeal to many sectors of Egyptian society that felt let down by the ruling regime. Egyptian society has been successfully Islamised in a generation, and this process serves as a model for Islamists in other states.

Competing with Islamists for legitimacy forced the state to make concessions to Islamist ideology on a variety of issues, including the acceptance of sharia as the main source of legislation. This provided Islamists with an opportunity to transform Egypt's judicial system and to use it to attack a wide range of norms and practices. As a result of the growing Islamist influence, central institutions of Egyptian life, including al-Azhar and other universities, the professional unions and the court system slipped away from secular regime control. Islamists penetrated the public and state sectors, including the educational establishment, and gained footholds in army, police, and government ministries. As one observer noted,

> Egypt's Islamist revolution by stealth has burrowed its way into the very heart of the institutions of the Arab world's largest and most important state… Leading institutions, once under complete government control, have begun to erode the state's secularist policies… Major institutions … are now in the hands of moderate Islamists [and in] neighborhoods and districts across the country popular sheikhs, free of government control, are making decisions on matters ranging from divorce to land ownership and the role of women in society.[303]

All this was achieved before the "Arab Spring", which, although started by young secular intellectuals, was soon taken over by Islamists, revealing the success of the Islamisation process in the previous decades.

Islamist Charities

Providing welfare was a vital part of the activity of Islamisers in Egypt and enabled them to engage in political activity as they sought to control all aspects of life in Egypt.[304] As Ali E. Hillal Dessouki, former Minister of Youth and Sport in the Mubarak government, noted, Islamists were

> seeking to gain the support of the average Egyptian one by one, inch by inch, through the provision of welfare facilities, Islamic schools, Islamic clinics, technical schools, economic institutions for profit, social insurance, monthly payments for the poor.[305]

The better quality of Islamist services in health, education, sport and finance was an indictment of the government's inability to provide basic services to its citizens and a vindication of the Muslim Brotherhood's slogan "Islam is the solution".[306]

Students' Associations

Beginning in the mid-1970s, Islamist student associations began to dominate student unions on most Egyptian campuses. As university infrastructure and services deteriorated, Islamists plugged the gap. Islamist associations provided students with all they needed, including photocopied textbooks, low-cost lecture notes and help with housing. Islamist student associations manipulated these services to further the process of Islamisation. Thus, they purchased minibuses to transport female students but offered this service only to women who wore the veil. To poor students who had trouble affording clothing, Islamists offered Islamic garments practically free of charge.[307]

Professional Syndicates and Unions

By the early 1990s, the Muslim Brotherhood had control of most professional bodies in Egypt. These included the syndicates representing doctors, engineers, scientists, pharmacists and lawyers. They provided members with a variety of much-needed services and expanded the scope of Islamisation.[308]

Censorship

Alongside the Islamists, al-Azhar University, the leading centre of Sunni Islamic learning, demanded ever-increasing Islamisation of society in the cultural sphere, promoting the Islamisation of school curricula. Al-Azhar and its Islamic Research Academy (IRA) were officially recognised by the government as having the authority to safeguard Islamic law and religion. This recognition enabled al-Azhar to exercise ever-stricter censorship on books, media and the arts, banning and confiscating many and labelling their authors as guilty of blasphemy or apostasy.[309] This led to harassment and even physical attacks. For example, the secular writer Farag Foda was murdered a few days after he was denounced by the authorities of al-Azhar in 1992.

Civil Society Activism

The diffuse nature of the Islamist infiltration of civil society helped Islamists avoid government prosecution, as it became increasingly difficult for the state to monitor them. A study of the Egyptian non-governmental sector explained that

> The government could not curtail Islamic charity organizations because they are the most dynamic organizations in civil society, and they reach people and regions that the state cannot.[310]

The success of Islamist infiltration contributed to isolating the Mubarak regime from the people and Islamising society. The changes in Egypt were so striking that long before the 2011 "Arab Spring" uprising, observers argued that the country was well on its way to becoming a near-Islamic state and that it was more Islamised than Iran. Egypt, long considered to be at the forefront of liberalism and secularism in the Arab world, was quietly being transformed into an Islamic society.[311] This fact became abundantly clear when the Islamists (the Muslim Brotherhood and the Salafists) gained a large majority of the votes in the first free elections to parliament in 2011-12.

In the presidential elections in June 2012, the Muslim Brotherhood candidate Muhammad Morsi won 51.7% of the votes, making him the first ever Islamist to be elected as head of state of an Arab country and putting the Muslim Brotherhood firmly in control of the Egyptian state. The secular-liberal activists who had instigated the revolution were confined to the side lines. The long years of grassroots work and Islamisation from below had finally paid off.[312] The Brotherhood moved to control all centres of power in Egypt, appropriating thousands of government posts to its members and allies. It released convicted terrorists from prison and allowed jihadists to return to Egypt and make the Sinai Peninsula their safe haven. The Brotherhood also used its militias to attack, torture and kill protesters and journalists and put the supreme constitutional court, newspaper offices, opposition parties' headquarters and the entire media under siege.[313] Morsi perceived democracy as a winner-takes-all system, packing the state with Brothers, granting himself almost unlimited powers and creating an upper house with an Islamist majority.[314] Many observers who had expected the Muslim Brotherhood to continue its pragmatic tactics when in power were taken aback by the Brotherhood's increasingly dictatorial manner, ignoring its critics, failing to reach out to other Egyptians and alienating its traditional allies. It seemed that the Brotherhood had shifted gear to its real core strategy and was engaged in an unabashed power grab that left no room for the pragmatism it had projected while in opposition.[315] As a result many of those who had originally voted for the Brotherhood turned against it and the military used the mass protests against Muslim Brotherhood misrule to justify its intervention on 3 July 2013, removing Morsi from power and banning the Brotherhood.

Lebanon

Following the civil war in the 1970s, Hizbullah, the radical Shia Islamist organisation notorious for suicide bombings and kidnappings, began to provide desperately needed social services, which the government had failed to provide, to the impoverished Shia community. Largely funded by Iran,

Hizbullah-affiliated associations now supply citizens with medical care, hospitals, housing, clean water, schools and jobs in its own enterprises. In addition to providing material aid, Hezbollah sponsors a wide range of recreational and communal associations and news services that help it attract supporters, spread its ideology and gradually reshape society from below. It has founded its own scout movement, summer camps and soccer league. It publishes a weekly newspaper and operates its own radio and TV stations.

Its civil society activities allow the movement to monitor the political attitudes of those they are assisting, as well as checking how dutiful they are in their Islamic religious observance. Hizbullah has thus been able to win hearts and minds and build its backing from the grass roots up. It has challenged and supplanted the weak central government in many vital areas. Finally, it chose to enter the electoral process and has gained a blocking minority in Parliament.[316]

Yemen

Yemeni society is traditionally tribal and sectarian. Islam in its Shia Zaydi or Sunni Shafii form has been extremely important. But the rise of Islamisation movements in recent years is now shattering the tribal system. There are four main Islamising political forces in Yemen: the Muslim Brotherhood, represented by the Islah party; Ansar Allah (the Shia Zaydi Houthis); various Salafi movements; and the Ansar al-Shariah movement, represented by Al-Qaeda in the Arabian Peninsula (AQAP). The Muslim Brotherhood is strongest in the political, social, educational, economic, security, media and diplomatic areas and also has the most followers.[317]

Sunni Islamists such as the Muslim Brotherhood and the Salafists, with Saudi support, have gradually changed the traditional Shafii Islam of Yemen, with its mystical Sufi elements, to a more puritanical Islamist Islam of the Brotherhood and Wahhabi types. Islah and Salafi Islamism are cooperating and competing with each other, and the result is the ever-increasing influence of Islamism in Yemeni society, culture and government. This trend sharpens hostility to Shia Zaydi Islam, which used to be dominant in Yemen and is trying via the Houthi Islamist movement to reassert itself, with Iranian help. So right across the various sects of Islam present in Yemen, there is a trend towards a fundamentalist Islamist type of Islam, whether Sunni or Shia, which radicalises its adherents and fuels the violence between the different communities.

The success of the "Arab Spring" in Tunisia and Egypt inspired mass demonstrations in the Yemeni capital, Sanaa, beginning in 2011. President Saleh was forced to step down, but his successor, Abed Rabbo Mansur Hadi,[318] did not act very differently. Islamisation in its various forms continued at a rapid pace, with the Islamising groups pressing for full implementation of sharia. The Joint Meeting Parties (JMP), which is a coalition of Islamists (including the Islah party), Nasserites and Cold War-era socialists, has emerged as the main political force in the country.[319] An important leader within Islah is Abdul Majid al-Zindani, who worked for many years with Osama bin Laden and supported Islamist terrorist causes.[320]

As in other countries affected by the "Arab Spring", the youthful crowds who initiated the demonstrations have been sidelined by established Islamising parties and politicians eager to maintain their power.[321] At the same time, the violent Islamisers of AQAP and their allies took advantage of the deteriorating conditions and the emerging power vacuum to overrun large swathes of territory, including several towns and cities in the south, pushing out government forces, establishing their own rule and implementing sharia.[322] They shifted from a strategy of small terrorist attacks to that of an armed insurgency, like the Taliban in Afghanistan, engaging in frontal attacks on Yemeni forces.[323]

Violence is now endemic in Yemen, perpetrated not only by AQAP, but by all competing Islamising forces eager to gain dominance in the state. Shia Iran and Sunni Saudi Arabia support the groups nearest to them in ideology and see Yemen as part of the regional conflict between Shia Islamism and Sunni Islamism that is engulfing the whole Middle East.

ISLAMISATION FROM ABOVE

Governments, under the influence or control of Islamisers, can progress the Islamisation of state and society by changing the constitution and legal system to comply with sharia.

Pakistan

General Zia ul-Haq (president 1977 to 1988) was sympathetic to the Islamist party Jamaat-i-Islami (JI)[324] and initiated a policy of radical Islamisation, including laws, public policy and popular culture. This process can be seen as a case of the systematic propagation of Islamism from above. The Zia regime's vision of the place of Islam in state and society drew heavily on Islamist ideology, which they were able to use to shore up state power and expand it domestically and regionally. The alliance between Islamists and the military gave legitimacy to military rule and justified the suppression of democratic forces by claiming to be building an Islamic order.[325]

Zia introduced extensive reforms to constitution and law that made Islamist interpretations of Sunni Islam the state ideology and made sharia the basis of its legal system. Under his rule, an Islamic legal code was issued by decree, to be applied by sharia courts. Interest-free banking was introduced, and commissions were formed for the Islamisation of the economy and education.[326] Zia's Islamisation drive and support for militant groups made Pakistan an important ideological and organisational centre of the global Islamist movement.[327] The process of Islamisation was continued under President Nawaz Sharif, who passed the Enforcement of Shari'ah Act in 1991. In 1998 the Fifteenth Amendment Bill (known as the Shariat Bill), which would have turned Pakistan into an Islamic dictatorship, was passed by the National Assembly but did not get through the Senate.

The Pakistani military favoured the creation of multiple jihadi groups to fight against India in Kashmir and the Soviet Union in Afghanistan. Leaders of these groups, even those banned after 11 September 2001, enjoy virtual immunity from the law and continue to propagate their militant ideologies, while Islamist terrorism has become widespread.[328] Islamist movements and their jihadi organisations have become increasingly powerful and are not content with a secondary role in national affairs. They have infiltrated state and army institutions and influenced a younger generation of military officers who have absorbed the Islamist ideology and its commitment to jihad.[329]

Under Islamist pressure, freedom of speech was constitutionally "subject to any reasonable restrictions imposed by law in the interest of the glory of Islam". This obviously impinged on the freedom of religion of the non-Muslim minorities.[330]

Under Zia, severe amendments were added to Section 295 of the Pakistan Penal Code, often called the "Blasphemy Law". Under these new provisions, desecration of the Quran became a crime carrying a punishment of life imprisonment (295-B, added in 1982), while defiling the name of Muhammad became a crime carrying a punishment of death or imprisonment for life and a fine (295-C, added in 1986). On 30 October 1990, the Federal Shariat Court ruled that the life imprisonment option was "repugnant to the injunctions of Islam" and that the President of Pakistan must amend the law so that it conformed with Islam. If this had not been done by 30 April 1991, said the judgment of the Federal Shariat Court, the words "imprisonment for life" in Section 295-C should cease to have effect on that date.[331] In December 2013 a Contempt of Court case was brought before the Federal Shariat Court by a lawyer who argued that the 1990 ruling had not been implemented and that the court should now issue orders to rectify this, which it duly did.[332]

Non-Muslims are particularly vulnerable to accusation under this law, because cases often come down to one person's word against another's about what was said at a certain place on a certain date. There is a tendency for Muslim judges, even in the civil courts, to give greater weight to the word of the Muslim accuser. This is in line with what sharia says about the value of a Muslim's testimony being twice that of a non-Muslim's. Some judges also apparently take more notice of the testimony of a devout-looking Muslim than of the testimony of other Muslims, as on 2 November 1992, when Gul Pervaiz Masih became the first Christian to be convicted under Section 295-C. Only one prosecution witness, the bearded Sajjad Hussain, spoke against him, while other Muslims spoke in his defence, but the judge ruled that

In my view the prosecution has succeeded to prove the guilt of the accused beyond any reasonable doubt. I see no mitigating circumstances in favour of the accused nor any such is pointed out to me, therefore, the accused is convicted and sentenced to death... Sajjad Hussain is a young man of 21 years of age, student of the 4th year with a beard and outlook of being a true Muslim and I have no reason to disbelieve him.[333]

Gul Pervaiz Masih was sentenced to death but acquitted on appeal.

Muhammad is greatly venerated by Muslims in the sub-continent. As a result, individuals accused of defiling the name of Muhammad – even if acquitted by the courts – usually find themselves under attack by Islamic extremist groups and individuals.[334] (Gul Pervaiz Masih had to leave Pakistan and move to another country.) Defence lawyers and judges dealing with blasphemy cases are often threatened.[335]

Sudan

President Nimeiri introduced sharia in 1983 in alliance with the Muslim Brotherhood under Hasan al-Turabi. Mahmoud Muhammad Taha, an Islamic scholar and leader of the Republican Brothers movement, was condemned to death as an apostate and executed in 1985 for his efforts to reinterpret the Quran in a more liberal way and thus reform Islam. Following General al-Bashir's military coup of 1989, the National Islamic Front of al-Turabi came to power and, in the constitution of 1991, sharia was again enforced and a formal Islamic state effectively created. The use of sharia as the basis of law and government has since become ever more explicit.[336] The government treats Islam as the state religion and has declared that it must inspire the country's laws, institutions, and policies. Non-Muslims are forbidden to share their faith, and Section 126 of the Sudan Criminal Law 1991 makes apostasy from Islam a criminal offence punishable by death in accordance with sharia.[337] As a result, discrimination against non-Muslims has been institutionalised; the government has tried to Islamise them and has violated their basic human rights.[338]

The long civil war (1983-2005) was fought by the Arab and Islamic government in Khartoum as a jihad to Islamise and Arabise the mainly non-Muslim and African South and to enforce sharia on its population. It caused untold suffering, with an estimated two million Southerners being killed and five million displaced. Following the independence of South Sudan in 2011, non-Muslims in the northern state now face increased pressures from the authorities there (see page 126).

Malaysia

While Muslims comprise only some 61% of Malaysia's population, Malay Muslims are given a superior status as the original indigenous people of West Malaysia (*bumiputra*, sons of the soil).[339] As *bumiputra*, Malays have many political and economic advantages over non-Malays, and in this way the authority of Islam is entrenched. The legal definition of "Malay" includes a list of characteristics, one being that the person is a Muslim. In the decades since independence, the *bumiputra* advantage has become ever more enshrined in law and in programmes of affirmative action.[340] The constitution declares Islam as the sole official state religion and, in addition, parliamentary and state constituencies have been drawn up in such a way as to give greater political weighting to rural areas where the majority of the Malays live.[341]

Islamic revivalist movements (known as *dakwah*, i.e. *dawa*) emerged in the 1970s and developed many Islamic activities. The opposition Parti Islam Se-Malaysia (PAS) challenged the ruling United Malay National Organisation (UMNO) by taking as its official goal the establishing of sharia. UMNO responded by trying to present itself as more Islamic[342] and took steps to Islamise society through the creation of new institutions and through the introduction of Islamic banking. In the 1980s, state-led Islamisation continued with the creation of institutions for Islamic studies. Clerical traditions were strengthened and efforts made to Islamise the interpretation of the law. Key organisations, such as the Pusat Islam (officially the Department of Islamic Development, JAKIM) and the Yayasan Dakwah, which coordinate official *dawa* activity, report directly to the Prime Minister's Office.[343]

Sharia courts have jurisdiction over the personal lives of Muslims and operate alongside the civil system. Civil courts do not have the authority to intervene in sharia cases. As Malaysia becomes increasingly Islamised, the religious authorities have become more assertive, emboldened by the lack of proper oversight.[344]

Two Malaysian states have passed *hudud* laws, which impose the penalties that Muslims believe are specifially ordained by Allah for certain crimes, such as amputation for theft or flogging for drinking alcohol. Both states have included the death penalty for apostasy from Islam, although this cannot be enforced because it would contravene provisions in the Federal Constitution and related acts. Kelantan State passed such laws in 1993, and Terengganu State passed similar laws in 2002.[345] Malaysia is in an advanced stage of transformation into an Islamic state.[346]

Given the ongoing need to compete with the more Islamist opposition, the Malaysian government continues to favour Islam as the national religion and to restrict the activities of other religions, limiting the religious freedom of non-Muslims. The rights and freedoms of the mainly non-Muslim Chinese and Indian minorities (who make up nearly 40% of the population) are being eroded.[347]

It is against the law in most states of Malaysia to write, speak or preach against Islam, and it is illegal for a Muslim to leave Islam. It is also almost impossible for non-Muslim religious groups to obtain additional land for places of worship, schools and cemeteries, and there are limits on the publication and distribution of Christian literature.[348]

In May 2007 Lina Joy, a Christian convert from Islam, lost a court battle to remove the word "Muslim" from her identification card, even though the Malaysian constitution guarantees freedom of religion. The previous month, a Hindu man was forcibly separated from his Muslim wife of 21 years and their six children after religious officials ruled their marriage invalid. (Sharia does not allow a Muslim woman to marry a non-Muslim man.) All female police officers are now required to wear the Islamic headscarf at official functions, regardless of their religion.[349]

Censorship is widespread. Since 1971, at least 1,517 books and other publications have been added to Malaysia's banned list, including many Christian publications. Operating under the Printing Presses and Publications Act 1984, the Publication and Quranic Text Control Division is in charge of the process.

The Federal Territories Islamic Affairs Department (JAWI) acts as an Islamic religious police, imposing censorship and ensuring that Muslims comply with Islamic dress codes and fast during Ramadan. Officials are also reported to patrol the parks looking for young, unmarried Muslim couples holding hands or cuddling (the crime of *khalwat*) and to raid night clubs trying to catch Muslims drinking alcohol. At present, these rules apply only to Muslims. But Malaysian sharia legal experts at a seminar in 2008, partly organised by the Sharia Judiciary Department, proposed that the ban on *khalwat* should be extended to non-Muslims caught committing *khalwat* with a Muslim.[350]

ISLAMISATION THROUGH REVOLUTION

In Islamic revolutions, political change precedes societal and cultural transformation: the state is captured, and the new regime then begins constructing a new Islamic order.

Iran

The majority of Shia Muslims believe in the future return of the Hidden Imam. This is the twelfth Shia Imam, who disappeared as a child in Iraq in AD 874 and is expected to reappear at the end of time as the *mahdi*, a saviour who will set up the final worldwide Islamic rule of righteousness.

Ayatollah Khomeini (1900-1989) introduced a radical new interpretation of Shia Islam, the *velayet-e-faqih* (guardianship of the jurist) doctrine. This taught that supreme political leadership of an Islamic state belongs to the leading cleric as the representative of the Hidden Imam. Following huge demonstrations against the Shah, Ayatollah Khomeini returned to Iran in 1979 to establish an Islamic Republic. The Iran-Iraq war which quickly followed (1980-1988) served to consolidate the new regime, as nationalistic fervour was added to Islamic rhetoric. Most Iranians united under the regime against the foreign enemy, and those who opposed the regime were labelled enemies of the nation and brutally crushed.

Mahmoud Ahmadinejad, President of Iran from 2005 to 2013, has an activist belief in the *mahdi's* imminent return and placed this belief at the centre of Iran's domestic and foreign policy while he was in power. Ahmadinejad considered it to be his government's responsibility to pave the way for the *mahdi*. It seems that he felt that part of this preparation was to build the perfect, powerful Islamic state, which could be handed over to the *mahdi* when he appeared, who would then use it to fulfil his programme. For Ahmadinejad, the whole purpose of the Iranian Revolution was to prepare the way for the *mahdi*. In fact, to some extent, all of Iran's leaders since the Revolution have believed they are actively preparing the way for the Hidden Imam's second appearance.

Since the 1979 Iranian Revolution, Shia Islam has been the state religion and sharia has formed the basis of the Iranian constitution and legal system. Article 4 of the constitution states that

All civil, penal financial, economic, administrative, cultural, military, political, and other laws and regulations must be based on Islamic criteria. This principle applies absolutely and generally to all articles of the Constitution as well as to all other laws and regulations.

In the Islamic Republic real power rests not with the parliament or the president, but with the Supreme Guide, who is seen as the representative of the Hidden Imam and of Allah's sovereignty on earth. The Supreme Guide has final authority according to the doctrine of *velayet-e-faqih*, and in practice he does indeed have almost unlimited powers.[351] He does not need the approval of the majority, and he takes precedence over the traditional democratic divisions of power, the legislature, judicial and executive, all of which he supervises.[352] He is also commander-in-chief of the armed forces. Houshang Sepehr, an Iranian revolutionary now living in exile, called the Islamic Republic of Iran "a Caliphate disguised as a Republic".[353]

The constitution lays down in Article 2 the foundations of the political system. These include, among others, God's rule (*hakimiyya*) and law (sharia), belief in divine revelation and its "fundamental role in setting forth the laws", and belief in the imamate and its continuous leadership. The constitution thus excludes non-Muslims from an ideological commitment to the state. It also excludes non-Shia Muslims, who do not accept the necessity of the Shia imamate.[354]

In Article 99, the constitution gives the Guardian Council responsibility for supervising elections. This power is used by the ruling elite to screen and pre-select the candidates who stand for election. Elections are thus reduced to a choice between those already approved by Supreme Guide and his close circle.[355]

Although the constitution guarantees freedom of belief, various laws place limits on religious freedoms. These restrictive and often contradictory laws are found in the Penal Code, the Theologians' Law (a body of law dealing with offences committed by clerics) and the Public and Revolutionary Courts' Procedural Law. A basic flaw in many of these laws is the absence of clear definitions of key concepts such as "state security", "propaganda" and "insulting Islam". Under Article 513 of the Penal Code, offences classified as "insult to religion" can be punishable by death or prison terms of between one and five years. Articles 6 and 26 of the Press Code forbid writings "containing apostasy and matters against Islamic standards [and] 'the true religion of Islam'…" In cases where there are no specific codified laws, judges can deliver *fatwas* based on authoritative Islamic sources.[356] In recent years there have been many cases of arbitrary detention, unfair trial and imprisonment under these clauses, following the expression of conscientiously held beliefs.[357]

While the state recognises Christianity, Judaism and Zoroastrianism as official religions with limited freedoms to worship within their communities, apostasy from Islam is a crime. The government has created a threatening atmosphere for nearly all non-Shia religious groups, most notably for Baha'is, as well as for Sufi Muslims, Protestant Christians, Jews, Sunni Muslims and Zoroastrians. Shia adherents who do not share the government's official religious views also face harassment and intimidation.[358]

The Islamic clerical ruling elite is virulently hostile to the Baha'i faith, which they consider a heresy that should be eliminated; there has been severe persecution of the Baha'i community ever since 1979. In the first six years following the Iranian Revolution, over 200 Baha'is, mainly community leaders, were executed. Baha'i institutions have been disbanded, property confiscated and holy places and cemeteries desecrated. Baha'is cannot hold government jobs, enforce legal contracts, practise law, collect pensions, attend universities or practise their faith. They have been deprived of all civil rights.

Christians form a separate electorate, not eligible to vote for Muslim representatives, but only for three Christian representatives to the Majlis (Parliament). Under the present Islamic regime, Christians and their institutions are intensively regulated and subjected to intrusive interference by the

Ministry of Information and Islamic Guidance, the Ministry of Religious Affairs and Endowments and the Ministry of the Interior and its notorious State Secret police.

Religious freedom continues to deteriorate as imprisonment, harassment, intimidation and discrimination based on religious beliefs increase. Many church buildings have been forcibly closed, especially those serving congregations of converts from Islam. One convert, pastor and evangelist, the Rev. Hossein Soodmand, was executed on 3 December 1990. Other church leaders have had death sentences passed on them but not implemented, and several have been mysteriously murdered. Seven Baha'i leaders had their sentences re-extended to the original 20 years after having had them reduced to 10 years in 2010. The government arrested them in 2009 for "espionage for Israel, insulting religious sanctities, and propaganda against the Islamic Republic".[359]

— 9 —

DAWA THROUGH JIHAD

Dawa is linked to jihad, as both have the same aim: to spread Islam and its dominion. This raises the important question of the definition of jihad itself. The concept of jihad has been part of Islam since it began. The Arabic word literally means "striving", and Muslims interpret this in a variety of ways including (1) personal spiritual struggle for moral purity, (2) trying to correct wrong and support right by voice and actions, and (3) military war against non-Muslims with the aim of spreading Islam. It is noteworthy that the second interpretation directly overlaps with the "commanding of good and forbidding of wrong" aspect of *dawa*.

However, the violent interpretation of jihad is also closely linked with *dawa*. As we have already seen, the early Islamic state would give an invitation (*dawa*) to non-Muslim enemies to convert to Islam or accept *dhimmi* status. (The *dhimmi* option was not available to pagans.) When they refused to do either, the Muslims waged jihad against them. So Islam was to be imposed by persuasion if possible, by force if not. Likewise, all forces hindering the spread of Islam and its dominion had to be fought and eradicated. After a Muslim victory, the non-Muslims, now living under Islamic rule, could be converted more easily with the help of the Islamic state and its institutions.

This doctrine of early Islam remains a guiding principle of 21st century Islamists such as the Taliban.

...this is the purpose of offensive jihad – to eliminate all elements that are acting as obstacles for the rest of the people converting to Islam; this is because when the people will see the open system of Islam and the peace that it brings, they will all willingly embrace Islam (History bears witness to this).[360]

Or, more succinctly:

Jihad is *Dawah* with force.[361]

While *dawa* can be propagated by peaceful means of persuasion, jihad enables it to function freely to its fullest extent. *Dawa* is most effective when the state enforces sharia and supports *dawa* with all its resources. Thus Islamist movements like the Muslim Brotherhood see themselves as committed to both *dawa* and jihad, or rather see both as different stages in the same enterprise. Fathi Yakan, leader of al-Jama'a al-Islamiyya, the Lebanese branch of the Muslim Brotherhood, explains the synergy between jihad and *dawa*:

It [*dawa*] is a call for Jihad since it calls for preparation for Jihad by all its forms and means so that truth may have the force to protect it and that the Da'wah may be able to face the challenges and surmount the barriers... Force is the surest way to establish the truth and how beautiful it would be if truth and force went side by side. Thus Jihad for the spread of Islam and the protection of the holy places of Islam is another obligation which Allah made compulsory on the Muslims...[362]

Sheikh Abdul Azeez ibn Abdullaah ibn Baaz, stated:

The truth has been spread through the correct Islamic *da'wah*, which in turn has been aided and supported by *jihaad* whenever anyone stood in its way... Thus it was *jihaad* and *da'wah* together which helped to open the doors to victories.[363]

The Dutch government has recognised clearly the intimate connection between *dawa* and jihad, noting that some organisations concentrate on *dawa*, some on armed jihad, and some combine the two. Commenting on this flexibility of approach, their 2004 intelligence report says:

The choice of Dawa-oriented groups for non-violent activities does not always imply that they are non-violent on principle. Often they simply do not yet consider armed Jihad expedient for practical reasons (Jihad can be counterproductive or impossible because of the other side's superiority) or for religious reasons (the Jihad against non-believers is only possible when all Muslims have returned to the "pure" faith).[364]

The unbroken spectrum between *dawa* and jihad, overt and covert, are shown in the Dutch government's diagram reproduced opposite page 73.

A striking illustration of the overlap between the two is the fact that Dr Yusuf Al-Qaradawi, described as being "active in the field of da'wah and the Islamic movement for more than half a century",[365] has also written a book of 1,439 pages[366] about the ethics of how a Muslim army should conduct a war. There is no doubt that his book is very practical military study, saying, for example, that the *umma* must have weapons of mass destruction as a deterrent, but should use them only if a nation is subject to an existential threat.[367]

We have already seen that jihad is not only the striving for personal holiness, not only war in the cause of Islam, but also includes everything Muslims do to bring the world under sharia, the law of Allah. In the words of Pakistani Brigadier S.K. Malik:

> *Jehad* is a continuous and never-ending struggle waged on all fronts including political, economic, social, psychological, domestic, moral and spiritual to attain the objectives of policy.[368]

Thus jihad is intimately linked not only with the classical Islamic concept of *dawa* but also with the modern Islamist concept of Islamisation. The eight-step outreach process described in the Malaysian *dawa* manual described above ended with making the new Muslim (6) understand the need to establish an Islamic state under sharia, i.e. for Islamisation, (7) understand the need for continual jihad and (8) become an effective witness for Islam, i.e. engage in *dawa*. (See page 21.)

Islam claims that, as it is the last revealed and final religion, Allah has promised Muslims the whole world as their territory for a global Islamic state. Key Quranic verses on this theme are:

> God has promised, to those among you who believe and work right-eous deeds, that He will, of a surety, grant them in the land, inheri-tance (of power), as He granted it to those before them; that He will establish in authority their religion - the one which He has chosen for

them; and that He will change (their state) after the fear in which they (lived), to one of security and peace: 'They will worship Me (alone) and not associate aught with Me. If any do reject faith after this, they are rebellious and wicked. (Q 24:55)

Before this We wrote in the Psalms after the Message (given to Moses): "My servants, the righteous, shall inherit the earth." (Q 21:105)

Mawdudi wrote frankly about Islam's global political aim:

Islam wishes to do away with all states and governments anywhere which are opposed to the ideology and programme of Islam... Islam requires the earth – not just a portion, but the entire planet.[369]

And according to Ismail Raji al-Faruqi, the potential Islamic state even includes outer space:

Islam asserts that the territory of the Islamic state is the whole earth or, better, the whole cosmos since the possibility of space travel [is] not too remote. Part of the earth may be under direct rule of the Islamic state and the rest may yet have to be included; the Islamic state exists and functions regardless. Indeed its territory is ever expansive. So is its citizenry, for its aim is to include all humankind. If the Islamic state is at any time restricted to a few of the world's population, it does not matter as long as it wills to comprehend humanity.[370]

But this ideological vision must be made a reality by the actions of Muslims (in early Islam, always by conquest). Land that has become part of the Islamic state is considered purified and dedicated to Allah, and such lands must never be given back to unbelievers.

A modern Islamist writes:

...the Kuffar [unbelievers, non-Muslims] are not allowed to establish a ruling system on earth because the earth belongs to Allah and only his righteous slaves are allowed to inherit it.[371]

Among the wide variety of Islamic doctrines, there has been a strand of radicalism and violence in much of Islam's traditional theology, ideology and history. Like other Islamic concepts, it is based on passages in the Islamic source texts (including the Quran and *hadith*), on Muhammad's example, and on early Muslim history. Bernard Lewis noted that:

> From the earliest times, the reported events of Islamic history, supported by the precepts of Islamic tradition and law, reflect two distinct and indeed contradictory principles. The one we have called authoritarian and quietist; the other might be called radical and activist... the radical activist tradition is also old and deep-rooted, and is acquiring new significance in our day, with the emergence of the idea of an Islamic Revolution, and of leaders and movements devoted to its accomplishment... The exponents of both traditions naturally looked to the life and teachings of the Prophet for guidance and inspiration; both concentrated their attention on the political actions which the Prophet found necessary to undertake in order to accomplish his religious mission.[372]

Because the Islamic source texts of Quran and *hadith* contain many passages encouraging violence, intolerance and contempt for non-Muslims, they have provided a strong motivation and justification throughout the ages for any Muslims seeking to further the power of Islam by aggression and violence. As the well-known Egyptian scholar Nasr Hamid Abu Zayd has noted:

> If we follow the rules of interpretation developed from the classical "science of Koranic interpretation", it is not possible to condemn terrorism in religious terms. It remains completely true to the classical rules in its evolution of sanctity for its own justification. This is where the secret of its theological strength lies.[373]

Numerous verses in the Quran command or commend fighting against non-Muslims, especially in the parts of the Quran that were "revealed" to Muhammad towards the end of his life. There are also many peaceable verses, but these, being dated earlier than the belligerent ones, are considered by most Islamic scholars to be abrogated i.e. cancelled out and overruled.[374]

A favourite verse of Islamists is known as the "Sword Verse", which begins:

> But when the forbidden months are past, then fight and slay the Pagans wherever ye find them... (Q 9:5)

The principle of military jihad is also based on the example of Muhammad's own life, and of the early caliphs who succeeded him as leaders of the *umma* and expanded the Islamic empire way beyond the bounds of the Arabian peninsula. Later, during the Abbasid caliphate, this strategy was codified in the form of the sharia doctrine of jihad. At this time the Islamic scholars also compiled the *maghazi*, which are a record of Muhammad's military excursions and battles as described in the early sources.

Military jihad continued to be practised up to the time of the Ottoman and Mughal Empires and their jihads into the heart of Europe and all of India respectively. Islamic history also shows repeated cycles of puritanical revivals, such as those of the Almoravids (1040-1147) and the Almohads (1121-1269) in North Africa, the Wahhabis in Arabia (since the mid-18th century), Usuman dan Fodio (1754-1817) in West Africa, the Mahdi (1845-1885) in Sudan and many more. These have all practised aggressive jihad as part of their programmes of reinstating original Islam and expanding its territorial base.

Only under severe constraints, when non-Islamic power was overwhelming, could the jihad imperative be put on hold for a while, for example, under Western colonial rule. This concession derived from sharia principles of *darura* and *maslaha* which permit the breaking of sharia principles when Muslims are weak and Islam is in danger. Such suspension of jihad, however, was always temporary, and jihad could be reactivated at any time if Muslims considered that their strength was enough to change the balance of power and reassert Islamic dominance. Violent jihad is an important aspect of the resurgence of Islam since the 1970s and is fuelled by the growing dominance of Islamism across the Muslim world.

Jihad and the expansion of Islam through war are not viewed by Muslims as aggression, but as the Allah-ordained method of attaining ultimate peace under the rule of Islam. The wars to spread Islam are not described by the Arabic word for war, *harb,* but by *futuh,* literally "opening" (i.e. opening of the world to Islam). Non-Muslims who stand in the way of the spread of Islam, creating obstacles to its mission (*dawa*), are the ones held responsible for the resulting state of war. The obstinate refusal of non-Muslims to accept Islam is viewed as aggression, because they hinder Islam in its Allah-ordained path to victory.[375]

DAWA THROUGH VIOLENCE
AND THREATS

As we have seen, for Islamists good is defined as what is good for Islam and its spread, while evil is any opposition to it. As a logical extension of this, many believe that violence can be good if it is used to advance and empower Islam.

Through the centuries, Muslim societies have tended to view the use of violence or the threat of violence as an effective method for keeping society in check as well as for the expansion of Islam. Even moderate Muslims usually seem to accept the need for violence against infidels, apostates, those who criticise Muhammad, and others they would consider enemies of Islam. This supportive attitude makes the use of violence an available option and a constant threat to all who disagree with them. In Muslim-majority states, this constant threat of violence limits freedom of expression and makes liberals reluctant to speak out.

In the West violent Muslim protests and riots are sometimes organised to try to force non-Muslim governments to accept Islamic demands. Such protests occurred in many countries following the Rushdie affair in Britain in 1989,[376] the Pope's Regensburg speech in 2006[377] and the Danish cartoons of Muhammad in 2005-2006.

There have also been targeted assassinations of individuals, such as Theo van Gogh in the Netherlands (2004), who had made a film about the treatment of women in Islam, and attempted attacks on the Danish cartoonist and his publishers in Scandinavia for depictions of Muhammad. Non-Muslim governments usually respond by conceding to radical Islamic demands.

The fear of further violence creates an atmosphere of excessive political correctness and self-censorship by non-Muslims in the West, and the result is that Islam gains a privileged position in Western society, culture and state in which it is never criticised or restrained. Could this be why Her Majesty's Chief Inspector of Constabulary refused to name the communities "from other cultures" living in the British Midlands who have their own form of justice, which they run without involving the British police (see page 50)?[378]

VIOLENT ISLAMISTS: JIHADISTS

Violent radical groups wage a constant campaign of terror against a variety of targets: the regimes in their own Muslim-majority states, Western states, especially the US and their interests and citizens worldwide, progressive and liberal Muslims accused of heresy and proclaimed as infidels worthy of death, Israel and Jews in general, and so on. Some focus on what Islam calls the "near enemy": Muslim rulers and regimes. Others focus on the "far enemy": the US, the UK and Israel, for example, and all other non-Muslim regimes.

Using a process called *takfir*, some condemn their more moderate fellow-Muslims as infidels or apostates. The significance of this is that sharia decrees a death penalty for adult male apostates and for all infidels (pagans). Therefore those who have been classified as infidels or apostates can then be lawfully killed, at least in the view of the *takfiris* who have condemned them. This process is applied to liberal and progressive Muslims, to more secular Muslim governments and even to whole Muslim societies that the radicals consider to be insufficiently devout. This kind of reasoning allows violent jihadists to legitimise – in their own minds – the horrors of the indiscriminate killing of Muslim innocents, as in the Algerian civil war and in Iraq post-2003.

The extent of activity by violent Islamists across the world, especially that involving suicide (or "martyr") operations, is phenomenal. The range stretches from Pakistan and Afghanistan through Iraq, Syria and Yemen to Somalia, Nigeria, Algeria and Kenya. The terror they unleash is evident in daily news bulletins that recount suicide bombings, assassinations and shootings across the globe.[379] The call for jihad has a powerful emotive attraction that constantly brings in new recruits from all over the Muslim world, replenishing the many fighters killed in the various fronts.

RELIGIOUS "CLEANSING"

Islamist violence and threats of violence are causing whole populations of non-Muslims to flee their homelands. In some cases this policy appears to be deliberate; the Islamists intentionally seek to "cleanse" a country of its non-Muslim population in the religious equivalent of ethnic cleansing.

Iraq

Following the downfall of Saddam Hussein in 2003, Islamist militant groups, both Sunni and Shia, targeted indigenous Christians in a programme of sustained violence that included kidnapping, assassination and bombing of churches. This resulted in the displacement of about half the country's Christian population. Many of the Christians received threats by letter, phone call or SMS, telling them to convert to Islam, leave or be killed.* It was clearly the intention of many of the militants to use intimidation and violence to rid the country of a Christian presence.

Syria

As the "Arab Spring" unfolded in Syria, the rebels became increasingly dominated by radical Islamist jihadi groups. These factions repeatedly attacked the Christian population, accusing them of supporting the ruling Assad regime and using violence to intimidate them and cause them to flee. Christians were threatened, kidnapped and killed. Church buildings and clergy were particular targets, which indicates that their faith was a significant reason for the attacks. Thousands were driven from their homes by the rebels.[380] At the time of writing, many have fled to Lebanon[381] or further afield, in what may prove to be only the beginning of a Christian migration on the scale already seen in Iraq. Ironically, many of the Christians who fled the anti-Christian violence in Iraq a few years earlier had found safety and

---

* Some were offered a fourth option of paying the traditional Islamic *jizya* tax, and thus acknowledging their inferior status relative to Muslim citizens. As we have seen, according to classical Islam, Jews and Christians who refused to pay *jizya* were no longer protected by the Islamic state and therefore could be killed by the Muslims.

security in Assad's Syria; they then had to face religious cleansing once more, this time in their country of refuge.

Nigeria

The modern resurgence of Islam has radicalised many Nigerian Muslims. Modern Islamism fits well with the traditional Northern Nigeria model of revival, creation of an Islamic state under sharia, and jihad, which was first exemplified there by Usuman dan Fodio. Following the imposition of sharia in twelve northern states (1999-2001), radical Islamists have been demanding the Islamisation of all Nigeria, including the South, which is predominantly Christian.

The militant group known as Boko Haram, now linked to al-Qaeda in the Maghreb, includes Christians as one of its main targets. In recent years they have been responsible for countless violent attacks on Christian churches, villages and individuals, which have led to thousands of deaths and to the displacement of huge numbers of Christians in the North. Boko Haram have actually stated that they are engaged in a war on Christians in Nigeria, and Nigerian Christians believe that the group are coordinating attacks with the aim of eradicating Christians from certain parts of the country, in which an Islamic state is to be proclaimed.[382] This statement was followed by vicious attacks on churches and Christians in the North and in Middle Belt states.

Sudan

In 2011, six years after the end of the long and bitter civil war, South Sudan became an independent state, the population of which is mainly African and predominantly Christian. Sudan, the Arab and Islamic northern state from which the South seceded, reacted by embarking on a policy of stripping over half a million Christians of their Sudanese citizenship and forcing them to move to South Sudan (from which most of them had fled during the civil war).[383] The Christians had already endured decades of oppression and brutality from the Sudanese government, which now announced that they must leave. President Omar al-Bashir made it very clear that they were not welcome, and the Sudanese authorities have stepped up the pressure on Christians by measures including the demolition of churches, the closing of Christian institutions, the arrest of Christians and the deportation of foreign Christian workers, in what appears to be a systematic campaign to eliminate the entire Christian presence in Sudan.[384]

Islamic Liberation Movements

Many Muslim states and organisations such as the powerful OIC support Muslim-minority demands for independence or autonomy as well as outright rebellions against non-Muslim central governments. There are problems of this kind in Kashmir, the Philippines, southern Thailand, the Xinjiang Province of China, Chechnya and elsewhere. The theological basis for such demands and rebellions is that Muslims believe they should never live under non-Muslim rule and they must always work to expand the area of territory that is under Muslim political rule. Insurgency and terrorism to support such causes are accepted as legitimate jihad, and funds, arms and fighters are provided by wealthy Muslim states and organisations.

Resistance to non-Muslim rule is considered a sacred duty in Islam. Western leftists often accept this view of Islamist activities as a valid liberation struggle.[385] Yusuf Al-Qaradawi expressed it clearly:

> The Islamic Movement should consider itself at the "beck and call" of every Islamic Cause and respond to every cry for help wherever that cry may come from. It should stand with Eritrea in its *jihad* against the unjust Marxist Christian regime … by Sudan against the treacherous Christian racist rebellion… It should support the Muslims of the Philippines against the biased Christian regime… it should also help the Muslims of Kashmir … support the Muslims of Somalia … mobilise the Muslims of the world for the Palestine Cause.[386]

Destabilisation of States

This is currently occurring in Nigeria, Ivory Coast, Kenya, the Philippines, India and elsewhere. Muslim minorities are urged to increase their power in the state and its institutions and to defy secular constitutions. Islamist jihadists destabilise the *status quo* by their violent and indiscriminate attacks on civilians. The population becomes polarised as the state increases its defensive measures and focuses on possible sources of terrorism in the Muslim population.

The Muslim minorities demand the implementation of sharia in Muslim-majority regions of the country. This demand is seen by Islamists as a prelude to imposing sharia on all the population.

Seizing Political Power by Military Force

Violent Islamists had a uniquely (so far) spectacular success in the Central African Republic (CAR) in March 2013 when the Seleka rebel group rapidly overwhelmed the government armed forces and seized political power. What is particularly striking about this incident is that Muslims are a relatively small minority in the CAR (15%). After months in which Seleka forces terrorised Christian targets, the non-Muslim population developed its own militias and, by early 2014, were actively retaliating. Some of these militias claimed to be Christian, although mainstream church leaders rejected this and called for Christians to respond with forgiveness, reconciliation and healing. On 20 January 2014, Catherine Samba-Panza (a Christian) was sworn in as interim president. She was chosen because she was seen as not being linked to either of the militias.[387]

Preventing Individuals from Leaving Islam

As we have seen, *dawa* operates partly at the level of personal religious belief: encouraging individuals to convert to Islam (see chapter 4). Equally important for increasing the number of Muslims is to prevent individuals from leaving Islam. Apostasy from Islam is viewed in sharia as a very serious crime, equivalent to treason against the *umma*. Adult male apostates are to be punished by death, and most schools of sharia also have the same penalty for adult female apostates. Those schools without the death sentence for women say that she must be imprisoned until she returns to Islam, and, according to Shia Islam, she must also be beaten with rods five times a day at the Islamic prayer times.

In Muslim states, religion is not usually a private matter as in the West, but is to some extent under state control as there is no division in Islam between state and religion. Freedom of religion is understood as a community affair, in which officially recognised religious minorities are guaranteed freedom of worship within their communities. The individual personal freedom to choose (i.e. change) one's religion is given only to non-Muslims who choose Islam; the converse is not allowed.

The ways in which Muslim-majority states seek to prevent conversion from Islam vary. A few include in their legal systems the death sentence for a Muslim who changes religion (Mauritania, Saudi Arabia, Sudan and Qatar, among others). State execution of apostates is also possible in Iran, because the law allows judges to apply sharia in areas where the law itself does not legislate. But these laws are rarely enforced.

In most Islamic contexts, there is no law to allow the official execution of an apostate for apostasy and quite often no law to punish them for leaving Islam at all. In such contexts, the authorities may find the convert guilty of another offence and punish him or her for that. Quite often this other offence is connected with the apostate's being considered a threat to public order. This is not simply a randomly chosen pretext; it is in fact quite logical within the Islamic worldview. Islam considers that a good citizen is a good Muslim. Since apostasy is seen as not only a crime against Allah but also political treason,* it is a threat to public order.[388] If public order offences are not invoked, the authorities may find other reasons for harassing converts from Islam, or for imprisoning them, perhaps with beatings and torture.

Interestingly, sharia sets out a whole range of punishments for apostasy, many of which would seem surplus to requirement if there were also a death sentence. These include dissolution of the convert's marriage, loss of custody of children, and loss of inheritance rights. Some of these are applicable today in various countries. For example, in Jordan a judge has the power to annul the marriage of a convert, transfer custody of the convert's children to a non-parent Muslim family member or make the children "wards of the state", transfer the convert's property rights to Muslim family members and deprive the converts of many civil rights.[389] In Malaysia, the penalty for leaving Islam varies from state to state. Converts may be sentenced to spend a fixed amount

---

* The comparison with treason is often made by Muslims seeking to explain and justify the severity of the penalty for apostasy. Dr Y. Zaki, a leading British Muslim (and incidentally a Scotsman who converted to Islam), argued on BBC radio that "Islam is not just a religion, it's a state, and Islam does not distinguish between sacred and secular authority ... apostasy and treason are one and the same thing." Since treason is traditionally punishable by death, he asserted, so too is apostasy. (*Sunday* programme, BBC Radio 4, 12 May 1991.)

Muhammad Iqbal Siddiqi, a popular Pakistani writer on Islam and Islamic law, uses exactly the same argument. He says that in Islam the foundations of the Kingdom of Heaven are first laid in the heart of the believer, and then "externalised in every phase of social set up i.e. in politics, in economics, in law, in manners and in international relations". Therefore, Siddiqi argues, to rebel against the Kingdom of Heaven within one's heart is also to commit "high treason against the Kingdom of Heaven on earth, the visible and concrete expression of the Kingdom of Heaven within the heart." He says there is nothing unusual in Islam punishing such treason severely. "In Islam religion is not a matter of private relationship between man and Allah, but is intertwined with society. So when he abandons Islam he in fact revolts against the authority of the Islamic state and society." (Muhammad Iqbal Siddiqi, *The Penal Law of Islam*, Lahore: Kazi Publications, 1979, pp. 108-109.)

of time in an Islamic rehabilitation centre, where pressure is put on them to return to Islam. In some states converts may face imprisonment, fines or caning.

The authorities can – and often do – discourage conversion from Islam simply by refraining from punishing any Muslim members of society who harass the convert. In fact, it is often the convert's own relatives who persecute them most severely, seeking to restore the family honour that has been lost by the shameful act of apostasy/treason. If converts can be dismissed from their jobs, attacked and even murdered, and their persecutors are not brought to justice, a clear message is sent that leaving Islam is an extremely dangerous decision.

This problem is made worse if the Islamic authorities (either sharia courts or individual Islamic clerics) issue a *fatwa* demanding the death of the apostate. The traditional Islamic way of expressing this is "His blood is permissible." Individual *fatwas* are not legally binding on the state but can be acted upon by any devout Muslim, and many Muslims would hold that the assassin is obeying sharia and therefore must not be prosecuted for the killing.

For some Muslim-majority states, a great merit of this approach, in which apostates are punished without the taking of any official action against them, is that it defuses potential criticism from the West.

PERSECUTION OF LIBERAL MUSLIMS

Heresy in Islam is almost as serious a charge as apostasy and is in fact very hard to distinguish from it. We have already seen how some violent jihadists use *takfir* to condemn other Muslims as apostates and thus make them legitimate targets for killing. A similar process takes place when state authorities condemn as heretics liberal Muslims who have wandered too far from the "true faith". Once they are classified as heretics, they can be punished and silenced.

The case of Dr Nasr Hamid Abu Zayd in Egypt is a good example.[390] Abu Zayd was a liberal-secularist academic who extended his linguistic research to the study of Islamic source texts, including the Quran. This enraged the Islamists. Islamist radicals declared he had blasphemed against Islam and called for his death. In 1993, seven Muslim lawyers brought a case of apostasy against him. Although he himself declared he was a Muslim, he was found guilty of apostasy by the Cairo Appeals Court on 14 June 1995 and ordered to separate from his wife. This ruling was based on the Islamic principle of *hisba*, which permits any Muslim to defend Islamic morals and behaviour. The landmark ruling against Abu Zayd, the first of its kind in modern Egypt, emboldened Islamists to file *hisba* lawsuits against other liberal and secularist Muslim intellectuals. It was an effective way of silencing them.

PERSECUTION OF CHRISTIAN MINORITIES

In the post-communist era, Islam has emerged as the main persecutor of Christians. In part this hostility must be due to the rise of radical Islam and the promotion of versions of Islamic theology that permit or even encourage violence against non-Muslims. But why are Christians such a target?

In Muslim-majority countries, Christianity is often seen as a "foreign religion", the religion of the hated Western colonial powers. When Muslims seek to retaliate against, say, Western air-strikes that accidentally kill Muslim civilians, the local Christians – unarmed and few in number – are the easiest target. Christians in Muslim-majority contexts are therefore bearing the brunt of the West's "war on terror".

Another reason why Christians are a prime target of Muslim persecution is that Christianity and Islam both actively seek to win new followers. Other world religions do not have such missionary zeal. So Christianity and Islam come head to head against each other in seeking converts. Many Muslim-majority countries have made the proselytising of Muslims illegal, and even where it is legal, it may often result in anti-Christian violence.

In the grand plan of Islamisation, the persecution of Christian minorities serves to encourage their conversion to Islam in order to escape harassment, discrimination and violence. In extreme cases, as we have already seen in Iraq, Syria and Sudan, severe persecution appears to be intended to cleanse a country of Christians altogether.

Anti-Christian violence is sweeping across the Muslim-majority world. If nothing is done to reverse the trend, this generation will witness the eradication of the Christian presence in many nations, with some being killed, others being internally displaced, and many fleeing to safe havens in the West. Everywhere, Christians are now living in fear of further attacks. They have no militias to fight for them and no one else to protect them. Western governments and churches seem unwilling or unable to help.

Anti-Semitism

Contemporary Islamism and its global Islamisation drive are closely linked to an especially virulent form of anti-Semitism. As a result, the Jewish populations of many Muslim-majority countries have dramatically dwindled in the last hundred years, as Jewish people have fled. Iraq and Egypt are notable examples.

— 11 —

Conclusion

There can be no doubt that the world faces a serious challenge of multi-faceted Islamisation, involving the economic, political, diplomatic, intellectual, ideological, legal and military arenas. Islamisation is incompatible with established secular orders of government, and is a direct threat to many freedoms and concepts of equality, tolerance and the worth of the individual. Islamisation seeks for Islam to be dominant and sharia to be enforced across the world. It gradually restricts individual human rights and freedom of expression. It suppresses creativity as censorship is allowed to stifle freedom of thought, and gives rise to an atmosphere of fear as religious police roam the streets and enforce uniformity of dress, behaviour and even thought.

Islamisers recognise that the long-term war of ideas is the ultimate battle-ground. The Islamist Saudi sheikh Abd al-'Aziz bin Salih al-Jarbu wrote that

> The battle with the disbelievers is a battle of beliefs. It is not a battle brought on by a dispute over some small piece of land, or a language difference, or military buildups, or economics, or modern technology, or cultural progression, or any of these other banners that constantly rise and fall. In fact, it is not even due to their enmity towards us! Rather, it is a battle based on belief and religion.[391]

Therefore the strategy to respond to the Islamising ideology must be equally comprehensive, must think equally long term, and must involve cooperation between the many groups opposed to Islamisation. Undermining the ideology of Islamisation is the only strategy that offers hope of a permanent solution to the threat it poses. For this it is essential to recognise that the legitimacy that Islamising ideology derives from classical Islamic theology, and also the sophisticated use of the media by Islamisers to embed their radical message into mainstream Islam.

It is important carefully to study and analyse Islamist ideology, history and practice, and the reasons for its wide appeal to ordinary Muslims, so as to devise strategies to counter its appeal. There is a need to develop a sophisticated strategic communications strategy to challenge Islamising doctrines.[392]

Governments of all persuasions, as well as the general public, must be made aware of the ongoing process of Islamisation unfolding globally. Its negative impact must be clarified, and strategies and tactics developed to limit its expansion and ensure equal rights and freedom of religion. The expansion of sharia must be stopped and limited to voluntary application by individuals in the private realm.

The two spheres most affected are society and politics. Efforts must be made to maintain or contend for a society in which freedom of religion is guaranteed by the constitution. The concepts of equal treatment for all, of individual value and of tolerance and respect for others, must be promoted. Any move to give sharia a role within the legal, economic or social system should be opposed. If sharia has already begun to be embedded in any of these systems, whether implicitly or explicitly, it should be reversed if possible.

There should be well thought out programmes to educate attitudes at a popular level about religions and to reshape what is generally understood about Christianity and Islam, and their respective teachings and histories. The major emphasis of this will be filmmaking, print, and televised and internet media. There should be a special focus on providing correct historical information for schools and children to counteract Muslim claims that Islam is the source of all that is good in Western and other civilisations, science and technology. There should be well researched and well argued debate about aspects of Islam that are opposed to concepts of human rights and individual freedoms and how these are directly related to fundamental distinctions within Islam between men and women, and Muslims and non-Muslims.

It is also vital to engage the political process to establish or defend the practice of ordered liberty. A main aim should be to prevent the "accidental" political and legal establishment of sharia or other aspects of Islamisation through governmental "interfaith" efforts that end up making Islam an "official" religion. Efforts must ensure that governments recognise individuals not according to group identity, whether religious, racial, gender or other, but as citizens deserving equal treatment under law. No level of government should allow "separate but equal" policies or laws, such as sharia-compliant finance, or those which grant special or privileged status according to membership in a religious group. Government must act within the scope of the limited powers prescribed by their constitution and ensure that foreign or competing laws or political movements do not displace it. A particular focus of attention should be upon resisting the advance of laws which suppress free speech, whether in the form of speech codes, "incitement to religious hatred", "religious defamation" or other so-called "hate-crime" laws directed against any unapproved public discussion or criticism of Islam. A related effort will be to neutralise the use or threatened use of the law for Islamisation (see pages 57–60) whether by Muslim groups or by Muslim individuals. It may be useful to become aware of and possibly sometimes act in conjunction with liberal Muslims, Muslim women's groups, Muslim academics, and Muslim politicians and others who have the same critical analysis of Islamism in certain areas.

The secular space must be maintained. It is recognised the the word "secular" is deeply offensive to Islamists. Perhaps a more useful term might be a "common" space in which all religions and none can co-exist based on a common citizenship. It is this that offers the best safeguard for human rights, religious liberty and full equality for all individual citizens sharing a common society.

— Appendix 1 —

Guide to the International Islamic Council for Daw'a and Relief (1994)

بسم الله الرحمن الرحيم

CUIDE TO
THE INTERNATIONAL ISLAMIC COUNCIL
FOR DAW'A AND RELIEF

(1415 * 1994)

The International Islamic Council
for Da'wa and Relief

CAIRO OFFICE

P.O.Box 1018
Tel.00 202 290 6159
F. 00 202 290 6217

AMMAN OFFICE

P.O.Box. 2074
Tel. 00 962 6 630239
F.   00 962 6 611950

GUIDE
TO
The International Islamic Council for Daw'a and Relief
General Directorate

RESOLUTION ON THE BY-LAWS
FOR
The International Islamic Council for Daw'a and Relief

Introduction

The religion of Islam is the seal of the Divine Messages, and Muhammad (Allah's peace and prayers be upon his soul) is similarly the seal of all the Prophets and Messengers. Allah sent him to all people in the world. Hence, his Daw'a was universal, unceasing in time, unlimited to any territory, and unrestricted to any race, color or category of human beings.

The Daw'a of Islam addresses all people in all times and places. "We have not sent Thee but to mankind entire, good tidings to bear and warning (against Sin)..." (Verse 28, Sura of Saba')

When the Prophet (may peace be upon him) passed away after delivering the message and fulfilling the trust, the sacred duty of Daw'a as "Fardh Kifayah", collective duty, went to his people ... to all the Muslims, rulers and ruled... carried out on their behalf by the Islamic elite of scholars and men of letters among them, in keeping with the Quranic guidance.

"It is not for the believers to go forth totally; but why should not a party of every section of them go forth, to become learned in religion and to warn their people when they return to them that perhaps they may beware". (Verse 132, Sura of Tawbah)

On this account, it is among the duties of the scholars and the jurists (Al-Fuqaha) who are well-versed in religious matters to propagate Islamic Daw'a, to explain its principles and to correct any misunderstanding of its conceptions, and to convey it to all people in the east and west and the remotest parts of the earth.

The message of Daw'a is among the greatest and noblest messages, especially as its ranges have so widely expanded and its scopes diversified, with the widening methods of demonstrating different contemporary schools of thought. It is to be equally noted nowadays that Islamic rules can be deliberately mixed up with incorrect ideas that are disseminated by God's enemies, which necessitated the assignment of groups of scholars to carry out the task of correcting misconceptions and straightening thoughts so that they conform with the correct criteria of the Islamic faith.

The difficulties of a preacher's mission, besides what has already been mentioned, may be aggravated by the incessant growth of the Muslim people and the spread of their societies all over the world. Besides the extended areas of their territories and countries, their diversified languages and environments all add to the aforementioned difficulties. That is why many institutions, organizations and associations in different countries bearing various nominations, were established to undertake Daw'a efforts, each on its own and according to its capabilities, without planning or coordination.

Consequently, some reformists of Daw'a called for coordination among these organizations, for the realization of optimum benefits on a wide scale so that efforts of all Daw'a institutions working in this field may be complemented.

These hopes have been frequently echoed by Islamic conferences in many sessions, mentioning among those gatherings the Fourth International Conference of Sirah and Sunna (life and traditions) of the Prophet (the Tenth Conference of Islamic Studies Academy), which was held in Cairo on 18-24 Safar, 1406A.H., corresponding to 1-7 November, 1985, the International Mosques Council Conference held in Mecca on 13-15 Safar, 1408A.H., corresponding to 6-8 October, 1987, and the Eleventh Conference of Islamic Studies (Islamic Daw'a Affairs) held in Cairo on 15-19 Rajab, 1408A.H., corresponding to 4-8 March, 1988, all of which discussed the following topics:

A- Coordination of activities of all bodies undertaking Islamic Daw'a and relief works.

B- The status of Islamic minorities in the world and the responsibilities of Muslims towards them.

C- Contemporary causes of the Islamic nation at large.

Among the decisions taken by the conference towards the first subject was the establishment of an International Islamic Council for Daw'a and Relief.

2

The Conference defined the functions of this Council and its sub-branches, and commissioned to Al-Azhar Al-Sharif, in collaboration with the Muslim World League in Mecca and the International Islamic Charitable Foundation in Kuwait, the task of preparing the draft of the By-Laws and Executive Regulations for the suggested Council and its branches.

Subsequently the Shaikh of Al-Azhar invited H.E. Dr. Abdullah Omar Nassif, Secretary General of the Muslim World League, and H.E. Shaikh Yusuf Hajji, the Chairman of the International Islamic Charitable Foundation in Kuwait, for a meeting held at Al-Azhar on Thursday 27 Sha'ban, 1408A.H., corresponding to 14 April, 1988. Discussions took place on the basic aspects of the By-Laws of the suggested Council, and its Executive Regulations.

The Founding Board of the Council was invited to a meeting in Cairo on Wednesday and Thursday 10th and 11 of Safar, 1408A.H., corresponding to 21 and 22 September, 1988, to consider the By-Laws which were adopted as follows:

3

Objects of the Council

Article 2 of the By-Laws sets out the objects of the Council as follows:

1- Study of ways and means that help the propagation of Islamic Daw'a in all parts of the world.

2- Examination and study of problems which encounter the Daw'a organs, suggestion of convenient solutions therefor, study of reports submitted by agencies working in Islamic Daw'a fields and issuance of recommendations concerning same.

3- Working on supporting religious values and adherence to them by different agencies of the public media.

4- Follow-up and study of the conditions of Islamic minorities and supporting them in the light of available studies and reports of Islamic centers on these minorities.

5- Reinforcement of efforts exerted for spreading Islamic Daw'a, acquainting foreign people with Islam, and realization of solidarity among Muslims everywhere in the world.

6- Protection of Islamic Daw'a and its means, the dissemination of true religious values and teachings, and obstructing anti-Islamic currents and antagonistic sects by all legitimate means.

7- Strengthening ties of acquaintance and solidarity between Muslim nations by means of coordination in holding conferences, symposiums, gatherings and Islamic youth camps.

8- Sending out preachers of Daw'a properly selected and trained for tasks of spreading true Daw'a and Islamic culture in different countries with special care for societies of Islamic minorities.

9- Allocation of academic scholarships for peoples and minorities in Islamic universities, institutes and schools, coordination of efforts of donors, securing the appropriate choice of students and due assurance of their well-being.

4

10- Preparing, printing and publishing the Holy Quran and translation of its content, as well as books, magazines, bulletins and newsletters which introduce Islam and expound its values and principles, together with such printed materials that contain enlightened defense of Islam against lies and fallacies fabricated with the purpose of mutilating Islamic principles, and the propagation and distribution of the Council's printed literature among people everywhere in various languages.

11- Following up and directing the help and relief grants submitted to Islamic nations stricken by natural calamities and public upheavals, in conformity with the principle of Islamic solidarity and mutual concerns among Muslims.

12- Encouragement and establishment of colleges, institutes and mosques to spread Islamic culture in different countries, and the establishment of training centers for the preparation and training of Daw'a preachers.

13- Follow-up and encouragement of those schools and mosques which specialize in teaching the Holy Quran by rote.

14- Providing studies, information and statistical data that can be useful for Council work.

15- Properly utilizing graduates of universities and institutes, by admitting them into centers for preparing and training Daw'a preachers and helping them thereafter to obtain appropriate employment.

5

Permanent Specialized Committees

Article 17 specifies that the following permanent committees shall be attached to the Council:

1- Education and Daw'a Permanent Committee, sitting at Al-Azhar Al-Sharif in Cairo.

2- General Relief Permanent Committee, sitting at the International Islamic Relief Organization in Jeddah.

3- Data and Follow-up Permanent Committee, sitting at the Muslim World League in Mecca.

4- Financing and Investment Permanent Committee, sitting at the International Islamic Charitable Foundation in Kuwait

5- Publication and Information Permanent Committee, sitting at the Muslim World League in Mecca.

The Council may establish other committees and specify their headquarters and choose the heads of such committees. The Council may move the headquarters of the committees according to work requirements.

The Presidency Board of the Council

Article 18 states that a Council presidency board shall be established consisting of the Council President, Council Vice-President, Secretary General and heads of the permanent committees established by the Council, and the heads of the member organizations approved by the Council.

6

Member Organizations of the Council

1- Al-Azhar Al-Sharif

Hon. Grand Imam Shaikh Jad El-Haqq Ali Jad El-Haqq, Shaikh of Al-Azhar and President of the Council.

Person to contact: Dr. Abdul Aziz Izzat Abdul Jalil
Address and telephone Nos.: Dirasa, Cairo.
Tel. 904797 - 924750, Fax 903974

2- Muslim World League/Mecca

Mr. Mohammad Bin Nasser Al-Aboudi, acting Secretary General

Person to contact: Mr. Mohammad Salim Hassan
Address: P.O.Box 537, Mecca.
Tel: 5445335, Fax 5436619 - 5435183

3- International Islamic Charitable Foundation/Kuwait

H.E. Shaikh Yusuf Hajji, Chairman

Person to contact: Dr. Badr Abdul Razeq Al-Mass
Address: P.O.Box 3434 Safat.
Tel. 2418025, Fax 2402817 Kuwait

4- International Islamic Relief Organization/Jeddah

Dr. Farid Yassin Qurshi, Head Supervisor of the Organization

Person to contact: Mr. Ibrahim Mohammad Dhahhar
Address: P.O.Box 14843 Jeddah.
Tel. 6519035, Fax 6518491

7

5- **Islamic Daw'a Organization (Munazamat Al-Daw'a Al-Islamiya)/ Khartoum**

Field Marshall Abdul Rahman Siwar Al-Dahab, Chairman of the Board of Trustees of the Organization

Person to contact: Mr. Mohammad Mousa Othman Al-Imam
Address: P.O.Box 199 Khartoum. Tel. 223477

6- **The General Islamic Congress for Jerusalem/Jordan**

H.E. Mr. Kamel Al-Sharif, Chief of the Executive Board of the Congress

Person to contact: Dr. Izzat Jaradat, Director General of the Congress
Address: P.O.Box 2074 Amman, Jordan.
Tel. 630239, Fax 611950

7- **Egyptian Awqaf Ministry**

H.E. Dr. Mohammad Ali Mahjoub, Egyptian Minister of Awqaf

Person to contact: Ministry representative Dr. Abdul Rasheed Abdul Aziz Salem, Undersecretary of the Ministry for Daw'a affairs
Address: Bab al Luq, Sabri Abou Alam Street.
Tel. 3938826, Fax 3936335 - 3900362

8- **International Association of Islamic Banks/Cairo**

H.H. Prince Mohammad Al-Faisal Al Saud, President

Person to contact: H.E. Ambassador Fuad Abdul Hamid Al-Khatib, Secretary General of the Association

Address: 45 Thawra Street, Masr Al-Gidida, Cairo,
Tel. 671728

8

9- **Human Relief Committee**
(Egyptian Medical Association)

Dr. Salem Najem, President of the Committee
Address: 42 Qasr Al-Aini Street, Dar Al-Hikma.
Tel. 3540738, Fax 3562751

10- **Islamic Relief Agency/Khartoum**

Dr. Said Abdullah Said, Director General of the Agency

Person to contact: Dr. Abdul Azim Mohammad Ali Mukhtar
Address: P.O.Box 3372 Khartoum.
Tel. 447630, Fax 447795

11- **International Islamic Union of Student Organizations/**
Khartoum

Dr. Sayyed Abdullah Taher, Secretary General of the Union

Person to contact: Mr. Al-Tayyeb Ahmad Hassan
Address: P.O.Box 3602 Khartoum.
Tel. 225699, Fax 225699

12- **National Relief Organization/Khartoum**

Dr. Alfaki Abdullah Alfaki, Secretary General of the Organization

Person to contact: Mr. Ahmad Abdul Wahhab Mohammad
Address: P.O.Box 2504 Khartoum. Tel. 45938

13- **Islamic Universities League/Morocco**

H.E. Dr. Abdullah Bin Abdul Muhsin Al-Turki, President

Person to contact: Dr. Idris Al-Alawi Al-Abdalawi, League
Secretary General
Address: P.O.Box 242 Akdal Rabat. Tel. 742-63 Morocco

9

14-   **Ministry of Awqaf and Religious Affairs/Morocco**

H.E. Dr. Abdul Kabir Al-Alawi Al-Madghari, Minister of Awqaf

Person to contact: Mr. Radwan Binshaqroun
Address: Rabat, Morocco. Tel. 62308

15-   **Morocco and Senegal Scholars Association/Morocco**

Hon. Mulai Mustafa Al-Alawi, Association President

Address: Rabat, Morocco, 4 Saadeh District. Tel. 755482

16-   **Iqra' Charity Foundation/Jeddah**

H.E. Dr. Mohammad Abdo Yamani, Foundation President

Person to contact: Mr. Hatem Qadi
Address: P.O.Box 10932.
Tel. 6710000, Fax 6694680 - 6673360

17-   **Headquarters of the Department of Scientific Research, Ifta',
Daw'a and Guidance/Riyadh**

Shaikh Abdul Aziz Abdullah Bin Baz, Chairman

Address: P.O.Box 11131 Riyadh.
Tel. 4595555, Fax 4597379

18-   **King Faisal Charity Foundation/Riyadh**

H.H. Prince Bandar Bin Saud Bin Khaled Al Saud, Foundation
Secretary General

Person to contact: Mr. Mohammad Abdul Rahman Kharashi
Address: P.O. Box 352 Riyadh.
Tel. 4652255 Fax 4656524

10

19- **World Assembly of Muslim Youth /Riyadh**

Dr. Mane' Bin Hammad Al-Jahni, Assembly Secretary General

Person to contact: Mr. Walid Mohammad Al-Dayel
Address: Prince Sultan Bin Abdul Aziz Street,
P.O. Box 10845. Tel. 4641669, Fax 4641710

20- **World Union of International Arab Islamic Schools/Riyadh**

H.H. Prince Mohammad Al-Faisal Al Saud, President.
Dr. Mahmoud Mohammad Al-Shawi, Secretary General

Person to contact: Mr. Ibrahim Nasreddine
Address: 25 Talat Harb Street Suite 6 Cairo
Tel/Fax 3939708
P.O. Box 13835 Riyadh. Tel. 4778019, Fax 6606061

21- **Al-Zakah House/Kuwait**

Dr. Abdul Qader Dhahi Ojeil, Director General

Person to contact: Mohammad Abdullah Al Jalahmeh
Address: P.O. Box 23865 Safat.
Tel. 5627700, Fax 5657885 - 5618630

22- **African Muslims Committee/Kuwait**

Dr. Abdul Rahman Hmoud Alsmit, Secretary General
Address: P.O.Box 23849 Safat.
Tel. 2467639, Fax 2439719 - 2528399

23- **Kuwait Relief Committee/Kuwait**

H.E. Mr. Jam'an Faleh Al-Azemi, President

Person to contact: Mr. Badr Nasser Al-Mutairi
Address: P.O. Box 13 Safat. Tel. 2466300, Fax 2449934

11

150

24- **Awqaf and Islamic Affairs Ministry/Kuwait**

H.E. Mr. Jam'an Faleh Al-Azemi, Minister

Person to contact: Mr. Badr Nasser Al-Mutairi
Address: P.O. Box 13 Safat. Tel. 2466300, Fax 2449943

25- **Social Reform Society/Kuwait**

Mr. Abdullah Suleiman Al-Atiqi, Secretary General

Person to contact: Mr. Walid Yusuf Al-Mir

Address: P.O. Box 4850 Safat. Tel. 2514180, Fax 2560523

26- **Revival of Islamic Heritage Association/Kuwait**

Mr. Khaled Sultan Bin Issa, President

Person to contact: Mr. Jassem Mohammad Al-Awn

Address: P.O. Box 5585 Safat. Tel. 5339068, Fax 5339067

27- **Islamic Daw'a Committee/Kuwait**

Mr. Majed Badr Al-Sayyed Hashem Rifai, President

Address: P.O. Box 66723 Bayan.

Tel. 2435604, Fax 2435628

28- **Charitable Assistance Committee/Kuwait**

Mr. Ahmad Abdul Aziz Mohammad Falah

Address: P.O. Box 65174. Tel. 2435879, Fax 2453906

12

29-   Ministry of Awqaf, Muslim Affairs and Sacred Sites/Jordan

H.E. Dr. Abdul Salam Al-Abbadi, Minister

Person to contact: Mr. Mohammad Khalil Lawzi
Address: P.O. Box 659 Amman. Tel. 666141, Fax 602254

30-   International Union of Islamic Medical Societies/Jordan

Dr. Ali Hawamdeh, Secretary General

Address: P.O. Box 2414 Amman. Tel. 693272, Fax 661773

31-   Social Reform and Guidance Association/Dubai, U.A.E.

Shaikh Mohammad Saleh Abdul Rahman Rayes, Secretary

Person to contact: Mr. Ahmad Yusuf Hassan
Address: P.O. Box 4663 Dubai. Tel. 665654, Fax 662071

32-   Charity Work Association/Ajman, U.A.E.

Mr. Salem Bin Ahmad Bin Abdul Rahman, Secretary General

Person to contact: Mr. Haydar Othman Ahmad
Address: P.O. Box 1286 Ajman. Tel. 422115, Fax 427444

33-   Ministry of Awqaf and Muslim Affairs/Abu Dhabi, U.A.E.

H.E. Mr. Mohammad Ahmad Khazerji, Minister of Justice and Muslim Affairs

Person to contact: Mr. Ahmad Mubarak Al-Kindi
Address: P.O. Box 2272 Abu Dhabi.
Tel. 323200, Fax 316003

13

34-   Reform Association/Bahrain

H.E. Shaikh Issa Bin Mohammad Abdullah Al-Khalifah, President

Person to contact: Mr. Issa Ahmad Abdul Rahim
Address: P.O. Box 22282 Muharraq.
Tel. 323990, Fax 332156

35-   Ministry of Awqaf and Islamic Affairs/Qatar

H.E. Shaikh Abdullah Bin Khaled Al Thani, Minister

Person to contact: Mr. Khalifah Bin Jassem Al-Kawwari
Address: P.O. Box 232 Doha. Tel. 466222, Fax 421816

36-   Islamic World Conference/Karachi, Pakistan

H.E. Dr. Abdullah Omar Nassif, Conference President
Hon. Shaikh Raj Mohammad Zafar Al-Hajj, Secretary General
Dr. Hamed Bin Ahmad Rifai, Assistant Secretary General

Address: P.O. Box 9028. Fax 6723997 Jeddah
Pakistan P.O.Box 5030 Karachi 74000 Pakistan.
Tel. 460712, Fax 92 21 466878

37-   Popular Islamic Congress/Iraq

Dr. Irfan Abdul Hamid Fattah, Secretary General

Person to contact: Mr. Riad Abdul Aziz Najem
Address: P.O. Box 4167 Baghdad. Tel. 4256424 Iraq

38-   Ministry of Awqaf and Religious Affairs/Iraq

H.E. Mr. Abdullah Fadhel, Minister

Person to contact: Mr. Riad Abdul Aziz Najem
Address: Baghdad, Iraq. Tel. 4169361

14

39-   Islamic Daw'a and Guidance Organization/Khartoum

Mulana Mr. Mohammad Othman Al-Marghani, President
Shaikh Taj Al-Sir Mahjoub Manoufli, Acting Secretary General

Person to contact: Shaikh Mohammad Said Ahmad
Address: 48 Giza Street Suite 32 Giza
Tel. 3487139, Fax 3491490

40-   Islamic Relief Organization/Birmingham

Dr. Hany El Banna, Director General
Address: 517-519 Moseley Road,
Birmingham-B12 QBX Q.K.
Tel 021-4403114, Fax 4464001

41-   Palestine and Lebanon Relief Fund/London

Mr. Issam Mustafa Yusuf, President
Address: P.O. Box 542 London E13 OOW.
Tel 450 2573, Fax 450 8092

The following organizations also participate in the activities of the Council:

**1-   Organization of Islamic Conference
(Islamic Solidarity Fund)/Jeddah**

H.E. Dr. Hamed Al-Ghabed, Secretary General

Person to contact: H.E. Mr. Al-Hadi Hneitesh
Address: P.O. Box 178 Jeddah. Tel. 6873880, Fax 6873568

2-   Islamic Development Bank/Jeddah

H.E. Dr. Ahmad Mohammed Ali, President

Address: P.O. Box 5925 Jeddah.
Tel. 6361400, Fax 6366871

15

Formation of the Specialized Committees
(according to the By-Laws)

1- Education and Daw'a Specialized Committee
under the patronage of Al-Azhar Al-Sharif/Cairo

The Education and Daw'a Specialized Committee consists of members representing the following bodies:

1- Al-Azhar Al-Sharif		Cairo
2- Egyptian Awqaf Ministry		Cairo
3- International Association of Islamic Banks		Cairo
4- Human Relief Committee (Egyptian Medical Association)		Cairo
5- Muslim World League		Mecca
6- Iqra' Charity Foundation		Jeddah
7- World Assembly of Muslim Youth		Riyadh
8- International Islamic Relief Organization		Jeddah
9- World Union of International Arab Islamic Schools		Riyadh
10- Al-Zakah House		Kuwait
11- Revival of Islamic Heritage Association		Kuwait
12- International Islamic Charitable Foundation		Kuwait
13- Ministry of Awqaf, Muslim Affairs and Sacred Sites		Jordan
14- Islamic Universities League		Morocco

16

15- Ministry of Awqaf and Muslim Affairs   **Morocco**

16- Popular Islamic Congress   **Baghdad**

17- Islamic Daw'a Organization
   (Munazamat Al-Daw'a Al-Islamiya)   **Khartoum**

18- International Islamic Union of Student
   Organizations   **Khartoum**

19- Islamic Daw'a and Guidance Organization   **Khartoum**

20- Qatar Charitable Society   **Qatar**

21- General Islamic Congress for Jerusalem   **Jordan**

2- <u>General Relief Specialized Committee</u>
<u>under the patronage of the International Islamic Relief Organization in</u>
<u>Jeddah</u>

The General Relief Specialized Committee consists of members representing the following bodies:

1- International Islamic Relief Organization   **Jeddah**

2- International Association of Islamic Banks   **Cairo**

3- Kuwait Relief Committee   **Kuwait**

4- Islamic Daw'a Organization
   (Munazamat Al-Daw'a Al-Islamiya)   **Khartoum**

5- International Islamic Charitable Foundation   **Kuwait**

6- Islamic Relief Agency   **Khartoum**

7- Human Relief Committee
   (Egyptian Medical Association)   **Cairo**

17

8- National Relief Organization   Khartoum

9- Charitable Assistance Committee   Kuwait

10- General Islamic Congress for Jerusalem   Jordan

11- International Union of Islamic
     Medical Societies   Jordan

12- Islamic Solidarity Fund   Jeddah

13- International Union of Islamic Banks   Jeddah

14- Palestine and Lebanon Relief Fund   London

3- Information and Follow-up Specialized Committee
under the patronage of the Muslim World League in Mecca.

The Information and Follow-up Specialized Committee consists of members representing the following bodies:

1- Muslim World League   Mecca

2- Al-Azhar Al-Sharif   Cairo

3- King Faisal Charity Foundation   Riyadh

4- Iqra' Charity Foundation   Jeddah

5- Islamic Daw'a Organization
     (Munazamat Al-Daw'a Al-Islamiya)   Khartoum

6- International Islamic Relief Organization   Jeddah

7- Ministry of Awqaf, Muslim Affairs
     and Sacred Sites   Jordan

8- Awqaf and Religious Affairs Ministry   Baghdad

18

9- General Islamic Congress for Jerusalem   Jordan

10- World Union of International Arab
    Islamic Schools   Riyadh

11- Charitable Assistance Committee   Kuwait

12- Human Relief Committee
    (Egyptian Medical Association)   Cairo

13- Islamic Daw'a and Guidance Organization   Khartoum

14- Morocco and Senegal Scholars Association   Morocco

4- <u>Finance and Investment Specialized Committee</u>
<u>under the patronage of the International Islamic Charitable Foundation</u>
<u>in Kuwait</u>

The Finance and Investment Specialized Committee consists of members representing the following bodies:

1- International Islamic Charitable Foundation   Kuwait

2- International Association of Islamic Banks   Cairo

3- Muslim World League   Mecca

4- King Faisal Charitable Foundation   Riyadh

5- Iqra' Charity Foundation   Jeddah

6- Human Relief Committee
    (Egyptian Medical Association)   Cairo

7- Social Reform and Guidance Society   Riyadh

8- World Assembly of Muslim Youth   Riyadh

9- Al-Zakah House   Kuwait

19

10- Popular Islamic Congress   Baghdad

11- Palestine and Lebanon Relief Fund   London

5- **The Publication and Information Specialized Committee**
under the patronage of the Muslim World League in Mecca

The Publication and Information Specialized Committee consists of
Members representing the following bodies:

1- Islamic World Conference   Pakistan

2- Muslim World League   Mecca

3- Al-Azhar Al-Sharif   Cairo

4- Revival of Islamic Heritage Association   Kuwait

5- Morocco and Senegal Scholars Association   Morocco

6- Popular Islamic Congress   Baghdad

7- General Islamic Congress for Jerusalem   Jordan

8- World Assembly of Muslim Youth   Riyadh

9- Awqaf and Islamic Affairs Ministry   Kuwait

10- Ministry of Awqaf, Muslim Affairs
and Sacred Sites   Jordan

11- Human Relief Committee
(Egyptian Medical Association)   Cairo

12- International Islamic Union of Student
Organizations   Khartoum

13- International Islamic Relief Organization   Jeddah

20

The Executive Board of the Council

The Executive Board of the Council is attached to the Secretary General of the Council, and operates under the supervision of the Secretary General. It consists of the following departments:

A-   Data, Documentation, Information and Research   Department.

B-   Financial and Administrative Affairs Department.

C-   Council Committees and Member Affairs Department.

D-   Public Relations Department.

E-   Administrative Secretarial Department.

Various divisions are attached to the above departments.

Address and telephone No. of the General Secretariat of the Council in Cairo

Address: 8 Qamar Street, Misr Al-Gidida, Cairo P.O. Box 1018

21

Telephone Numbers of the Offices
of the Member Organizations in Cairo

Shaikh Al-Azhar, President of the Council:	904797
	924750
Egyptian Minister of Awqaf:	938826
Muslim World League:	3606668
Islamic Daw'a Organization (Munazamat Al-Daw'a Al-Islamiya):	3497386
International Islamic Relief Organization:	3471140
	3474499
	3481176
Charity Work Association:	2597638
International Islamic Union of Student Organizations:	3497386
Iqra' Charity Foundation:	627062
Islamic Relief Agency:	2452340
Islamic Daw'a and Guidance Organization:	Tel. 3487139
	Fax 3491490
World Union of International Arab Islamic Schools:	8079393
International Association of Islamic Banks:	2906701
Kuwait Zakah House:	3602477
Human Relief Committee at the Egyptian Medical Association	Tel. 3562751
	Fax 3540738

22

— APPENDIX 2 —

INTERNATIONAL ISLAMIC COUNCIL FOR DAW'A AND RELIEF: RESOLUTION ON THE BY-LAWS (1994)

بسم الله الرحمن الرحيم

INTERNATIONAL ISLAMIC COUNCIL
FOR DAW'A AND RELIEF

RESOLUTION ON THE BY-LAWS

(1415 * 1994)

The International Islamic Council
for Da'wa and Relief

CAIRO OFFICE

P.O.Box 1018
Tel.00 202 290 6159
F. 00 202 290 6217

AMMAN OFFICE

P.O.Box. 2074
Tel. 00 962 6 630239
F.   00 962 6 611950

**RESOLUTION ON THE BY-LAWS
FOR
The International Islamic Council for Daw'a and Relief**

RESOLUTION ON THE BY-LAWS
FOR
The International Islamic Council for Daw'a and Relief

Introduction

The religion of Islam is the seal of the Divine Messages, and Muhammad (Allah's peace and prayers be upon his soul) is similarly the seal of all the Prophets and Messengers. Allah sent him to all people in the world. Hence, his Daw'a was universal, unceasing in time, unlimited to any territory, and unrestricted to any race, color or category of human beings.

The Daw'a of Islam addresses all people in all times and places. "We have not sent Thee but to mankind entire, good tidings to bear and warning (against Sin)..." (Verse 28, Sura of Saba')

When the Prophet (may peace be upon him) passed away after delivering the message and fulfilling the trust, the sacred duty of Daw'a as "Fardh Kifayah", collective duty, went to his people ... to all the Muslims, rulers and ruled... carried out on their behalf by the Islamic elite of scholars and men of letters among them, in keeping with the Quranic guidance.

"It is not for the believers to go forth totally; but why should not a party of every section of them go forth, to become learned in religion and to warn their people when they return to them that perhaps they may beware". (Verse 132, Sura of Tawbah)

On this account, it is among the duties of the scholars and the jurists (Al-Fuqaha) who are well-versed in religious matters to propagate Islamic Daw'a, to explain its principles and to correct any misunderstanding of its conceptions, and to convey it to all people in the east and west and the remotest parts of the earth.

The message of Daw'a is among the greatest and noblest messages, especially as its ranges have so widely expanded and its scopes diversified, with the widening methods of demonstrating different contemporary schools of thought. It is to be equally noted nowadays that Islamic rules can be deliberately mixed up with incorrect ideas that are disseminated by God's enemies, which necessitated the assignment of groups of scholars to carry out the task of correcting misconceptions and straightening thoughts so that they conform with the correct criteria of the Islamic faith.

The difficulties of a preacher's mission, besides what has already been mentioned, may be aggravated by the incessant growth of the Muslim people and the spread of their societies all over the world. Besides the extended areas of their territories and countries, their diversified languages and environments all add to the aforementioned difficulties. That is why many institutions, organizations and associations in different countries bearing various nominations, were established to undertake Daw'a efforts, each on its own and according to its capabilities, without planning or coordination.

Consequently, some reformists of Daw'a called for coordination among these organizations, for the realization of optimum benefits on a wide scale so that efforts of all Daw'a institutions working in this field may be complemented.

These hopes have been frequently echoed by Islamic conferences in many sessions, mentioning among those gatherings the Fourth International Conference of Sirah and Sunna (life and traditions) of the Prophet (the Tenth Conference of Islamic Studies Academy), which was held in Cairo on 18-24 Safar, 1406A.H., corresponding to 1-7 November, 1985, the International Mosques Council Conference held in Mecca on 13-15 Safar, 1408A.H., corresponding to 6-8 October, 1987, and the Eleventh Conference of Islamic Studies (Islamic Daw'a Affairs) held in Cairo on 15-19 Rajab, 1408A.H., corresponding to 4-8 March, 1988, all of which discussed the following topics:

A- Coordination of activities of all bodies undertaking Islamic Daw'a and relief works.

B- The status of Islamic minorities in the world and the responsibilities of Muslims towards them.

C- Contemporary causes of the Islamic nation at large.

Among the decisions taken by the conference towards the first subject was the establishment of an International Islamic Council for Daw'a and Relief.

2

The Conference defined the functions of this Council and its sub-branches, and commissioned to Al-Azhar Al-Sharif, in collaboration with the Muslim World League in Mecca and the International Islamic Charitable Foundation in Kuwait, the task of preparing the draft of the By-Laws and Executive Regulations for the suggested Council and its branches.

Subsequently the Shaikh of Al-Azhar invited H.E. Dr. Abdullah Omar Nassif, Secretary General of the Muslim World League, and H.E. Shaikh Yusuf Hajji, the Chairman of the International Islamic Charitable Foundation in Kuwait, for a meeting held at Al-Azhar on Thursday 27 Sha'ban, 1408A.H., corresponding to 14 April, 1988. Discussions took place on the basic aspects of the By-Laws of the suggested Council, and its Executive Regulations.

The Founding Board of the Council was invited to a meeting in Cairo on Wednesday and Thursday 10th and 11 of Safar, 1408A.H., corresponding to 21 and 22 September, 1988, to consider the By-Laws which were adopted as follows:

3

**THE BY-LAWS
FOR
THE INTERNATIONAL ISLAMIC COUNCIL FOR DAW'A AND
RELIEF**

Article 1

An international council shall be established which will be known as "The International Islamic Council for Daw'a and Relief" and shall be situated in Cairo.

Article 2

The Council shall coordinate and plan all matters related to the affairs of Daw'a and Relief in the world with special consideration to the following:

1- Study of ways and means that help the propagation of Islamic Daw'a in all parts of the world.

2- Examination and study of problems which encounter the Daw'a organs, suggestion of convenient solutions therefor, study of reports submitted by agencies working in Islamic Daw'a fields and issuance of recommendations concerning same.

3- Working on supporting religious values and adherence to them by different agencies of the public media.

4- Follow-up and study of the conditions of Islamic minorities and supporting them in the light of available studies and reports of Islamic centers on these minorities.

5- Reinforcement of efforts exerted for spreading Islamic Daw'a, acquainting foreign people with Islam, and realization of solidarity among Muslims everywhere in the world.

6- Protection of Islamic Daw'a and its means, the dissemination of true religious values and teachings, and obstructing anti-Islamic currents and antagonistic sects by all legitimate means.

4

7- Strengthening ties of acquaintance and solidarity between Muslim nations by means of coordination in holding conferences, symposiums, gatherings and Islamic youth camps.

8- Sending out preachers of Daw'a properly selected and trained for tasks of spreading true Daw'a and Islamic culture in different countries with special care for societies of Islamic minorities.

9- Allocation of academic scholarships for peoples and minorities in Islamic universities, institutes and schools, coordination of efforts of donors, securing the appropriate choice of students and due assurance of their well-being.

10- Preparing, printing and publishing the Holy Quran and translation of its content, as well as books, magazines, bulletins and newsletters which introduce Islam and expound its values and principles, together with such printed materials that contain enlightened defense of Islam against lies and fallacies fabricated with the purpose of mutilating Islamic principles, and the propagation and distribution of the Council's printed literature among people everywhere in various languages.

11- Following up and directing the help and relief grants submitted to Islamic nations stricken by natural calamities and public upheavals, in conformity with the principle of Islamic solidarity and mutual concerns among Muslims.

12- Encouragement and establishment of colleges, institutes and mosques to spread Islamic culture in different countries, and the establishment of training centers for the preparation and training of Daw'a preachers.

13- Providing studies, information and statistical data that can be useful for Council work.

14- Properly utilizing graduates of universities and institutes, by admitting them into centers for preparing and training Daw'a preachers and helping them thereafter to obtain appropriate employment.

5

Article 3

The Council consists of the institutions, organizations and associations whose memberships have been adopted by the Council, and they are:

1-	Al-Azhar Al-Sharif	In Cairo
2-	International Association of Islamic Banks	In Jeddah
3-	Al-Zakah (Islamic Compulsory Tithe) House	In Kuwait
4-	Al-Islah (Reform) Association	In Bahrain
5-	Al-Islah (Social Reform) Association	In Kuwait
6-	Al-Islah (Social Reform) and Guidance Association	In Dubai
7-	Revival of Islamic Heritage Association	In Kuwait
8-	Muslim World League	In Mecca
9-	Islamic Universities League	In Rabat
10-	Morocco and Senegal Scholars Association	In Rabat
11-	General Headquarters Departments of Cultural Research, Daw'a and Guidance	In Riyadh
12-	African Muslims Committee	In Kuwait
13-	Kuwait Relief Committee	In Kuwait
14-	Islamic Daw'a Organization (Munazamat Al-Daw'a Al-Islamiya)	In Khartoum
15-	Popular Islamic Congress	In Baghdad
16-	General Islamic Congress for Jerusalem	In Jordan

6

17-	Iqra' (Read) Charity Foundation	In Jeddah
18-	King Faisal Charity Foundation	In Riyadh
19-	World Assembly of Muslim Youth	In Riyadh
20-	International Islamic Charitable Foundation	In Kuwait
21-	International Islamic Relief Organization	In Jeddah
22-	Islamic Relief Agency	In Khartoum
23-	Islamic Daw'a Committee	In Kuwait
24-	Charity Work Association	In Ajman
25-	Human Relief Committee (Egyptian Medical Association)	In Cairo
26-	International Islamic Union of Student Organizations	In Khartoum
27-	National Relief Organization	In Khartoum
28-	World Union of International Arab Islamic Schools	In Riyadh
29-	International Union of Islamic Medical Societies	In Jordan
30-	Islamic World Conference	In Pakistan
31-	Charitable Assistance Committee	In Kuwait
32-	Islamic Daw'a and Guidance Organization	In Kuwait
33-	Islamic Relief Organization	In Birmingham
34-	Palestine and Lebanon Relief Fund	In London

7

35-	Al-Imam Al-Bukhari Society	In Morocco
36-	Islamic World Council	In London
37-	Qatar Charitable Society	In Qatar
38-	Muwaffaq Charitable Organization	In Khartoum
39-	Islamic Waqf Society for Education and Guidance	In Nigeria
40-	Britain Scholars Society	In Britain
41-	Indonesian Higher Council for Islamic Daw'a	In Indonesia

42-   Ministries of Awqaf and Islamic Affairs Departments of:

A-Arab Republic of Egypt.

B-The Kingdom of Morocco.

C-The Republic of Iraq.

D-The State of Kuwait.

E-The State of Qatar

F-United Arab Emirates.

G-The Hashemite Kingdom of Jordan.

Article 4

Every institution, group, or organization exercising activities in the scope of Islamic Daw'a and Relief outside the territories of its country is entitled to join the Council by application to be filed with the permanent General Secretariat of the Council, which application shall be submitted to the first meeting of the Council following the filing of the application.

8

Article 5

The Council consists of the Founding Members and those who join it thereafter, and Cairo will be the permanent headquarters for the Council's sessions. The Council may, however, by a majority of attending members, decide to hold session in any other location. The Sheik of Al-Azhar shall be the Chairman of the Council.

Article 6

The Council shall hold an annual session in Muharram, the first month of the Islamic calendar, by invitation from its Chairman, or his deputy in case of the Chairman's absence, to discuss its agenda in which the following subjects shall have priority:

1- Approval of previous session minutes whether ordinary or extraordinary.

2- Study and adoption of administrative and financial regulations and their amendment.

3- Study and adoption of the annual budget and final accounts.

4- Acceptance of new members in the Council.

5- Appointing one or more auditors for the forthcoming fiscal year and fixing his or their remuneration.

6- Adoption of the financial report of the previous year.

7- Election of the Secretary General of the Council in accordance with the provisions of these By-Laws.

8- Discussion of the Secretary General's report and reports of other committees on the activities of the Council during the previous year.

Article 7

The Council may convene an emergency meeting whenever there is a need for such meeting, by an invitation of the Chairman or that of at least five of

9

its members. The Council may not be convened except upon the approval of an absolute majority of the members attending such a meeting.

Article 8

The Council elects its Deputy Chairman for a term of four years, which term is renewable.

Article 9

Each member of the Council shall have one vote.

Article 10

Council decisions are binding upon all members whether passed unanimously or by absolute majority.

Article 11

Except in the cases stipulated in these By-Laws, decisions shall be passed by absolute majority of members present.

Article 12

The Council enjoys legal competence concerning the following:

A- Owning and disposing of movable and immovable property, contributions, subscriptions, wills and Waqfs which serve its goals.

B- Contracting power.

C- Judicial competence.

Article 13

The Council shall have a General Secretariat composed of a Secretary General and a sufficient number of staff.

10

Article 14

The Council shall choose one of its members to be the Secretary General for three years, renewable for one more term. The Secretary General shall be the legal representative of the Council, and shall represent the Council before other organizations, and shall preside over the executive staff of the Council.

Article 15

The General Secretariat, under the direction of the Secretary General of the Council, shall have the following duties:

1- Carrying out the preparatory works for conferences and sessions of the Council and other committees, and transmitting to Council members any decisions taken.

2- Requesting suggestions from members prior to the holding of the conference or the Council.

3- Carrying out the functions of the Secretariat of the Council, its meetings, conferences and other committees, and the dispatching of invitations to members.

4- Submission of an annual report to the Council on its performance.

5- Preparation of the draft budget and final accounts.

6- Arranging and typing the suggestions and dispatching same to members prior to the holding of the Council session or meeting, within not less than one month.

7- Execution of the Council's decisions and recommendations.

8- Delivery to members of the Council all information and suggestions received by the General Secretariat.

11

Article 16

The financial resources of the Council shall consist of the following:

1- Annual subscription for Council membership. Each member shall fix its subscription amount through a written admission sent to the Council Secretariat within a period not exceeding three months as from the date of ratification of these By-Laws by the Council, provided that the subscription amount shall be not less than US$3,000 (three thousand U.S. Dollars) annually.

2- Contributions, gifts, testamentary dispositions, and Waqf which the Council approves and which are in conformity with its purposes.

3- Returns on the Council's financial investments.

Article 17

The following specialized committees shall be attached to the Council:

1- Education and Daw'a Committee	In Cairo
2- General Relief Committee	In Jeddah
3- Data and Follow-up Committee	In Mecca
4- Financing and Investment Committee	In Kuwait
5- Publication and Information Committee	In Baghdad
6- Youth Committee	In Riyadh
7- Muslim Minorities Committee	In London

The Council shall select the heads of these committees and may establish other specialized committees as required by the work, and the Presidency Board shall name the heads of these committees and choose the headquarters thereof as the work requires.

12

Article 18

A- The Presidency Board of the Council shall consist of the Council Chairman, the Deputy Chairman, the Secretary General and the heads of the specialized committees formed by the Council, and the heads of the member organizations that the Council decides to include in the Presidency Board.

B- The Secretary General may upon the approval of the Chairman invite whomever of the heads of the member organizations to attend Presidency Board meetings, and in such case they shall have the rights of membership of the Presidency Board.

C- The Chairman shall represent the Council before governmental and international organizations and on official occasions.

Article 19

The Presidency Board of the Council shall undertake the following:

1- Follow-up of coordination between organizations, institutions and associations working in the field of Islamic Daw'a and Relief, and planning for such activities.

2- Follow-up of the execution of the Council's resolutions and recommendations.

3- General guidance and supervision of all committees and institutions working for the realization of the Council's aims.

4- Handling the important issues that are not included within the sphere of authority of the committees.

Article 20

The Education and Daw'a Committee consists of members representing the following bodies:

1- Al-Azhar Al-Sharif   In Cairo

13

2- International Association of Islamic Banks	In Cairo
3- Al-Zakah House	In Kuwait
4- Revival of Islamic Heritage Association	In Kuwait
5- Muslim World League	In Mecca
6- Islamic Universities League	In Rabat
7- Iqra' Charity Foundation	In Jeddah
8- Popular Islamic Congress	In Baghdad
9- Islamic Daw'a Organization (Munazamat Al-Daw'a Al-Islamiya)	In Khartoum
10- International Islamic Charitable Foundation	In Kuwait
11- World Assembly of Muslim Youth	In Riyadh
12- Ministry of Awqaf, Muslim Affairs and Sacred Sites	In Jordan
13- Awqaf and Islamic Affairs Ministry	In Morocco
14- International Islamic Relief Organization	In Jeddah
15- International Islamic Union of Student Organization	In Khartoum
16- Human Relief Committee (Egyptian Medical Association)	In Cairo
17- World Union of International Arab Islamic Schools	In Riyadh
18- Egyptian Awqaf Ministry	In Cairo
19- Islamic Daw'a and Guidance Organization	In Khartoum
20- Qatar Charitable Society	In Qatar

14

21- General Islamic Congress for Jerusalem   In Jordan

Article 21

The Education and Daw'a Committee specializes in the following matters:

-   Setting up plans and projects for transmitting Islamic Daw'a and spreading Islamic culture (incremental as well as annual plans and projects) to all people and submitting them to the Council for adoption.

-   Prescribing incremental targets for Daw'a preachers to meet.

-   Suggesting the establishment of educational and cultural institutions (vocational, educational and pedagogical) and supporting same, such as schools, universities, libraries, culture clubs and centers for preparing and training Daw'a preachers.

-   Preparing a chart of the needs of Muslims for preachers in different countries.

-   Suggesting a number of scholarships for applicants wishing to study in Islamic universities and schools and the conditions for granting such scholarships, laying down the bases for optimum utilization of such scholarships, and taking measures for surmounting difficulties encountered by students.

-   Proposing the best means and methods for developing the education and styles of Daw'a commensurate with the development of Daw'a institutes.

-   Studying specific problems facing Daw'a preachers in each country.

-   Follow-up of execution of Daw'a and education plans and propagation of Islamic culture.

-   Setting up programmes for preparing preachers and their training so that they shoulder the message of Daw'a, taking into account the diversity of Muslim environments in matters of conventions and

15

traditions, so that they may be able to establish and run appropriate centers for this purpose.

- The submission of an annual report to the Council on it activities in this scope, detailing achievements realized in the fields of education and Daw'a.

Article 22

The General Relief Committee consists of members representing the following bodies:

1-	International Islamic Relief Organization	In Jeddah
2-	International Association of Islamic Banks	In Cairo
3-	Islamic Solidarity Fund	In Jeddah
4-	Kuwait Relief Committee	In Kuwait
5-	Islamic Daw'a Organization (Munazamat Al-Daw'a Al-Islamiya)	In Khartoum
6-	International Islamic Charitable Foundation	In Kuwait
7-	Islamic Relief Agency	In Khartoum
8-	General Islamic Congress for Jerusalem	In Jordan
9-	Charitable Assistance Committee	In Kuwait
10-	National Relief Organization	In Khartoum
11-	Human Relief Committee (Egyptian Medical Association)	In Cairo
12-	International Union of Islamic Medical Societies	In Jordan
13-	Palestine and Lebanon Relief Fund	In London

16

14- Qatar Charitable Society   In Qatar

Article 23

The Relief Committee specializes in the following matters:

-   Setting up plans for collecting aid and relief contributions and the policy of their distribution in such a way as to fulfill the needs of needy Muslim individuals and universities, such as dress, food, homes, medicine and education. All these entail the establishment of hospitals, medical centers, cultural and educational institutions, clubs, libraries and other similar facilities so that a Muslim "personality" shall be guaranteed and developed religiously, medically, socially, economically and educationally.

-   Coordination with international relief agencies.

-   Preparing a list for the priorities of distributing the aid and relief among peoples of the Islamic World.

-   Study of applications received by the Council concerning aid.

-   The submission to the Council of an annual report on the Council's activities in this concern.

-   Follow-up of plans for aid and assistance.

Article 24

The Finance and Investment Committee consists of members representing the following bodies:

1- International Islamic Charitable Foundation   In Kuwait

2- International Association of Islamic Banks   In Cairo

3- Muslim World League   In Mecca

4- King Faisal Charity Foundation   In Riyadh

17

5- Iqra' Charity Foundation	In Jeddah
6- Popular Islamic Congress	In Baghdad
7- Social Reform and Guidance Association	In Dubai
8- World Assembly of Muslim Youth	In Riyadh
9- Al-Zakah House	In Kuwait
10- Human Relief Committee (Egyptian Medical Association)	In Cairo
11- Palestine and Lebanon Relief Fund	In London

Article 25

The Finance and Investment Committee specializes in the following matters:

- Preparing a general plan for collecting contributions and following up its execution.

- Forming sub-committees for collection of contributions from different countries, from religious sources, in the form of donations/contributions (in cash and in kind), aid/waqf/wills offered by individuals and bodies (private sector/governmental, international or local) so long as they do not conflict with the targets and purposes of the Council.

- Preparing a general plan for investment of the Council's money so that returns thereon will be employed in realization of the Council's aims, and the plan shall be submitted to the Council for adoption.

- The Committee is entitled to seek, for realization of its targets, the assistance of Islamic financial, economic and investment experts together with Sharia experts.

18

- Deliver an annual report about the amount of the Council's money and its returns.

Article 26

The Data and Follow-up Committee consists of members representing the following bodies:

1- Muslim World League	In Mecca
2- Al-Azhar Al-Sharif	In Cairo
3- Morocco and Senegal Scholars League	In Rabat
4- King Faisal Charity Foundation	In Riyadh
5- Iqra' Charity Foundation	In Jeddah
6- Islamic Daw'a Organization (Munazamat Al-Daw'a Al-Islamiya)	In Khartoum
7- International Islamic Relief Organization	In Jeddah
8- Iraqi Ministry of Awqaf	In Baghdad
9- Ministry of Awqaf, Muslim Affairs and Sacred Sites	In Jordan
10- Charitable Assistance Committee	In Kuwait
11- World Union of International Arab Islamic Schools	In Riyadh
12- General Islamic Congress for Jerusalem	In Jordan
13- Human Relief Committee (Egyptian Medical Association)	In Cairo
14- Islamic Daw'a and Guidance Organization	In Khartoum

19

Article 27

The Data and Follow-up Committee carries out the process of collecting and exchanging data, statistics and statements on all matters relating to the Council's mission from all countries of the world and Islamic centers abroad, then organizes the utilization of all such data and statistics and provides same to the Council and its committees so that they make use of them in formulating their decisions and recommendations.

Article 28

The Publication and Information Committee consists of members representing the following bodies:

1- Islamic World Conference	In Pakistan
2- Al-Azhar Al-Sharif	In Cairo
3- Revival of Islamic Heritage Association	In Kuwait
4- Muslim World League	In Mecca
5- Morocco and Senegal Scholars League	In Rabat
6- Popular Islamic Congress	In Baghdad
7- General Islamic Congress for Jerusalem	In Jordan
8- World Assembly of Muslim Youth	In Riyadh
9- Al-Awqaf Ministry	In Kuwait
10- Ministry of Awqaf, Muslim Affairs and Sacred Sites	In Jordan
11- International Islamic Relief Organization	In Jeddah
12- International Islamic Union of Student Organizations	In Khartoum
13- Human Relief Committee (Egyptian Medical Association)	In Cairo

20

Article 29

The Committee for Publication and Information specializes in the following matters:

1- Preparing plans and studies that guarantee the promotion of Islamic information in the audio-visual and print media.

2- The preparation of television and broadcasting projects that serve the Council's purposes.

3- Preparing plans and studies that guarantee the countering of propaganda hostile to Islam and Muslims.

4- Suggesting plans for coordinating between organizations and agencies working on Islamic information.

5- Coordinating the work of different agencies engaged in printing the Holy Quran and translating its contents into other languages.

6- Following up all publications hostile to Islam and refuting their false allegations.

7- Preparing subjects for studies and proposing writing books and coordinating between the organs undertaking these tasks in the following fields:

   a- Presenting Islam and exposing its principles for non-Muslims.

   b- Publishing books which introduce Islam and Islamic culture.

   c- Confronting the destructive currents that work against the faith of Islam and undermine true religious conceptions and values.

8- Suggesting names of studies and books that deserve to be translated to other languages.

9- Coordinating between organs working in the field of mass media in the Islamic World.

21

10- Building up coordination in the field of mass media concerning major Islamic causes.

Article 30

The Youth Committee consists of members representing the following bodies:

1-	World Assembly of Muslim Youth	In Riyadh
2-	Muslim World League	In Mecca
3-	Qatari Ministry of Awqaf and Islamic Affairs	In Qatar
4-	International Islamic Union of Student Organizations	In Khartoum
5-	Islamic World Council	In London
6-	Iqra' Charity Foundation	In Jeddah
7-	World Union of International Arab Islamic Schools	In Riyadh
8-	Ministry of Awqaf and Islamic Affairs	In Kuwait
9-	Social Reform and Guidance Association	In Dubai
10-	International Islamic Relief Organization	In Jeddah
11-	International Islamic Charitable Foundation	In Kuwait
12-	African Muslims Committee	In Kuwait
13-	Britain Scholars Society	In Britain
14-	General Islamic Congress for Jerusalem	In Jordan
15-	Islamic World Conference	In Pakistan/ Jeddah Office

22

16- Islamic Daw'a and Guidance Organization   In Khartoum

17- International Islamic Council for Daw'a and Relief   In Cairo

Article 31

The Youth Committee specializes in the following matters:

- Studying the problems of Muslim youth in light of Sharia and the spirit of Islam based upon the circumstances of the different environments and countries and establishing a joint vision of such problems and methods of solution.

- Investigation of the reasons for negative phenomena rife in certain youth trends and guiding the youth towards the values of balance, forgiveness and daw'a through wisdom and good advice.

- Encouragement of the movement of information and publication in various languages and the use of modern auditory, visual and print media to disseminate proper Islamic thought among the youth.

- Guiding specialized researchers to set out theoretical and practical education programs to exploit the potential of youth in supporting construction and development projects in the various Islamic countries.

- Setting up meetings, camps and seminars which include youth from the various Islamic countries for the purpose of introduction and strengthening the sense of belonging to the one nation of Islam, and improving the observance of Islam.

- Contributing to the establishment of playgrounds and athletic unions and the appropriate athletic competitions within the framework of Islamic Sharia and traditions.

- Strengthening the connection with the official and popular educational and media organizations and supplying them with beneficial cultural and leisure programs which nurture faith and the spirit of hard work and observance among Muslim youth.

23

- Establishing joint projects which benefit the youth movement among the concerned member organizations and presenting them to the Presidency Board to decide upon them on the basis of the policy of coordination among those organizations.

- Attempting to cooperate and coordinate with ministries and organizations concerned with youth in the countries of the Islamic World.

- Attempting to cooperate and coordinate with Islamic societies and organizations concerned with youth affairs on the international level.

- Preparing Muslim youth to contribute to daw'a and relief work through the daw'a and relief organizations of the Council and others.

- Attempting to provide educational grants and financial support for gifted Muslim students and attempting to coordinate among Islamic entities that provide such grants in the Islamic world.

- Working towards establishing a "Youth Fund" to provide financial support for various youth programs funded through Islamic governments and contributions of member organizations, donations and potential investment projects.

- Providing youth centers and hostels in the major cities of the world to serve as guest houses and education centers for Muslim youth in those cities, while attempting to exploit the houses available in some Islamic countries.

- Offering cultural, intellectual and training programs to prepare leaderships of Islamic youth activities administratively and actively.

- Preparing specialized seminars to study youth problems and matters of interest to youth and presenting recommendations to those entities supervising youth activities in the world.

- Attempting to cooperate and coordinate with international

24

organizations to provide a voice for Muslim youth in crucial matters especially those affecting the Islamic world.

- Continuing to carry out the existing plans and presenting an annual report on what has been achieved, and highlighting the problems encountered and methods of improving the work.

Article 32

The Muslim Minorities Committee consists of members representing the following bodies:

1-	Islamic World Council	In London
2-	Muslim World League	In Mecca
3-	Islamic Daw'a Organization (Munazamat Al-Daw'a Al-Islamiya)	In Khartoum
4-	Egyptian Ministry of Awqaf	In Cairo
5-	World Assembly of Muslim Youth	In Riyadh
6-	International Islamic Charitable Foundation	In Kuwait
7-	General Islamic Congress for Jerusalem	In Jordan
8-	Islamic World Conference	In Pakistan
9-	African Muslims Committee	In Kuwait
10-	Revival of Islamic Heritage Association	In Kuwait
11-	Britain Scholars Society	In Birmingham

Article 33

The Muslim Minorities Committee specializes in the following matters:

25

- Studying the affairs of Muslim minorities in the world and specifying organizational and administrative methods to identify their problems.

- Devising and preparing joint projects among member organizations which guarantee the preservation of the Islamic character through educational and media programs, to be presented to the Presidency Board of the International Islamic Council for Daw'a and Relief.

- Working to establish educational, cultural and youth organizations which include Muslim children to nurture them in an Islamic environment, by way of cooperating with the member organizations and philanthropist Muslims.

- Preparing specialized seminars and meetings which explore the situation of Muslim minorities and what they encounter, with the aim of arriving at a unified vision of their problems and methods of their solution.

- Organizing the relationship with Islamic governments to support cultural and social efforts exerted to protect the Muslim minorities and confirming their right to preserve their religion and Islamic traditions, and to guarantee coexistence and good neighborly relations with their nationals.

General Provisions

Article 34

The Council may discharge any member who refrains from carrying out its duties stipulated in these By-Laws. Such discharge shall be by a decision taken by a two thirds majority of members present.

Article 35

If a member decides to withdraw from Council membership, such member must submit this decision in writing to the Council Chairman three months prior to the Council session, and the Council shall decide on its request during the first session immediately after the member submitted its resignation.

26

Article 36

The amendment of the Council's By-Laws shall be effective upon the approval of two thirds of the Council members. Should such quorum not be realized, the suggested amendment shall be resubmitted to the Council in the following session, whereupon the vote of two thirds of the members present shall be sufficient for the passage of the amendment.

Article 37

Commissions and bodies applying for membership in the Council may be invited to attend the Council and committee meetings as observers until a decision is taken on their membership.

Article 38

Reports of committees shall be submitted to the Council's Presidency Board for decisions concerning such reports.

Article 39

The heads of the specialized committees shall inform the Secretary General of the suggested dates of meetings of their committees and their agenda of meetings so that he may coordinate between them.

The Secretary General shall notify all Council members of such coordination. Each member may attend any committee meeting and participate fully in its function.

Article 40

These By-Laws shall become valid and binding when the members have signed same. Each member may ratify same in the method applicable in that member's respective country.

Members of the Founding Board
[Signatures]

27

— Appendix 3 —

Coordination System of the International Islamic Council for Daw'a and Relief (1993, 1995)

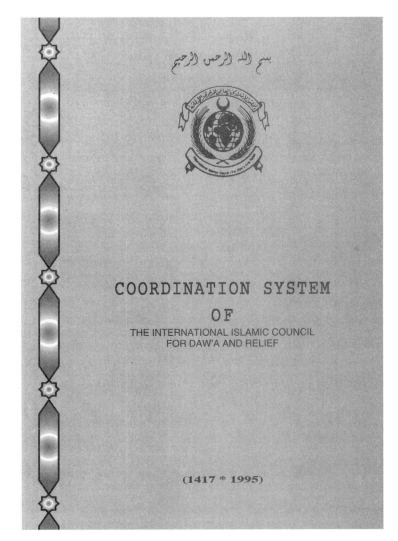

**Coordination System
of
The International Islamic Council for Daw'a and Relief**

1414 AH.*1993 AD.

Table of Contents

2

1- Introduction to the Coordination System

"Truly, Allah loves those who fight in His cause in battle array, as if they were a solid cemented structure". (Al-Saff, Aya 4)

"He it is that hath strengthened thee with his aid and with (the company of) the Believers; and (moreover) He hath put affection between their hearts; not if thou hadst spent all that is in the earth couldst thou have produced that affection, but Allah hath done it: for He is exalted in might, Wise". (Al-Anfal, Ayas 62-63)

"Stand straight and do not differ lest your hearts should differ". (A dignified tradition)

"Allah's aid is for the united group". (A dignified tradition)

Islam calls on Muslims to unify their world and assimilate their opinion. It urges the straightness of line and fights against disunity, differences and divisions. In the Holy Quran, in the tradition of the Prophet (Allah's prayers be upon him), and in the history of the early and good predecessors, there are commandments, warnings and lessons whose aims are comprehended by all those whose hearts are opened, by Allah's grace, to the light of faith; those that surmount desire and worldly non-lasting temptations... When Muslims abided by Allah's orders, they ascended to real glory and were conveyors of goodness, peace and guidance for all humanity; but when they shunned righteousness, differences aggravated, and, becoming badly divided, they brought misery unto themselves and the world at large.

The leaders of Islamic popular movements became aware of these facts and they found that among the means leading to the coveted unity was coordination in thought, effort and action on a stable and disciplined basis. They also found the advantage of the transference of Daw'a and relief work from the local sphere to the world sphere, without prejudicing the distinctive national features of each organization. Hence, there emerged, for the first time, the idea of the International Islamic Council for Daw'a and Relief. The notion was that those cooperative sister organizations comprise the elites of Muslim thinkers and large sectors of peoples. They enjoy amicable relationships with governments and leaders, and possess such informational capabilities that give them the advantage of influencing those sides, and direct them towards the unification of Muslim attitudes which shall undoubtedly serve their concerns and those of the world at large.

Despite the belief that coordination can be very useful as a method for unifying aims and goals, a certain ambiguity still hovered around this conception and its practical scope. It also engulfed the framework suggested for the working of such a large project and whatever institutions were necessary to carry out this weighty idea. Now, our intention through this coordinating system for the International Islamic Council for Daw'a and Relief, has been to answer the questions posed above, so that the features of this plan may become clear in relation to the geographical divisions and administrative responsibilities of the Council, and so that each participating party recognize its duty and try to accomplish it to the best of its abilities.

-3-

196

It is needless to mention that the stronger organizations should come to the aid of the ones with lesser capabilities and undertake a share of their development, especially when the abler sides perceive the burdens and the obstacles of those less fortunate, that obstruct the expansion of their activities. Unless such essential need is realized, the concept of coordination, and the whole idea of the Council, and all the hopes attached thereto, become mere jabber, subject with time to setbacks, despair and hopelessness .

It shall become clear from these papers that each institution and each individual has an important role to play in this endeavor. It is similar to a complete body, where the whole structure collapses by the collapse of a part of it, just as the honored prophetic tradition says, "Muslims in their fraternity, mutual mercy and compassion are like to a body where the complaint of a single member of it makes the whole body rally with feverishness and watchfulness". True are the words of Prophet (Allah's prayers be upon him).

May Allah, glorified be His name, straighten our way and bestow success on us all.

Kamel Al-Sharif
Secretary General
International Islamic Council for Daw'a and Relief.

4

2.   General Principles for the Coordination System

First: Prevention of duplication and contradiction in the work of member organizations, which lead to an unnecessary waste of effort and money, and paves the way for harmful competition and the rise of disagreements. This shall be achieved by specific definition of roles and scope of work through Council institutions where all participate on various levels.

Second: Creation of joint projects especially in the scope of relief, in which more than one organization participate so that there will emerge capable and sustained institutions with permanent resources which guarantee subsistence for those dependent upon them, and providing them with scientific, technical, and fiscal capabilities necessary to secure a good life.

Third: Entrance to zones stricken by political or natural catastrophes in a disciplined manner free from improvisation and unrestricted competition which cause harmful and destructive allegiances of a tribal, intellectual or secular nature detrimental to the general benefit and set the stage for the rise atheist or secular ideas under the pretext of restoring security and stability.

Fourth: Providing of information and data on the prevalent local circumstances in distressed areas and a description of existing trends and obstacles, which will be at the disposal of member organizations and their delegates so that their work may be systematic and continuous, and so that each new effort is added as a layer onto the previous layer, thus avoiding contradiction.

Fifth: The foundation of a wide communications network connected to a unified direction center so that this center shall duly become a pressure source for supporting such Islamic causes as Palestine, Bosnia and Kashmir and others, and provide studies, statistics and documents on these causes and others which shall be at the disposal of member organizations so that they may effect activities of the following type:-

   A. Publication in mass media.
   B. Despatching cables and declarations.
   C. Sending local and international delegations.

Sixth: The establishment of scientific institutions and training centers of unified curricula with the purpose of graduating preachers who abide by Islamic methodology of preaching faith in Allah by wisdom and good advice,...free from the influence of narrow religious sects, political parties and other beliefs, so that those trainees shall be exposed to modern cultures and know the languages and traditions of countries where they work.

Seventh: Reviewing the distribution of preachers in different countries during the joint meetings held by the Council committees, organizations and symposiums so that the overcrowding of preachers in one country while others lack them because of the lack of coordination is avoided. It is also

5

vital that work of relief and Daw'a should be linked wherever possible and as the circumstances of each country may allow, and according to the country's special situation based on studies prepared by Council staff.

Eighth: The creation of a Muslim intellectual current on the basis of the Quran and Sunna, which current tends towards the unification of the Muslim attitude through wisdom and good advice offered to Muslim leaders and peoples alike. This shall be achieved by the development of a publishing agency supervised by the Council. Such intellectualism shall have to be promoted through the available mass media, or through new media channels established for that purpose. It shall be organized by mutual work of member organizations through the specialized Council committees.

Ninth: The more power this International Islamic Council acquires, the more respect and importance it acquires among Muslims, and consequently, the more momentum it gains to mediate for peace among the faithful, governments and organizations alike. This shall also cause it to attain more authority and prestige in contacting non-Muslims, which has become a message the importance of which is deeply felt and appreciated.

Tenth: To face up to the hostile campaigns launched against Islam and Muslims in political and intellectual arenas. There shall have to be prepared scientific research on each of the topics raised. Plans shall have to be laid for cooperation among Muslim centers. New institutions may be established for following up such hostile propaganda. There shall have to be established a central leadership with substance and prestige, in order to establish contacts to promote understanding among nations based on truth, justice and mutual respect.. No doubt, the success of the coordination concept and the cooperation of all in supporting it is the first step for the foundation of that Islamic leadership.

Eleventh: So long as the basic aim is the establishment of a popular world organ for implementation of the purposes intended by the establishment of International Islamic Council for Daw'a and Relief, it is really necessary that the aforementioned organizations should help one another. It will not serve coordination purposes that an organization be established where another one is functioning except in cases of real necessity. We ought also to give priority for directing financial or moral support to member organizations or through them so that the ultimate goals of the coordination process may be realized.

6

3- The Role of the Presidency Board

The Presidency Board of the Council plays a principal role in the coordination process by virtue of the powers granted to it by the Council and by virtue of the presence in it of the heads of specialized committees and chairmen of member organizations, who are entitled to take decisions and distribute roles and follow-up through the General Secretariat of the Council. The role of the Presidency Board may be defined as follows:-

First: The Presidency Board shall meet about once every three months at a location agreed by the Board members to keep pace with the execution of the decisions of the Founding Board.

Second: Additionally, the Presidency Board reviews the projects submitted to it from three sources:-

A. Those submitted by the specialized committees.
B. Those submitted directly by the General Secretariat.
C. Those submitted by a Board member.

Third: The Presidency Board studies reports submitted by the General Secretariat on urgent Islamic causes between sessions of the Founding Board, in order to take the necessary steps.

Fourth: The Board moves as a unit or by delegating any of its members to try to resolve disputes and reconcile parties in conflict.

Fifth: The Board requests the Secretary General and some members of the Presidency Board or organizations chairmen to conduct political contacts with states, foreign organizations and bodies.

Sixth: The Board shall control the development of financial and administrative affairs during intervals between Presidency Board sessions and meetings of the Founding Board.

7

4-   The Role of the General Secretariat

The General Secretariat of the International Islamic Council for Daw'a and Relief is the executive apparatus of the Council within the framework of the comprehensive coordination process. It adopts the following coordinating methods and styles under the supervision of the Secretary General and by way of the Director General of the Council:-

1- Sections of the General Secretariat shall be in accordance with existing member organizations so that there shall be specialization in keeping pace with organization activities. They sort reports received from organizations or from communications delegates and benefit from them in the coordination process.

2- Sections shall exist on the basis of the specialized Council committees. They shall receive the reports and recommendations of these committees, which they scrutinize and suggest instruments for their implementation. They shall then be submitted to the Secretary General and the Director General so that they may follow up the execution procedures.

3- The Studies and Research Section in the General Secretariat shall prepare periodic reports on the development of various Islamic causes so that the General Secretariat may submit same to the various Council organs and its specialized committees and member organizations to benefit from them in their action.

4- The General Secretariat shall carry out due contacts with specialized committees and organization members suggesting informational campaigns or pressure means or political contacts for the support of Islamic causes.

5- The General Secretariat shall issue such bulletins and magazines and publications as reflect the activities of organization members, their scope of work and the attitude of the Council vis-a-vis all causes, with the purpose of establishing a unified understanding among organization members towards Islamic causes.

6- Receiving delegation reports sent by organization members, sorting them and placing them at the disposal of any new delegations that are sent out, to ensure continuity and prevent contradiction or unnecessary overlap in their work.

7- Following up political contacts in causes decided by the Founding Board or the Presidency Board, especially which relate to reconciliation and participation in the efforts of organization members.

8- Representing the Council in conferences and symposiums and general meetings held by organization members and reporting the results of such meetings to organization members through Council channels.

8

201

9- Preparation of annual reports for the General Secretariat to be submitted to the Founding Board including a summary of the outcome of Council efforts and the efforts of its organs, with special concentration on development of the coordination process and whatever progress or obstacles it may encounter.

10- Follow-up of committees chairmen and communications delegates in writing or by direct contact to remind and urge them to implement the decisions and recommendations taken jointly by the Founding Board and the Presidency Board, and to cooperate with them in surmounting obstacles.

11- Cooperation with the heads of the specialized committees in the preparation of an agenda for their work and notifying organization members of the times and places of meetings, and representing the Council in such meetings.

12- Following up work on the ratification of states and international organizations of the By-Laws of the International Islamic Council for Daw'a and Relief, preparation of adequate documents for that purpose, to establish a popular international Islamic collective qualified to serve the goals of the Council.

13- Receiving statements from member organizations on causes and attitudes which concern such organizations in their own countries, or within the framework of their specializations, accompanied with such suggestions as they may deem appropriate for guaranteeing cooperation of organization members in such causes. The General Secretariat shall circulate such statements and suggestions on organization members. It shall also undertake the role required from it so that a serious international interest in Council work by member organizations shall be secured.

Remark: The limited financial capabilities of the General Secretariat still hinder it from recruiting cadres and technical staff capable of bearing a maximum load of such responsibilities. Nevertheless the nucleus of the essential coordinating staff has been realized.

9

5-   The General Role of the Specialized Committees

A. Specialized Committees

Article (17) of· the By-Laws of the Council provides for the establishment of the following permanent committees:-

1- The Education and Daw'a Committee, located at Al Azhar in Cairo.

2- The General Relief Committee, located at the International Islamic Relief Organization in Jeddah.

3- The Data and Follow-up Committee, located at the Muslim World League in Mecca.

4- The Financing and Investment Committee, located at the International Islamic Charitable Foundation in Kuwait.

5- The Publication and Information Committee, located at the Muslim World League in Mecca.

The Presidency Board has recommended to the Founding Board the amendment of the By-Laws to enable the Presidency Board to form other committees and relocate them as required.

B. Committees and Coordination

It was quite clear from the beginning . that the specialized committees shall have a basic role in the coordination process. Practice has further highlighted the importance of this role for the following major reasons:-

1- The broad dimensions of fields of work and the long distances are such that it is impossible to concentrate work in the General Secretariat alone.

2- The nature of the work requires high levels of specialization, academic knowledge and extensive work experience which are more available in one principal organization.

3- It is presumed that an organization that embraces one of the committees is capable financially and technically and in the field of manpower, and it can provide such capabilities, which are not available to the General Secretariat of the Council.

4- The committee chairmen and delegates, being attached and active within the organization, can visit regions of activities, contact other organizations, and as such, they are in a position that allows them to perform sustained follow-up.

10

5- The nature of work necessitates sustained coordination among member organizations in various fields.

C. Means of Coordination

In order that the specialized committees may perform their role of coordination among their members and with the main body of the International Islamic Council for Daw'a and Relief, and on the assumption that there is full access among specializations and each field can serve the others, and since experience and information are supposed to be at the disposal of all, the following have been decided:-

1- The formation of a complete secretariat for the specialized committee in the organization that embraces the said committee, so that officials shall be made available to the secretariat, in addition to communication channels and an adequate budget. (The General Secretariat has repeatedly reminded of this point).

2- Establishing an archive for each member organization, within the said secretariat, comprising all required data and information on activities of organization members so that information shall always be updated.

3- The committee shall hold at least three ordinary sessions per year, and may also meet in emergencies. In all cases, the committee shall meet by a request from its chairman or two of its members. The chairman shall specify the place and time of the meeting, and shall notify the General Secretariat of the meeting wthin an adequate time prior to such meeting.

4- The secretariat shall send to the members the meeting agenda and the matters proposed for discussion, at least one month prior to the meeting, so that they may be able to prepare their studies and ideas on the matters to be discussed, and send them to secretariat prior to the meeting.

5- Administrative preparations such as entrance visas and such shall be made in advance with ample time, so that no unforseen circumstances shall adversely affect the meetings and their results.

6- The secretariat shall prepare working papers for the matters stated in the meeting agenda from among the organization studies or research sent by member organizations of the Committee prior to the meeting.

7- The meeting shall have to be attended by chairmen of member organizations, or responsible delegates from them authorized on behalf of their organization to be committed to whatever decisions or recommendations issued by the committee.

11

8- The secretariat shall be particular towards receiving periodical reports from member organizations on the running of their work in executing the said decisions and recommendations.

9- The committee's secretariats shall be careful to send copies of their decisions to the General Secretariat, the Central Studies and Research Center for keeping, and to be assisted in following-up and for efficiency of efforts of member organizations.

D. Objectives

1- The object of the meeting shall be explicitly defined, and it shall have to issue practical decisions and recommendations conforming to the available capabilities of member organizations. These decisions and recommendations shall have to be accompanied by a description of practical implementation methods, so that unimplemented decisions shall not be accumulated in a way that mars the seriousness of the whole work.

2- Among the objectives of meetings is the formation of a unified understanding of the nature of current problems in regions, and their positive and negative aspects, so that each region carry a load proportionate to its capabilities.

3- Meetings aim at prevention of duplication and the waste of funds in unnecessary administrative expenditure, the setting up of more profitable projects, the unification of systems and equipment in various regions and the equitable distribution of support among regions.

4- Meetings also aim at developing collection methods and financial support of Daw'a and relief activities provided by the Council and the member organizations.

5- The secretariat shall be attentive, through directives promulgated by the committee chairman who values what is published, to strengthen relations with general information committee, and other mass media organization to promote public activities which raise the confidence of the public and broaden and encourage public awareness.

6- The secretariat shall prepare for the specialized committee chairman drafts of periodic reports for the Presidency Board and an annual report to the Founding Board, about committee activities and member organizations in their fields of work so that they may help in drawing up a general strategy for the International Islamic Council for Daw'a and Relief.

12

6.   Working Committees, Coordination System and Procedures

A. The Education and Daw'a Committee

Coordination System

The coordination system of the Education and Daw'a Committee depends on the following criteria:

1- Adoption of a unified system of Daw'a in its fundamentals, by wisdom and good advice.

2- The foundation of a training center for prayer leaders (Imams) and preachers in light of the above system.

3- Laying down of a unified plan for re-distribution of men of Daw'a and their spreading in various Muslim communities.

4- Proliferation of typical Islamic schools for preparation of prechers, the spread of Daw'a and education of Muslim minorities.

5- Laying down a plan for scholarships and the appointment of proficient and specialized teachers.

6- Carrying out major joint projects.

7- Laying down plans for Daw'a suitable for the circumstances in each intended region.

8- Reinforcing Islamic culture curricula in all educational institutes of all levels.

9- Foundation of Islamic centers for promulgation of Islamic education in Muslim communities and various provinces and regions.

10- Training teachers and workers in Islamic education in Muslim centers and schools.

Examples of Decisions

A. The Committee recommended the necessity of carrying out a field study to pinpoint imam and preacher training centers in various parts of the world, especially those sponsored by organization members of the Council, recognition of their capabilities, fields of their interest and their programs, in preparation for a choice of centers adequately qualified to become regional training centers.

B. Encouraging Islamic centers in the West to lay down programs and activities addressed to it, and directed for unification of the Muslims and

13

their approaches to reinforce their future roles in those societies and their success in spreading Daw'a among non-Muslims.

C. Referring the suggestion for the foundation of a permanent fund to financially support students coming to study in Islamic countries who run out of funds, to one of the organizations so that it may study it thoroughly and submit it as a suggestion to the Council Presidency Board.

<u>Suggested Procedures</u>

Coordination in the general scope of Daw'a requires the performance of procedures that can be summed up as follows:-

1- Each organization undertakes to inform the Council General Secretariat about its plan and programs for Daw'a, including preparations made and the site or countries where its Daw'a men are working.

2- The General Secretariat shall ascertain all preaching and guidance missions sent by member organizations and prepare a survey of all regions that are in need of such missions, and then undertakes to circulate the results of this work among concerned organizations for defining their roles in light of their interests and capabilities.

3- The General Secretariat shall lay down a medium-term plan (3-5 years) for scholarship and mission programs in light of the needs of Muslim minorities and countries on the one hand, and on the other hand, in light of the capabilities of member organizations and their priorities in the filed of scholarships. The master plan shall then be circulated among member organizations to include it in their programs.

4- Each organization shall provide the General Secretariat of the Council with annual reports on preachers, teachers and scholars and the schools they sponsor so that they can be utilized in planning, follow-up and evaluation work.

5- The General Secretariat shall try to benefit from services of full-time experts or part-timers for preparation of studies, reports, plans, and evaluation of programs and activities in this field.

6- Each organization shall provide the General Secretariat with a statistical work on the number of schools, teachers and Islamic centers sponsored by it. It shall also provide reports on such schools concerning their curricula and their scope of regional interest.

7- The General Secretariat of the Council shall prepare a comprehensive report on schools and Islamic centers and circulate it among member organizations so that they may benefit form it in preparing their plans and future programs.

14

8- The Council General Secretariat shall request the services of a number of full-time experts who work with member organizations to assist in laying down unified curricula for Islamic education at all levels and programs.

B. The General Relief Committee

Coordination System

The system of relief work depends on a number of principal references among which are the following important ones:-

1- Foundation of regional coordination offices to manage Islamic relief work adequately.

2- Broadening the base of relief work so as to cover all Muslim regions.

3- Diversification of relief works for the sake of satisfying the needs of all societies and communities.

4- Studying various methods of collection and expansion of resources of relief agencies.

5- Requesting Muslim governments to support popular Islamic relief activities.

6- Discussing difficulties that hamper relief work and trying to remove them.

7- Establishing joint warehouses for member organizations for the storage of basic commodities.

8- Undertaking joint projects that secure the flow of a fixed income for relief beneficiaries.

Examples of Decisions

1- The necessity of cooperation with monitoring organizations in performance of works of member organizations in fields of Daw'a and elief and trying to strengthen contacts with monitors to deepen such participation and strengthening it.

2- Accrediting offices of member organizations in certain countries and regions as offices of other organizations functioning in the same region whenever this may be possible.

3- Unification of facilities for storing relief materials in emergency regions for the sake of realizing cooperation and perfecting coordination, and saving on expenses of storage, administration and security.

15

4- Benefiting from centers and capabilities of some member organizations when functioning in their own countries, in order to increase mobility of such organizations and invigorate their zeal and help them to take on assistance work without their incurring any additional financial burdens.

5- Care for cooperation with governmental efforts whenever such formal cooperation is available so that Islamic work gain more effectiveness and positiveness on both official and public levels.

Suggested Procedures

Coordination of relief work requires the implementation of certain procedures, distinctive among which are the following:-

1- Each organization shall provide the General Secretariat of the Council with a comprehensive report including its relief programs, the regions where it functions, the group targeted by its programs, and the branches and offices working for it.

2- The General Secretariat prepares a report ascertaining relief works by region. The report shall be circulated among member organizations to supply them with full information, thus enabling them to coordinate work among them.

3- The General Secretariat shall prepare a census of international bodies undertaking relief work with the purpose of getting acquainted with their programs and fields of work, and shall provide such information to member organizations so that they may benefit from their experiences or cooperate with them on clear and well-defined bases.

C. The Data and Follow-up Committee

Coordination System

1- Establishing a data base at the Information Center with which all member organizations shall be linked during a specific time period.

2- Accrediting studies and research in collecting, documenting and storing data at the Information Center.

3- Facilitation of informational exchanges among various member organizations.

Examples of Decisions

1- Establishing branches of the information network within each member organization.

16

2- Provision of periodic reports concerning the organization and its variables and programs to the Information Center.

3- The necessity for displaying special care for information centers so that the Education and Daw'a Committee may be linked through Al-Azhar with the Muslim World League. Other organizations shall be linked to the aforementioned Information Center, and all necessary equipment and technicalities shall have to provided.

Suggested Procedures

1- Each organization shall undertake to establish an information data base on its premises according to technical specifications circulated by the Information Center.

2- The General Secretariat shall undertake, in coordination with Information Center, a training course for those organization delegates responsible for the branches of the Central Information data base, with the purpose of facilitating the use of the data base and benefiting from it.

D. The Financing and Investment Committee

Coordination System

1- Expansion of the base of the sources of financing.

2- Development of financial sources by investments.

3- Urging Islamic financial institutions to support the Council and finance its programs.

4- Establishment of investment projects that guarantee the continuous financing of the Council.

5- Cooperating with Islamic financial institutions for the support of general Islamic activities.

Examples of Decisions

1- Creation of sources that rely on Islamic Waqf for the benefit of the Council.

2- Benefiting from Waqf securities for Council support.

Suggested Procedures

1- Each member organization shall contact financial institutions and businessmen on the local level to acquaint them with the International

17

Islamic Council and its programs so that they may participate in financing the Council.

2- Launching contribution campaigns organized by the Financing and Investment Committee by contacting major Islamic financial institutions in the world.

3- Appointing representatives of the Council in Muslim countries to represent it in various activities especially in financial affairs.

E. The Publication and Information Committee

Coordination System

The coordination system of information depends on the following:-

1- Establishing regional information centers especially in the European continent.

2- Laying down programs for the preparation and training of Islamic information staff.

3- Accrediting research and studies on various Islamic causes to be used in information programs.

4- Issuance of periodicals, magazines and informational bulletins.

5- Accrediting research and studies for discussing Islamic topics and disseminating them by means of publication and printed materials.

6- Issuance of a series of Islamic-oriented publications to combat destructive doctrines and trends and to refute false and fabricated propaganda against Islam, its values and principles.

Examples of Decisions

1- Realization of complementation of periodicals, magazines and specialized bulletins issued by member organizations.

2- Publication of books and printed materials to acquaint the world with Islamic thought and to answer and refute cultural campaigns against it.

3- Exchange of periodicals and printed materials among member organization.

4- Formation of joint delegations of member organizations to be invited to participate in or attend international meetings and Islamic conferences.

18

5- Reinforcing cooperation between the Council on the one hand, and International and Islamic institutions on the other.

6- Supporting specialized symposiums organized by member organizations by participating in and financing such symposiums.

7- Preparation of comprehensive studies and reports on Islamic causes so that they might be used in meetings and international conferences and symposiums in which either the Council or a member organization may participate.

8- Monitoring anti-Islamic films and conceptions adversary to Islam and Muslims in various mass media channels and printed materials, ascertaining their sources, and replying to them.

Suggested Procedures

1- The Council General Secretariat shall identify information centers and acquaint itself with their tasks, programs and technical capabilities and manpower.

2- The General Secretariat of the Council shall request one of the member organizations or a committee of experts to lay down programs for the preparation and training of Muslim information staff. Such programs shall be tendered to Arab and Islamic universities and to Islamic information centers.

3- Requesting one or more of the member organizations to work on the preparation of information programs in the fields of education and Islamic culture representing an original Muslim point of view and submitting some to mass media (broadcasting and television) in Islamic countries to supplement their role in providing sound Islamic principles and values to people, free from political and intellectual points of conflict.

4- Each member organization shall provide the General Secretariat with periodical reports on its activities and programs to be exploited by mass media channels that are available to the Council.

5- The General Secretariat shall make a census of periodicals and bulletins published by member organizations and begin an effort to make their goals and scopes of interest well-known, and circulate this information among organization so that they may be utilized in the exchange of information and technical know-how.

6- Each organization shall support such periodicals through subscribing in them.

7- Each organization shall provide the Council with its annual plan of publication and issuance of book series and translations so that they may

19

be collected and distributed to member organizations to avoid duplication of publication or translation.

8- The Council General Secretariat shall lay down a medium-term plan (3-5 years) for developing and enriching the publication and translation work in the scope of Islamic thought and culture.

9- In coordination with specialized committees, the Council General Secretariat or member organizations shall form suitable delegations to participate in international or Islamic conferences and contact governments concerned with a current Islamic cause.

10- The General Secretariat shall hold seminars specialized in each cause which a number of experts shall attend, to try and establish a vision or an objective analysis of the cause and the advisable methods for its solution, and reports on such a Muslim cause shall be circulated among member organizations.

11- The General Secretariat shall seek the services of one or more experts for the preparation of studies on certain Islamic causes that require urgent review by the Council, so that such review may be utilized in information or for contacts with concerned governments or international agencies.

12- The General Secretariat shall issue communiqués on emergency causes and circulate them among member organizations to be used in information campaigns in support of such Islamic causes on a country level.

13- Member organizations shall arrange for delegates to contact concerned embassies for dealing with any Islamic cause, and shall send cables and memoranda to various international organs for the sake of formulating a public opinion pressure group for helping such cause and putting it within a cadre of world attention.

14- Each organization shall be at freedom to use various kinds of locally available mass media channels, to make known Islamic causes and direct to them the attention of local opinion.

15- Each organization shall undertake to send detailed reports on its activities enumerating all efforts exerted by it in the scope of each of the current Muslim causes to the Council General Secretariat, so that such circulation shall be widely made and be utilized in reports, publications and mass media channels.

20

7-   Regional Coordination

Broad Lines for Regional Coordination Offices

With the passage of four years of the life of International Islamic Council for Daw'a and Relief, and the subsequent attempts of regional organizations to establish coordination offices in Peshawar, Sudan and others, there has arisen a dire need for encouraging expanded regional coordination of a more comprehensive nature within the Council, for the confirmation of unity of Islamic work in the field of Daw'a and relief, and to affirm the message of the Council and its goals of promoting coordination among member organizations, and establishing joint projects. In light of prior experience, the Council Presidency Board and its Founding Board resolved to establish regional coordination offices to realize the aforementioned purposes. The Council Secretary General was commissioned to draw the broad lines of the work of the regional coordination offices in such a way as to guarantee free play for the offices without prejudice to the Council unity or hampering the movement of comprehensive coordination or encourage the emergence of regional divisions.

Starting from those recommendations and on the basis of the aforementioned criteria, I hereby submit the project of regional coordination offices of the International Islamic Council for Daw'a and Relief.

First: Definitions

The Council: The International Islamic Council for Daw'a and Relief.

The Founding
Board: The Founding Board of the International Islamic Council for Daw'a and Relief.

General Secretariat: The General Secretariat of the International Islamic Council for Daw'a and Relief

Office: Regional Coordination Office.

Director: Director of the Regional Coordination Office.

President: President of the Regional Coordination Office.

Second: General Rules

1- The Office functions within one of the Council member organizations by recommendation of the Council Presidency Board and a resolution of the Founding Board.

2- The Coordination Office shall direct the work of organizations within the region according to the general policy defined by the International Islamic Council for Daw'a and Relief within the region, so that no duplication or contradiction shall occur.

21

3- The Founding Board shall authorize the Presidency Board to establish Regional Coordination Offices on the basis of the abovementioned principles, provided that it shall present such resolution to the Founding Board in its first meeting for ratification.

4- The organization that embraces an Office shall enjoy special provisions, good relations with local authorities and people in that country.

5- Member organizations of the International Islamic Council for Daw'a and Relief shall be considered, together with their offices outside such region, as branches of the Regional Coordination Office, so that duplication and contradiction are avoided, certain expenditures spared, local energies exploited and coordination efforts confirmed.

6- The Office shall be under the chairmanship of the organization within which the Office is established, and that organization shall bear the expenses of the Office.

7- The Board of Directors of the Office shall be formed of the heads of the member organizations who hold membership in it, to supervise the work of the Office.

8- The Board of Directors shall set a special budget for the Office, to be financed by the member organizations.

Third: Office Tasks

The office shall carry out the following tasks:-

1- Observing the implementation of decisions taken by the Presidency Board, the Founding Board and the committee working in that region attached to Council.

2- Recommending to the Presidency Board and the Founding Board and working committees such work and projects suggested by member organizations, who are represented in the Office.

3- Representing member organizations before concerned authorities or others within the region.

4- Coordinating delegation travels and deciding their tasks and zones of activity, arranging reports on such activities, and sending copies of same to the General Secretariat and information centers attached to the Council for the benefit of other members.

5- Receiving assistance in cash and in kind sent by member organizations in the Council for the benefit of needy regions, and drawing joint plans to benefit from them, organizing regional contribution collection for the benefit of joint

22

projects among member organizations, opening special accounts for the Office, access to the funds therein to be according to an accountancy system decided by the Board of Directors for use in the joint projects, in coordination with the chairman of theb Financing and Investment Committee of the International Islamic Council for Daw'a and Relief.

6- In the Coordination Office there shall be established a regional information office which shall be linked to the Jeddah Information Office and the Cairo Information Office as closely as possible.

Fourth: Board of Directors

1- The Board of Directors of the Regional Coordination Office shall be formed of the chairmen of that region's member organizations.

2- The Board shall supervise all administrative and financial activities of the Office.

3- The Board shall be presided over by the chairman of the organization which the Founding Board accepts as the location of the Coordination Office.

4- The Board shall appoint the Office Director and the staff. It shall also decide their salaries, duties and privileges.

5- The Board shall convene once a month and may hold emergency meetings. In all cases the Chairman of the Board shall send out invitations for meetings.

6- Any printed stationery or otherwise shall bear the name of the member organization together with name of the International Islamic Council for Daw'a and Relief.

7- The Board shall select a secretary for the Board from among communications officers accredited by organizations.

Fifth: Office Staff

1- The Director of the Regional Coordination Office shall be a full-time officer. The Board shall decide his salary and office tasks.

2- The Office Director shall preside over the secretarial system of the Regional Coordination Office.

3- The secretary shall record the minutes of Board meetings and shall send copies of same to the General Secretariat. The secretary shall oversee the implementation of such procedures and he shall dispatch copies of the minutes of meetings to the General Secretariat and information centers.

23

4- Directors of Coordination Offices shall attend the Founding Board meetings and also meetings of special committees of the International Islamic Council for Daw'a and Relief.

5- The Office Director shall take the necessary measures for publishing the activities of member organizations in magazines and periodicals of the Council and member organizations.

6- The Director shall recommend to the Board works and projects submitted by member organizations for final decisions on them, and then refer them to the Presidency Board of the International Islamic Council for Daw'a and Relief or to its specialized committees or to the Founding Board.

7- The Office Director shall supervise the development of the plan for collecting contributions and subscriptions related to the International Islamic Council for Daw'a and Relief.

Sixth: The coordination project shall be submitted to the Founding Board for approval.

Seventh: The General Secretariat shall promulgate unified executive regulations organizing the work of the Regional Coordination Office .

24

8. System of Communications Delegates

A communications delegate is a link between the organization which he represents and the General Secretariat in Cairo, the Information Committee, and the Muslim World League Information Center in Mecca.

As this delegate is fully aware of the goals of the International Islamic Council for Daw'a and Relief and as he is completely aware of the organizational goals which he represents, his basic task is to supplement the movement of coordination, cooperation and follow-up between member organizations in fields of Daw'a and relief through the General Secretariat of the Council in Cairo. This is performed by a number of procedures and methods hereunder summarized:-

1- The Communications Delegate shall keep abreast of the affairs of the International Islamic Council during the meetings of his organization so that he may be able to present the Council's suggested projects, decisions, recommendations and such messages as are available to him, to his organization, or adopt any other administrative method to inform his organization of such matters, in order to facilitate the coordination process which the Council wishes to promote among organizations.

2- The Communications Delegate shall send a weekly message to the General Secretariat including:-

    A- A copy of the organization's decisions which he represents on matters related to the Council, the joint projects suggested by his company in the fields of Daw'a and relief and such decisions as his organization wishes to communicate to the General Secretariat.

    B Brief or detailed reports on:-

        1- the most important activities of his organization in affairs of Daw'a and relief.

        2- other important Islamic activities taking place in the region of his organization in matters of Daw'a and relief.

        3- important anti-Islamic activities undertaken by Christianizing parties, sects and other believers who digress from Allah's way.

    C- Authenticated news that concern Islamic scientific activities that are under way in his region.

    D- News and requirements of Islamic minorities.

    E- Notifying the General Secretariat of any change in the basic information about his organization (addresses, telephone numbers and other communications channels).

25

F- Completed data sheets.

G- Following up the implementation of the decisions of the Founding Board or of the Presidency Board of the Council which were endorsed by the organization which he represents.

It is evident that the General Secretariat will use these weekly messages as follows:-

- Documentation of their data and storing them at the information Center in the General Secretariat in Cairo, so that they may be used as background for decision-making or for submitting information services to members.

- Enriching the Muslim World League Information Center in Mecca with information and reports incoming from member organizations.

- Submit briefs of reports and information and joint projects reported by member organizations to the Presidency Board so that the Board may be fully aware of the status of public Islamic work, in which all organizations participate in conducting. This shall facilitate decisions on various matters, and shall assist in achieving coordination and proper planning.

- Notification of the permanent Council committees, each in its field of specialization, of the contents of the weekly messages of the Communications Delegates regarding joint projects to be studied, and submitting same to the Presidency Board for mutual coordination and execution follow-up.

- Publication of important news concerning public Islamic work through such publications be they fortnightly or quarterly, or in newspapers, magazines and periodicals, in addition to attempting to publish same in the publications of other organizations for further dissemination of such information.

3- The Communications Delegate shall undertake to follow up the responding to correspondence from the General Secretariat and other organs of the Council, and shall provide information and clarifications requested by them in accordance with the regulations adopted by the organization he represents.

4- To facilitate the job of the Communications Delegate, the presidency of the organization shall enable him to contact the information unit in his organization asking its officials to collect, sort and preserve information by traditional methods in the first stage, until the provision of a modern communication means to each information unit, as already decided.

5- The Communications Delegate shall exert his best effort to strengthen the ties of his organization with information systems and modern local mass media according to a plan he draws with the knowledge and review of his organization's administration and by notification of the General Secretariat, in addition to providing the General Secretariat with copies of such publications for the benefit of the Council's activities.

6- The Communications Delegate may suggest anything that may strengthen ties among member organizations and between them and the General Secretariat in a way that serves cooperative and coordinating targets which can encourage the establishment of joint projects in scopes of Daw'a and relief on a worldwide basis.

7- The Communications Delegate shall try to locate the sources of information serving Islamic relief and Daw'a activities and notify the General Secretariat about them. These include reference books, illustrated books, publications, and information centers. He shall also notify the General Secretariat about such sources so that they may secure them or deal with them in the appropriate manner.

8- The Communications Delegate shall supply the Information Center of the General Secretariat with the printed materials of his organization and other illustrated bulletins expounding on its achievements.

9- The Communications Delegate shall supply the Information Center of the General Secretariat with the information that the latter requires including the "identity cards" of Muslim personalities or of foreign hostile personalities and their intellectual product, so that the General Secretariat may benefit from them and transfer those to the Central Information Office. He shall also supply the General Secretariat with information on conferences, meetings and activities carried out by member organizations so that the General Secretariat may invite other organizations to participate in them.

10- Member organizations shall endeavor to obtain financial support and manpower services for the office of the Communications Delegate, so that he may discharge the tasks aforementioned. He may notify the General Secretariat of any obstacles that hamper such an endeavor.

11- All activities of the Communications Delegate shall be carried out through the organization or institute that he represents in accordance with working directives in effect there. He shall not perform any individual activity, because the purpose of the establishment of the position of Communications Delegate is to strengthen the working relationship among the organizations of the International Islamic Council for Daw'a and Relief and the General Secretariat, for the purpose of realizing worldwide, unified Islamic work.

27

— APPENDIX 4 —

ISLAMISATION THROUGH DEMOCRACY
IN MUSLIM-MAJORITY NATIONS

MOROCCO

King Mohammed VI has pursued a two-track strategy of encouraging non-violent Islamists who support the monarchy to participate in politics, while suppressing violent jihadists and Salafis.[393] The Islamist Justice and Development Party (PJD) is a political party that has competed in Morocco's parliamentary elections since 1997 and has become entrenched in Morocco's political process. In 2002, the PJD became the country's leading opposition party, winning 42 of 325 seats in Morocco's parliament, making it the third largest group in the national legislature. Some analysts believe that although the party has agreed to work within the democratic political system, it remains committed to establishing an Islamic state under sharia in Morocco.[394]

Following popular protests in 2011 demanding reforms, King Mohammed VI offered a new constitution, which was endorsed on 1 July 2011 in a referendum. Under the new constitution, the king no longer holds the title "Commander of the Faithful" and is obliged to appoint a prime minister from the majority party in parliament. In the November 2011 elections, the PJD won the largest number of parliamentary seats (107 of 395 seats) and formed a coalition government on 3 January 2012, with its leader, Abdelilah Benkirane, as Prime Minister.[395] It is too early to know how much pressure the PJD will bring on the system to undo previous reforms of sharia family law and to accommodate traditional sharia.

ALGERIA

In Algeria, the Islamic Salvation Front (FIS), a movement similar to and allied to the Muslim Brotherhood, entered the political process as a party. The Islamists were able to use their success in civil society and impressive record of social responsibility and welfare to mobilise supporters and construct a powerful political machine. The movement's civil society associations became the support network of the new political party, which was able to attract a broad base of support across the country. FIS won the first round of elections in 1992 before it was stopped by the FLN (Front de Libération Nationale) government and the military. Only the suspension of the voting and the imposition of martial law prevented the FIS from taking full control of the country. A brutal civil war followed, in which, it is estimated, at least 100,000 people died (1991-2002).[396]

TUNISIA

Tunisia is the most secular of the Arab states and has a significant middle class and civil society. The Ben Ali regime (1987-2011) allowed Islam some role in public life but suppressed the Islamists and their political structures.

Following the ousting of President Ben Ali by the "Arab Spring" uprising in January 2011, the Islamist Ennahda (*al-Nahda*) party experienced a revival as its elderly founder Rachid Ghannouchi returned from exile. In the November 2011 elections for a Constituent Assembly, Ennahda gained 41% of the seats, and its party leader Hamadi Jebali became prime minister of a coalition government.

The liberal and independent National Authority for the Reform of Media and Communications (INRIC) accused the new government and the Ennahda party of trying to control the media to ensure that it spread the government's message, ideology and misinformation. The government failed to implement previous decrees to protect journalists. Reporters without Borders, the largest press freedom NGO in the world, complained about state censorship and takeover of the media.[397] There was also increasing Salafi activity, including attempts to impose Islamic dress codes and other sharia rules by force on the street and on university campuses.[398] The ruling Ennahda party refused to prosecute the Salafi excesses and violence and in some cases actually encouraged them, allegedly owing to the considerable financial and political support given to the movement by Saudi Arabia and Qatar.[399] In January 2014, the Ennahda government handed power to a caretaker administration, pending elections for a new government to be held by the end of the year. In the same month, Tunisia agreed a new constitution, which is generally supportive of human rights, although it has some internal contradictions.

EGYPT

Until the "Arab Spring", the Muslim Brotherhood was never allowed to organise as a political party; instead it forged alliances with other parties to gain access to the National Assembly and set up members as independent candidates. In the 2005 Majlis (parliamentary) elections, the Muslim Brotherhood gained 19% of the vote despite the stacking of the process against them.[400]

After the fall of President Mubarak in 2011, the Muslim Brotherhood set up the Freedom and Justice Party and contested the parliamentary elections, in which it gained 47% of the vote, which gave it a leading role in the new system. The Muslim Brotherhood and the Salafists together won more than 70% of parliamentary seats. Finally, Muhammad Morsi, a prominent Muslim Brotherhood member, won the presidential elections.

The Freedom and Justice Party (FJP) and the two Salafi parties (Nour and Asala) used their majority on the 100-member Constituent Assembly to Islamise several articles of the 1971 constitution. The changes proposed by the Islamists to the constitution could have paved the way for the introduction of *hudud* punishments and could have laid the foundation for a theocratic state, if passed. The Islamists introduced an article that ruled, "It is strictly forbidden to speak ill of the Divine Self or the Prophets of God, the Mothers of the Believers [Wives of the Prophet Mohamed] and the Wise Caliphs." According to Egyptian secularists, this article could have been used to impose strict censorship and criminalise anyone who questioned traditional Islamic interpretations.[401] The final draft was not as extreme and was accepted in a referendum in December 2012. It was criticised as being undemocratic and too Islamist, allowing clerics to intervene in the lawmaking process and leaving minority groups and women without proper legal protection.[402]

Following mass demonstrations against the authoritarian attempts by President Morsi and the Muslim Brotherhood to force the pace of state

Islamisation, and also against his failure to improve economic and social conditions for impoverished Egyptians, the military intervened on 3 July 2013. Morsi was deposed; many Muslim Brotherhood leaders were arrested; and the Brotherhood was banned.

Later that month, interim President Adly Mansour started the process of creating another new constitution, which was accepted by an overwhelming majority of those who participated in a referendum on 14-15 January 2014. Almost twice as many votes were cast in favour of Mansour's constitution as had been cast in favour of Morsi's constitution.

The new constitution reversed the Islamisation process and removed most of the additions that Morsi had inserted. It enshrines the equality of all citizens and prohibits discrimination on the grounds of religion, belief, sex, race and other factors. Christians and other minorities are granted greater political representation. In a significant shift, the new constitution grants "absolute" freedom of belief, although the freedom to practise religion and establish places of worship is limited to the followers of Islam, Christianity and Judaism. Although retaining Article 2, which states that the principles of sharia are "the primary source of legislation", it omits the precise definition of "principles" that Morsi had introduced and that had opened the way to applying literal and archaic interpretations of sharia. Political parties based on religion are banned.

PALESTINE

The Palestinian Hamas,[403] an offshoot of the Muslim Brotherhood, gained popularity through its participation in the violent *intifadas* against Israel, specialising in mass suicide bombings against civilians. It also built an infrastructure of social welfare and educational agencies. It entered the political process in the Palestinian Authority in 2005, and in the January 2006 Palestinian Legislative Council (PLC) elections, Hamas won 74 out of 132 seats, with the ruling Fatah party winning only 45, and the three liberal parties winning only six seats.

However, frustrated by the impediments placed in its way by the Fatah faction, Hamas moved to violence. In 2007, it seized control of the Gaza Strip from the Palestine Liberation Organisation, displacing security forces loyal to the secular President Mahmoud Abbas. After the civil war ended, Hamas declared the "end of secularism and heresy in the Gaza Strip". Gaza human rights groups accuse Hamas of restricting many freedoms. Since the

2007 coup, the Gaza Strip has shown the hallmarks of a process of "Talibanisation", such as happened in Afghanistan under Taliban rule. Hamas has imposed strict rules on women, discouraged activities commonly associated with Western or Christian culture, oppressed non-Muslim minorities, imposed sharia, and deployed religious police to enforce these laws. According to Human Rights Watch, the Hamas-controlled government of Gaza stepped up its efforts to Islamise Gaza in 2010, efforts that included the repression of civil society and severe violations of personal freedom.[404] Hamas is gradually turning the Gaza Strip into a Taliban-style Islamic entity.

Lebanon

Hizbullah is a good example of an Islamist movement operating simultaneously in different modes: terrorist group, national resistance movement and political party. It has infiltrated society, built up its own armed forces and alternative infrastructure as a virtual state within a state and participates in elections and government.

Hizbullah was founded in the early 1980s as a Shia Islamist jihadist movement, trained by the Iranian Revolutionary Guard and calling for an Islamic state in Lebanon. Following the 1990-1991 Gulf War, Hizbullah transformed itself into a political party, while keeping its military forces and weapons and its special links with Iran and Syria. Its political mode became even more important following the Israeli withdrawal from southern Lebanon in 2000, which deprived Hizbullah of its justification for continuing to operate as an independent militia. Indeed, it sees its deeper political engagement as the best way to safeguard its armed status. At the same time, it continued its terrorist attacks against Israel, engaged in international terrorism, mainly against Jewish targets, and assassinated several Lebanese opposed to its policies.

Hizbullah first participated in elections in 1992 winning eight parliamentary seats. In 1996 it won ten seats; in 2000 it won eight; in 2005 it won 14. In alliance with other pro-Syrian and anti-Western parties, it attempted to gain a blocking minority. After Syria's withdrawal from Lebanon in 2005, Hizbullah, seeking to protect its interests, agreed to enter the government, obtaining three seats in the cabinet.[405] However, the UN Special Tribunal for Lebanon (STL), which was investigating the 2005 murder of former Lebanese Prime Minister Rafiq al-Hariri, implicated senior Hizbullah members in his killing. In 2006, the Hizbullah members left the cabinet in protest against a cabinet vote approving the creation of an international tribunal to try suspects in the assassination of Hariri.

Following the 2006 Israeli invasion of Lebanon, Hizbullah emerged as the most popular Lebanese movement, committed to "resistance". However, in May 2008, it turned its weapons on fellow Lebanese as its forces imposed their control over the streets of Beirut for a few days. Hizbullah fighters torched the offices of the pro-Hariri TV station Future TV and newspaper Al-Mustaqbal and then drew back to let the message sink in that Hizbullah is the dominant force in Lebanon.[406]

In the 2009 elections, Hizbullah won 12 seats, and with its allies failed to get a majority in parliament. The March14 anti-Syrian coalition gained 71 of the 128 seats, and Sa'ad Hariri of the anti-Syrian coalition formed a government. Hizbullah decided to join the government and received two cabinet posts. In 2010, Hizbullah broke up the governing coalition in order to secure the establishment of a government that would take a firm stance against the STL. Its preferred Sunni candidate, Najib Mikati, replaced the March 14 leader, Sa'ad Hariri, as prime minister. The new government was dominated by Hizbullah and its allies.[407]

Hizbullah have supported the Assad regime (which is Shia, like Hizbullah) in the uprising in Syria that began in 2011. This stance has reduced Sunni Muslim support in Lebanon for Hizbullah. Many Sunni Lebanese had previously supported Hizbullah because of its firm stand against Israel but now see it in the camp of the Shia enemy. Sunni jihadi groups have begun to fight Hizbullah with assassinations and suicide bombings.

JORDAN

The Islamic Action Front (IAF) functions as the political wing of Jordan's Muslim Brotherhood and has a long history of competing in elections and occasionally participating in the government. It is allowed to operate in many social spheres and run candidates for parliament, often criticising government policy (especially on cultural and Islamic issues), as long as it does not pose a direct challenge to the regime. The Jordanian regime makes sure the IAF operates in a framework deliberately designed to keep it a minority. The regime keeps a close eye on the IAF and several times has arrested some of its leaders. IAF leaders prefer to participate in the system rather than try to overthrow it, assuming that more can be gained by constantly pushing for Islamisation from within the system. Because of its electoral strength and good organisation, it has now become the only viable opposition. It is allied to t he much weaker leftist and nationalist parties. IAF deputies used their parliamentary seats to call for the implementation of sharia, to condemn cultural practices they consider un-Islamic and to oppose the peace with Israel.

The Muslim Brotherhood's position on these issues tends to be hard and uncompromising. The Jordanian government prohibits the Brotherhood's supporters from giving some sermons and regulates the content of those sermons that are allowed. It has shut down newspapers associated with the movement and more recently has passed legislation restricting the issuing of *fatwas* without official permission.

The IAF's 2003 platform called for the application of sharia, identifying it as a religious obligation and basic goal of the party. The IAF also opposed the American war in Iraq in very strong terms. Some of the more extreme IAF members praised the Jordanian-born Islamist militant Abu Musab Al Zarqawi, who was killed in an attack by US forces in Iraq in 2006. Four IAF Members of Parliament (MPs) who attended his funeral in 2006 were arrested and charged with inciting violence.

IAF members can be divided into "hawks" and "doves", who sometimes criticise each other in public. They differ on their attitudes toward the Jordanian system, the role of Islam, and Palestine. Doves function as a "loyal opposition", keen to participate in the political process and not to overthrow it, content with a slow and gradual process of building a greater role for Islam in public and political life. Hawks express no loyalty to the throne, are in a hurry to see sharia implemented and view parliamentary elections as a means, not an end.

Over the past two decades, the Jordanian regime has gradually come to regard the Islamist movement as its most significant domestic rival. The main debate among Jordan's ruling elite seems to be whether to treat the Islamist movement as a security challenge to be dealt with by repression, or a political one to be contained, co-opted, harassed and managed rather than completely suppressed.[408]

TURKEY

The Islamist Welfare Party, representing the radical Islamist Milli Gorus movement, won power in the 1995 elections under Necmettin Erbakan. It invoked Islamism and expressed anti-Western and anti-Semitic attitudes as it tried to forge closer links with Iran, Libya and Syria. These policies alienated the secular political elite and the military, and in 1997 the National Security Council removed the Welfare Party from power. The Welfare Party then re-emerged as the Justice and Development Party (AKP), defined as a secular party on the model of European Christian-Democratic parties. It won the 2002 elections by a landslide, obtaining 34% of the votes, and formed the new Turkish government under Recep Tayyip Erdogan (the former Mayor of Istanbul). To gain legitimacy, the AKP initially defined itself as "conservative democratic", placed a strong emphasis on democracy and human rights, advocated European Union (EU) membership, supported globalisation and rejected anti-Western attitudes.

This shift, however, proved to be merely tactical, to ensure that the AKP remained in power and could gradually engage in its Islamisation campaign.[409] It manipulated the EU accession process, which required Turkey to reduce the powers of the military and lift restrictions on freedom of expression, so as to weaken the centres of radical secularism that had existed in the judiciary, at high levels of the state bureaucracy, in the mainstream media and especially in the military.[410] While pledging its loyalty to the secular state system, it has been quietly changing the political atmosphere in Turkey in an Islamist direction, weakening the secular forces of the military, judiciary and press, and aligning Turkey with states such as Iran and Saudi Arabia, distancing itself from the US and encouraging anti-Christian attitudes. It is gradually placing Islamists in positions of authority in all government institutions. The EU was utilised as a natural ally in efforts to decrease the power of the military and to achieve a system of democratic governance, within which Islamic social and political forces would be regarded as legitimate players.[411]

In its early days of power, the AKP was wary of revealing its Islamist-rooted political vision. But as time went on, this vision became apparent as the AKP began to follow an agenda that aims to replace the secular Kemalist elite and transform Turkey into a religiously conservative Islamic society. The military has been weakened by the arrest of several high-ranking generals on charges of conspiracy against the state. Islamists are being placed in influential positions in education, the media, the police and the judiciary. Many journalists have been arrested on trumped-up charges so as to subdue the media. Turkey is now playing a much more active role in the OIC. The AKP was allied for some time to the hugely influential Gülen movement, an international religious and social movement led by Fethullah Gülen, which has had a great impact in Turkey and increasingly across the world as well, through an extensive network of schools, universities, charities, student associations, newspapers and radio and TV stations.[412]

Turkey is a model both for the gradual Islamisation of a state from below (before the accession to power of the AKP) and Islamisation from above, as the ruling AKP infiltrates all state and civic institutions with its followers and weakens all possible opponents, such as the military, judiciary and media.

In the drive for a Sunni Islamisation of Turkey, Erdogan has caused splits in the national cohesion of Turkey. He has pursued an on-off relationship with the large Kurdish minority, alternately responding to their demands and then rejecting them again; the result is great mutual suspicion. He also alienated the Shia Alevis, who resented both the increasingly Sunni character of society and the aggressive attitude of the Turkish state to the ruling Syrian regime, dominated by their co-religionists, the Alawis.[413]

PAKISTAN

Most Islamising parties originated when Pakistan was part of British India and argued against the creation of a homeland for South Asian Muslims. They would have preferred Indian Muslims to remain part of the Muslim community in India, linked to the global *umma*, rather than live in a smaller, independent, nationalistic Pakistan.

However, with the creation of Pakistan in 1947, they organised themselves to accommodate the new reality, unwelcome though it was, and adapted their goals to focus on the constitution and politics of the new nation so as to give it a stronger Islamic identity.

Pakistan's Islamic parties operate within the democratic system and participate in elections. Their impact was relatively limited during Pakistan's first decades, but the secession of Bangladesh (formerly East Pakistan), with Indian help, in 1971 increased their influence, as Pakistan reeled from the trauma and sought for a unifying identity to strengthen its position versus the victorious India, always regarded as Pakistan's enemy. Islam was the natural unifying factor, and part of the response was an increasing Islamisation of society. This Islamisation was reflected in the creation of many *madrasas* and greater support for militant Sunni Islamist groups.[414]

Various Islamic and Islamist factions, all dedicated to the Islamisation of Pakistan, began to compete for official patronage by the government. Islamic clerical elites built up political parties, expanded their *madrasa* networks and founded their own armed militias. Co-opted by the military and by various

Pakistani governments, these have brought Pakistan to the point where Islamic extremism threatens the foundation of state and society.

Some 25 Islamic and Islamist parties participate in Pakistani politics. Their electoral power has been relatively low, never reaching beyond a combined 12% of the seats in the National Assembly. But despite this modest performance, they have succeeded, because they have had support from the various military regimes, which utilised them to weaken the main democratic parties, to exclude secular politicians from power and to maintain a centralised state controlled by the military. Empowered by the military, Islamists and Islamic parties have created a climate of extreme religious intolerance, which makes it hard to have a stable democratic government. They have become well armed and well financed, wielding considerable influence within different branches of government.[415] They have large networks of mosques and *madrasas* serving as recruiting grounds for their organisations, which often benefit from military patronage.[416] All such parties, in spite of the violent disagreements between them, aim at a full implementation of sharia in Pakistan, and all of them support the infamous blasphemy law.[417]

INDONESIA

The Prosperous Justice Party (PKS) was founded in 1998 after the resignation of long-serving Indonesian President Suharto. It came out of the Islamist *tarbiyah* (education) movement, which saw a new opportunity to influence the nation through politics, once Suharto was no longer in power, and therefore created an official political party. PKS was widely seen in Indonesia as the "*dawa* party", which seems to have been an accurate reflection of its hopes to implement what an Indonesian academic[418] describes as "a pristine Islam in the country's social, economic and political spheres". In its early years it stood out from other Indonesian political parties because of its orderly rallies and its anti-corruption stance. But its reputation began to fade after the 2004 election, and unprecedented corruption allegations were made in 2013 against Luthfi Hasan Ishaq, its former president.[419] Even its supreme leader, Hilmi Aminuddin, was questioned by the Corruption Eradication Commission.[420] But for the fact that they were discovered to be somewhat less pure than they had claimed, the PKS would have gained considerable political power.

GLOSSARY

ablutions – washing the body, especially as part of a religious ceremony.

Ahmadiyya – a Muslim sect, originating in 19th century India, regarded as extremely heretical by other Muslims.

al-amr bi'l m'aruf wa'l nahy 'an al-munkar – commanding right and forbidding wrong.

Allah – the Arabic word for God.

Ayatollah – literally "sign of Allah". A term of honour for a religious leader in Shia Islam.

Bahai – a world religion that developed out of the Twelver Shia Islam in Iran. Founded by Bahaullah (1817-1892) who proclaimed himself Mahdi in 1863. Bahaism is now a separate universalistic religion with its own scripture, which stresses the brotherhood of all peoples, equality of the sexes, and pacifism. Considered heretical by orthodox Muslims.

Barelvi – An important Sunni movement originating in the Indian subcontinent in the 19th century that follows the teachings of Sayyid Ahmad Barelvi (1786-1831). Barelvis practise a traditional form of Islam in which Sufism and veneration of Muhammad have an important role. Largest Muslim movement in Pakistan.

bismillah – "in the name of Allah".

caliph – the Sunni title for the supreme ruler of the Muslim community, cf. imam.

da'ee – Islamic missionary.

darura – necessity. According to sharia, extreme necessity transforms the unlawful into the lawful.

dawa – literally "call" or "invitation" [to Islam] i.e. Islamic missionary work.

Deobandi – radical movement very influential in south Asia and Afghanistan. Rejects all Western influence and seeks to return to classical Islam. In recent years has become militant.

dhimma – literally "protected". The status of Jews, Christians and Sabeans in an Islamic state. They were permitted to live and keep their own faith in return for payment of *jizya* and keeping various humiliating regulations.

dhimmitude – the cowed and submissive behaviour typical of those who are subject to *dhimma*. The term was coined in 1982 by the Lebanese President and Maronite militia leader Bachir Gemayel, but it was introduced into Western discourse and popularised by the historian Bat Ye'or.

dua – supplicatory prayer (not ritual prayer).

episteme – the body of ideas that determine the knowledge that is intellectually certain at any particular time.

fard ayn – an individual personal duty.

fard kifaya – a communal duty.

Fatimids – Isma'ili dynasty based in Cairo, ruling from 969 to 1171.

fatwa – an authoritative statement on a point of Islamic law.

fiqh al-aqaliyyat al-Muslimah – Muslim minority jurisprudence.

futuh – literally "opening". Used to refer to wars to spread Islam, because they were opening the world to Islam.

hadith – traditions recording what Muhammad and his early followers said and did. Some are considered more authentic and reliable than others. cf. *sunna*.

hakimiyya – Allah's sole sovereignty and rule over human society in all things as Lord and legislator. No other authority can be recognised. Thus all legal and political systems must be based on Allah's revealed law (sharia). Humankind does not legislate but merely submits to, obeys, interprets and implements sharia.

harb – war

hijab – literally "partition" or "curtain", hence modesty. Often used to mean the woman's headscarf covering neck and hair.

hijra – migration. Muhammad's flight from Mecca to Medina in 622, which was used as the starting point of the Islamic calendar.

hisba – duty of Muslim individuals and states to "command good and forbid evil", i.e. to ensure that Allah's commands (sharia) are implemented in all society.

hudud – fixed punishments for certain crimes as specified in the Quran, e.g. amputation for theft, flogging for drinking alcohol. (Arabic singular *hadd*.)

ibadat – unchangeable sharia rules pertaining to humankind's duties to God, mainly regarding ritual and worship. cf. *muamalat*.

IIIT – International Institute for Islamic Thought.

ijma – the consensus of Muslim scholars on any given subject. Used in *ijtihad*.

ijtihad – the process of logical deduction on a legal or theological question, using the Quran and *hadith* as sources, from which sharia was created.

imam – the Shia term for the supreme ruler of the Muslim community (equivalent to the Sunni caliph). The same term is used by Sunni Muslims for the prayer leader at a local mosque, similar to a Christian parish priest or church pastor.

imamate – the role of imam, or the area ruled by an imam.

intifada – literally "shaking off". Used of the two Palestinian uprisings in 1987-93 and 2000-05.

Isa – the Quranic name for Jesus.

Islamisers – may be defined as all Muslims who believe in the imperative of spreading Muslim hegemony in the world, no matter what their religious or ideological background.

Islamism – the view of Islam as a comprehensive political ideology that aims to establish Islamic states under sharia wherever possible. It is characterised by zeal, activism and a desire to follow sharia in minute detail. Also called "Islamic fundamentalism" or "political Islam".

Isma'ilis – a secretive Shia sect who infiltrated normal Muslim society. Also called "Seveners". Today they are found mainly in India and Pakistan.

jahiliyya – the time of ignorance (meaning before Islam), especially in pre-Islamic Arabia.

jamaa – group or organisation (*jamaat* – group or organisation of).

Jamaat-i-Islami (Jamaat-e-Islami) – influential Islamist Pakistani political party established in 1941 in Lahore (now Pakistan) by Sayyid Abul A'la Mawdudi, one of the main founding figures of Islamism, whose goal is an Islamic state under sharia. Jamaat-e-Islami is the largest Islamist political party in Bangladesh.

jihad – literally "striving". The term has a variety of interpretations, including (1) spiritual struggle for moral purity, (2) trying to support right and correct wrong by voice and actions, (3) military war against non-Muslims with the aim of spreading Islam and Islamic rule.

jilbab – full-length outer garment for Muslim women.

jizya – a tax payable by non-Muslims (*dhimmi*) within an Islamic state. Various practices designed to humiliate the payer were associated with this tax.

kanisa – church.

khalwat – used in Malaysia to mean the crime of close proximity with the opposite sex.

madrasa – Islamic religious school.

maghazi – a record of Muhammad's military excursions and battles compiled from the early sources.

mahdi – the awaited End Time deliverer.

majlis – literally "sitting place", used to denote a gathering. Often used for parliament, or a legislative assembly, or a special council.

maslaha – public good, a principle in interpreting and applying sharia that takes into account the intention of the lawgiver (Allah) for the good of the Muslims.

Mecca – the Arabian city where Muhammad lived until the age of 52, now the holiest city in Islam.

Medina – Muhammad and his first followers migrated from Mecca to Medina in 622 because of persecution. cf. *hijra*. At Medina Muhammad established and led the first Islamic state, where Islam developed into a more aggressive form.

muamalat – flexible social and inter-personal rules of sharia, as distinct from the unchangeable rules of worship (*ibadat*).

Mughal – the Arabic and Persian form of "Mongol". Conventionally used to describe the Muslim dynasty that ruled large parts of India from the early 16th to mid-18th century. Also spelled "Mogul".

Muslim Brotherhood – the first modern Islamist grassroots movement, founded in Egypt in 1928 by Hasan al-Banna, which has become the largest and most influential international Islamist organisation in the world.

MWL – Muslim World League.

niqab – opaque veil covering a Muslim woman's face except the eyes.

ontology – the study of the nature of being (a branch of metaphysics).

Ottomans – a Turkish clan who established a principality in Anatolia around 1300. By military conquest, their territory expanded into an empire, which was the dominant Muslim power for some six centuries. The Ottoman Sultanate was abolished in 1922 and the caliphate in 1924.

People of the Book – those who have their own revealed scriptures. The term is applied to Jews, Christians, Sabeans and sometimes Zoroastrians.

Pillars of Islam – the five obligatory duties of a Muslim.

qiyas – analogical reasoning, used in *ijtihad*.

Quran – a series of "revelations" that Muhammad believed God gave him over the period 610 to 632.

rashidun – the rightly guided ones, used of the first four caliphs following Muhammad as leaders of the Muslim community. Their rule covered the period 632 to 661.

riba – some contemporary Islamists consider this to mean any kind of interest on money lent, but the traditional meaning was "extortionate interest".

risala – role and message of the messenger/apostle.

Sabeans – follows of John the Baptist. Considered in the Quran to have a revealed religion and thus to be in the same category as Jews and Christians, i.e. not pagans.

sabr – patience and perseverance in striving for the goal. This term is often used in Islamist discourse, especially by the Muslim Brotherhood, who support a gradualist method.

Salafism – Salafi Muslims believe in returning to the ways of their "pious ancestors", the *salaf*, such as Muhammad and his immediate successors, who practised a pure form of Islam.

Sassanid or Sassanian – a Persian dynasty founded in AD 224. It was destroyed by the Arab Muslims in 637-651.

Shafii – a Sunni school of sharia, founded by Imam Muhammad bin Idris ash Shafii (died 820).

shahada – testimony, particularly reciting the Islamic creed. Also legal testimony in a court of law. Also martyrdom.

sharia – Islamic law.

sheikh – literally "old man" or elder. This title can be given to heads of religious orders, Quranic scholars, jurists, those who preach and lead prayers in the mosque and Sufi saints. It is also used for a village elder or tribal chief.

Shia – a minority sect of Islam, which broke away from the main body in 657. They believe that the rightful successor to Muhammad was Ali, his closest relative. A majority in Iran, Iraq, Azerbaijan and Bahrain. cf. Sunni, Isma'ili, Zaydi.

sira – biography of Muhammad, usually referring to authoritative early accounts (Ibn Ishaq, al-Tabari and others).

Sufism – Islamic mysticism.

sunna – literally "a trodden path". The actions and words of Muhammad as recorded in the *hadith*. Some Muslims also include the actions and words of Muhammad's early followers who knew him personally.

Sunni – literally "one of the path". The largest sect in Islam, comprising 80-90% of Muslims today, who follow the elected successors of Muhammad. cf. Shia.

Tablighi Jamaat – the largest Islamist fundamentalist reform movement in the world, first established in 1926 in British India by Muhammad Ilyas to prevent Muslims from drifting into Hinduism. It is engaged in systematic *dawa* work among Muslims everywhere, seeking to revive individual faith and piety along Deobandi theology. Revival of personal Islam is considered the best *jihad* and it stresses persuasion and peaceful means. However due to its size it was infiltrated by the Pakistani intelligence to recruit individuals to fight in the *jihad* against Soviet troops in Afghanistan. This helped establish a violent element within the movement.

tafsir – the Islamic science of the explanation of the Quran; Quranic commentary.

takfir – the act of declaring that another Muslim is not a genuine believer but an infidel.

Taliban – literally "students" or "seekers". The ultra-conservative Islamic movement that had political power in Afghanistan from 1996 to 2001.

taqiyya – the practice of concealing one's true beliefs in times of danger. This doctrine is very strong in Shia Islam but also present in Sunni Islam.

tawhid – unity, oneness. Basic doctrine of Islam, declaring the absolute oneness of Allah.

umma – the Islamic nation; the whole body of Muslims worldwide.

velayat-e-faqih – literally, guardianship of the jurist. Vice-regency of the Islamic jurists, i.e. government by the Islamic jurists. A doctrine devised by Ayatollah Khomeini (1900-89), the architect of the 1979 Islamic Revolution in Iran.

Wahhabism – strictly puritanical form of Sunni Islam, founded in the 18th century, predominant in Saudi Arabia.

zakat – compulsory alms-giving to help the poor of the Muslim community and, according to some Islamic scholars, to help extend Islamic rule. One of the five pillars of Islam.

Zaydi – "Fiver" Shia sect that ruled North Yemen for many centuries.

Zoroastrianism – the pre-Islamic religion of Persia, strongly ethical and with both monotheistic and dualistic aspects.

BIBLIOGRAPHY

Abdelmassih, Mary, "Egyptian Muslim Ring Uses Sexual Coercion to Convert Christian Girls: Report", *Assyrian Christian News Agency,* 13 July 2011, http://aina.org/news/20110712201559.htm, viewed 9 May 2014.

Abdurrahman, Abuhuraira, *Method of Islamic Da'wah,* Johor Baru, Malaysia: Perniagaan Jahabersa, 2003.

Abul-Fadl, Mona, *Where East Meets West: Appropriating the Islamic Encounter for a Spiritual-Cultural Revival.* Herndon, Virginia: The International Institute of Islamic Thought, 1992.

Abul-Fadl, Mona, "Contrasting Epistemics: Tawhid, the Vocationist and Social Theory", *The American Journal of Islamic Social Sciences,* Vol. 7, No. 1, 1990.

Abul-Fadl, Mona, *Introducing Islam from Within: Alternative Perspectives,* Leicester: The Islamic Foundation, 1991.

Abul-Fadl, Mona "Islamization as a Force of Global Cultural Renewal or: The Relevance of the Taw d Episteme to Modernity", *The American Journal of Islamic Social Sciences,* Vol. 5, No. 2, 1988.

Abul-Fadl, Mona, *Rethinking Culture, Renewing The Academy: Tawhidi Perspectives,* Contrasting Episteme Collection Mona M. Abul-Fadl © Draft under Review Restricted Circulation/ GSISS Library/ In House Collection 1, http://muslimwomenstudies.com/Rethinking%20Culture -part%20A%20&%20B-cpy.pdf, viewed 28 April 2014.

Abdul-Hussain, Hussain, "Hezbollah: The State within a State", *Current Trends in Islamist Ideology*, Vol. 8, 21 May 2009.

Adamu, Adamu and Michelle Faul, "Few voters in Nigerian state amid Islamic uprising", *Associated Press*, 28 December 2013, http://news.yahoo.com/few-voters-nigerian-state-amid-islamic-uprising-094737998.html, viewed 20 January 2014.

Ahmed, Akbar S., *Postmodernism and Islam: Predicament and Promise*, London: Routledge, 1992.

Ahmad, Khurshid, "Economic Development in an Islamic Framework" in Khurshid Ahmad (ed.), *Studies in Islamic Economics*, Leicester: The Islamic Foundation, 1980.

al-Ahsan, Abdullah, *OIC The Organization of the Islamic Conference: (An Introduction to an Islamic Political Institution)*, Herndon, Virginia: The International Institute of Islamic Thought, 1988.

Ahsan, M. Manazir, "Dawa and Its Significance for the Future" in Merryl Wyn Davies and Adnan Khalil Pasha, eds., *Beyond Frontiers: Islam and Contemporary Needs*, London: Mansell Publishing 1989.

Akhbar al-'Alam al-Islami, No. 908 (January 14, 1985), summarised in Ekkehard Rudolph, "The Debate on Muslim-Christian Dialogue as Reflected in Muslim Periodicals in Arabic (1970-1991)" in Jacques Waardenburg ed., *Muslim Perceptions of Other Religions: A Historical Survey*, New York, Oxford University Press, 1999.

"The AKP Government's Attempts to move Turkey from Secularism to Islamism (Part III): PM Erdogan: Islam is Turkey's Supra-Identity", *MEMRI,* Special Dispatch Series No. 1086, February 7, 2006, http://www.memri.org/report/en/print1600.htm, viewed 13 May 2014.

"All Foreign Gifts", Federal Student Aid, an office of the US Department of Education, 5 April 2013, http://studentaid.ed.gov/sites/default/files/fsawg/datacenter/library/ForeignGift04052013.xls, viewed 15 May 2014.

'Amr Khalid, in an interview on Dream 2 TV, 10 May 2008, quoted in *MEMRI Special Dispatch Series,* No. 2003, 27 July 2008.

Ansari, Humayun, *'The Infidel Within': Muslims in Britain Since 1800,* London, Hurst & Co., 2004.

Ansari, Humayun, *Muslims in Britain,* London: Minorities Rights Group International, 2002.

Anwar, Zainah, "What Islam, Whose Islam? Sisters in Islam and the Struggle for Women's Rights" in Robert Hefner, ed., *The Politics of Multiculturalism*, Honolulu: University of Hawai'i Press, 2001.

Article In Issue III Of English-Language Taliban Magazine 'Azan' Declares Modern Muslim Countries 'Dar-ul-Kufr,' 'Dar-ul-Harb,' Says Conversion Is Forbidden In Islam, 'Offensive Jihad' Is Essential To Implement Islamic Sharia Worldwide, *MEMRI Special Dispatch*, No. 5428, 30 August 2013, http://www.memri.org/report/en/print 7385.htm, viewed 6 May 2014.

Asian Human Rights Commission, *The State of Human Rights in Pakistan in 2012*, 2012, p. 8. http://www.humanrights.asia/resources/hrreport/ 2012/ahrc-spr-008-2012.pdf/view viewed 7 March 2014.

Aydin, Senem and Ru en Çakır, "Political Islam in Turkey", Centre European Policy Studies (CEPS) Working Document No. 265, April 2007.

Ayubi, Nazih N., "Islamic State", in John L. Esposito, ed., *The Oxford Encyclopedia of the Modern Islamic World*, New York; Oxford University Press, 1995.

Badawi, M. A. Zaki, *Islam in Britain: a Public Lecture 1981,* London: Ta-Ha Publishers, 1981.

Bakar, Osman, "Islam, Ethnicity, Pluralism and Democracy: Malaysia's Unique Experience", in *Islam, Democracy and the Secularist State in the Post-Modern Era*, Burtonsville, MD: Center for the Study of Islam & Democracy (CSID), 2001.

Baldwin, Tom, "Barack Obama offers open hand to Muslims", *The Times*, 28 January 2009.

Bangash, Zafar, ed. *In Pursuit of the Power of Islam: Major Writings of Kalim Siddiqui,* London: The Open Press, 1996.

"Bangladesh coalition party vows Islamic state", *Reuters*, 10 April 2001.

"Bangladesh SC rejects Jamaat's plea against disqualification", *The Hindu*, 5 August 2013.

Barillas, Martin, "Nigeria: Islamist terrorists threaten to abduct Christian women to teach fear of Islam", *Spero News,* 9 March 2012.

"Barnabas Aid Response to the Yale Center for Faith and Culture Statement", 30 January 2008,http://www.barnabasfund.org/US/News/Archives/ Barnabas-Fund-Response-to-the-Yale-Center-for-Faith-and-Culture-Statement.html?p=7, viewed 12 May 2014.

Barnabas Fund, "Sharia Courts in the UK: what do they mean?", *Barnabas Aid,* March/April 2009.

Bartolucci, Valentina, "Morocco's silent revolution", *openDemocracy,* 17 January 2012, http://www.opendemocracy.net/valentina-bartolucci/ moroccos-silent-revolution, viewed 13 May 2014.

Bat Ye'or, *Islam and Dhimmitude: Where Civilizations Collide*, Madison, New Jersey: Fairleigh Dickinson University Press, 2002.

Baxter, Sarah, "Obama reaches out to Muslims", *The Sunday Times,* 18 January 2009.

Beaumont, Peter, "Mohamed Morsi signs Egypt's new constitution into law", *The Guardian*, 26 December 2012, http://www.theguardian.com/world/2012/dec/26/mohamed-morsi-egypt-constitution-law, viewed 14 May 2014.

Berman, Sheri, "Islamism, Revolution, and Civil Society", *Perspectives on Politics*, Vol. 1, No. 2, June 2003 https://docs.google.com/a/barnard.edu/viewer?a=v&pid=sites&srcid=YmFybmFyZC5lZHV8c2hlcmktYmVyb WFufGd4OjE1OGYzOGI5MTljZjUzNWU, viewed 13 May 2014.

"Bishop attacks 'Muslim hypocrisy'", *BBC News,* 5 November 2006, http://news.bbc.co.uk/1/hi/uk/6117912.stm, viewed 15 May 2014.

Bitar, Zaher, "Dubai Chamber to attract world Islamic business anchors", *Gulf News*, 29 September 2013, http://gulfnews.com/business/general/dubai-chamber-to-attract-world-islamic-business-anchors-1.1237067, viewed 6 February 2014.

"Blast kills dozens as Yemen violence rages", CBS News, May 21, 2012, http://www.cbsnews.com/news/blast-kills-dozens-as-yemen-violence-rages/, viewed 13 May 2014.

Bodi, Faisal, "Koranic codes", *The Guardian,* 24 July 1999, http://www.theguardian.com/comment/story/0,,279722,00.html, viewed 12 May 2014.

"Boko Haram issues three-day ultimatum to Christians", *AFP*, 2 January 2012, http://www.vanguardngr.com/2012/01/boko-haram-spokesman-threatens-christians-troops/#sthash.1VvYWuqo.dpuf, viewed 13 February 2014.

"Boko Haram raid kills dozens in Nigeria", *Al-Jazeera*, 12 February 2014, http://www.aljazeera.com/news/africa/2014/02/boko-haram-raid-kills-dozens-nigeria-201421221431015516.html, viewed 13 February 2014.

Boone, Jeb, "Yemen's Transition: Who's Who in the Yemeni Opposition", The Jamestown Foundation, *Militant Leadership Monitor (MLM)*, Vol. 2 Issue 12, 30 December 2011.

Boroumand, Ladan, "The Untold Story of the Fight for Human Rights", *Journal of Democracy*, Vol. 18, No. 4, October 2007.

Boswell, Alan, "Darfur Redux: Is 'Ethnic Cleansing' Occurring in Sudan's Nuba Mountains?", *TIME World*, 14 June 2011, http://www.time.com/time/world/article/0,8599,2077376,00.html, viewed 16 May 2014.

Brandon, James and Salam Hafez, *Crimes of the Community: Honour-Based Violence in the UK*, London: Centre for Social Cohesion, 2008.

Brown, Cameron S., "Waiting For The Other Shoe To Drop: How Inevitable Is An Islamist Future?", *The Middle East Review of International Affairs*, Vol. 10, No. 2, June 2006, pp. 108-119.

Brown Nathan J., "Jordan and its Islamic Movement: The Limits of Inclusion?" Carnegie Endowment for International Peace, Democracy And Rule Of Law Project, Number 74, November 2006, http://carnegieendowment.org/files/cp_74_brown_final.pdf, viewed 6 May 2014.

Burke, Jason, "Britain stops talk of 'war on terror'", *The Observer*, 10 December 2006.

Byrnes, Sholto, "Creeping Islamisation: Observations on Malaysia", *New Statesman*, 6 September 2007, http://www.newstatesman.com/society/2007/09/malaysia-religious-muslim, viewed 13 May 2014.

Caldwell, Christopher, "Islamic Europe?", *The Weekly Standard*, 4 October 2004, http://www.weeklystandard.com/Content/Public/Articles/000/000/004/685ozxcq.asp, viewed 16 May 2014.

Callick, Rowan, "Christians 'emptied from the Middle East", *The Australian*, 6 October 2012, http://www.theaustralian.com.au/news/world/christians-emptied-from-middle-east/story-e6frg6so-1226489418086, viewed 15 May 2014.

Cameron, David, "Why I Want London To Be One Of The Great Capitals of Islamic Finance", *Linkedin*, 29 October 201. http://www.linkedin.com/today/post/article/20131029170632-146036479-why-i-want-london-to-be-one-of-the-great-capitals-of-islamic-finance, viewed 16 May 2014.

"Canada Condemns Sudan's Deteriorating Human Rights Situation", *International Business Times*, 4 March 2013, http://ca.ibtimes.com/articles/441741/20130304/sharialaw-canada-sudan-amputation-human-rightswatch.htm, viewed 16 May 2014.

"Catherine Samba-Panza chosen as CAR's new interim President", *AFP*, 21 January 2014, http://www.the-star.co.ke/news/article-151614/catherine-samba-panza-chosen-cars-new-interim-president#sthash.7VH XxiXc.dpuf, viewed 10 March 2014.

Center for Security Policy, "Muslim Brotherhood Strategy for North America: An Explanatory Memorandum on the General Strategic Goal for the Group in North America", http://www.centerforsecuritypolicy

.org/wp-content/uploads/2014/05/Explanatory_Memoradum.pdf, viewed 13 May 2014.

Center for the Study of Islam and Democracy, "Islam, Democracy and the Secularist State in the Post-Modern Era", Burtonsville, Maryland: Center for the Study of Islam & Democracy (CSID), 2001.

"Channel 4 to broadcast Call to Prayer during Ramadan, Channel 4", 2 July 2013, http://www.channel4.com/info/press/news/channel-4-to-broad cast-call-to-prayer-during-ramadan, viewed 14 May 2014.

"Christian proselytizing activities in Sudan are limited, says minister", *Sudan Tribune*, 17 April 2013, http://www.sudantribune.com/spip.php ?article46270, viewed 16 May 2014.

Chye, Kee Thuan, "Will There Be Justice for Sabah?" *MSN Malaysia*, http://news.malaysia.msn.com/community/blogs/blog-will-there-be-jus tice-for-sabah,viewed 12 May 2014.

Citizens for National Security, *Council on American-Islamic Relations: Its Use of Lawfare and Intimidation*, Boca Raton, Florida: Citizens for National Security, October 2013.

Coleman, Clive, "One UK legal system? Think again", *The Times*, 2 December 2006.

Coleman, Isobel, "Gender Disparities, Economic Growth and Islamization in Pakistan", *Council on Foreign Relations*, July 2004, http://www.cfr.org/asia-and-pacific/gender-disparities-economic-growth-islamization-pakistan/p7217, viewed 12 May 2014.

Collier, Myles, "Abduction of Christian Girls Increased in Egypt Since Regime Change", *The Christian Post*, 17 April 2013, http://global .christianpost.com/news/abductions-of-christian-girls-increased-in-egypt-since-regime-change-94130/, viewed 9 May 2014.

Conesa, Pierre, "Background to Washington's War on Terror: Al-Qaida, the sect", *Le Monde Diplomatique*, January 2002, http://mondediplo .com/2002/01/07sect, viewed 13 May 2014.

Connolly, Kate, "Row threatens Cologne's mega mosque", *The Guardian*, 5 March 2012, http://www.theguardian.com/world/2012/mar/05/row-over-cologne-mega-mosque, viewed 14 May 2014.

Cosgrove-Mather, Bootie, "Many British Muslims Put Islam First, NRO: Survey Shows Many More Loyal To Fellow Muslims Outside U.K.", CBS News, 14 August 2006, http://www.cbsnews.com/stories/2006/08/ 14/opinion/main1893879.shtml, viewed 16 May 2014.

Curtis, Michael, Islam and Free Speech: OIC vs. Universal Declaration of Human Rights, *The Gatestone Institute*, 8 February 2012, http://www.gatestoneinstitute.org/2828/islam-free-speech-oic, viewed 3 April 2012

Dallal, Ahmad S., "Ummah", in John L. Esposito, ed., *The Encyclopedia of the Modern Muslim World,* Vol. 4, pp. 267-270, New York: Oxford University Press, 1995.

Davies, Merryl Wyn and Adnan Khalil Pasha, eds., *Beyond Frontiers: Islam and Contemporary Needs,* London: Mansell Publishing, 1989.

Davis, Jacquelyn K. and Charles M. Perry, "Rethinking the War on Terror, Developing a Strategy to Counter Extremist Ideologies: A Workshop Report", March 2007, http://www.ifpa.org/pdf/Rethink_WOT.pdf, viewed 14 May 2014.

"Dawah", Oxford Islamic Studies Online, http://www.oxfordislamicstudies .com/articles/opr/t236/e0182, viewed 14 January 2014.

"Death only penalty for blasphemer: Shariat Court", *The International News* [Pakistan], 5 December 2013, http://www.thenews.com.pk/Todays-News-13-27076-Death-only-penalty-for-blasphemer-Shariat-Court, viewed 16 May 2014.

Deedat, Ahmad, in *Akhbar al-'Alam al-Islami,* No. 1115, 27 March 1989.

Dempsey, Martin E., Memorandum for Chiefs of the Military Services, Commanders of the Combatant Commands, Chief, National Guard Bureau, Subject: Review of Military Education and Training Curriculum, CM-0098-12 in *Responses to 30-Day Review of Military Education and Training Programs,* 24 April 2012, http://www.dod.mil/pubs/foi/ joint_staff/jointStaff_jointOperations/12F1160_FINAL_RESPONSE_ DOCSs_30Day_review_militaryEducation_and_training_programs-6-1-12.pdf, viewed 16 May 2014.

DeYoung, Terri, "Arabic Language and Middle East/North African Studies, University of Indiana, 1999, http://www.indiana.edu/~arabic/arabic_ history.htm, viewed 17 August 2011.

El-Din, Gamal Essam, "Dogma rules: Islamists on the Constitutional Assembly are steamrolling through constitutional drafts that will turn Egypt into a non-civil state", *Al-Ahram Weekly,* Issue No. 1108, 26 July - 1 Aug 2012.

Dobie, Kathy, "Black, Female and Muslim: The Premiere Statewide Islamic Sisters' Friendship Conference, the Malcolm Shabazz Mosque, 116th Street, Harlem", *The Village Voice,* 28 May 1991.

Effendy, Bathiar, "PKS Fiasco and the End of the 'Da wah' Party?", *The Jakarta Post,* 19 August 2013.

Elkholy, Abdo A., *The Arab Moslems in the United States: Religion and Assimilation*, New Haven, Connecticut: College & University Press, 1966.

Ellis, Carl, *S.O.S Saving Our Sons: Confronting the Lure of Islam With Truth, Faith & Courage,* Chicago, Illinois: Imani Books, 2007.

Embong, Abdul Rahman, "The Culture and Practice of Pluralism in Postcolonial Malaysia" in Robert W. Hefner, ed., *The Politics of Multiculturalism: Pluralism and Citizenship in Malaysia, Singapore, and Indonesia,* Honolulu: University of Hawai'i Press, 2001.

Erlich, Reuven, "The Use of Mosques for Military and Political Purposes by Hamas and other Terrorist Organisations and Islamic Groups", *Think-Israel,* 1 March 2009, http://www,think-israel.org/erlich.terrorists mosques, viewed 6 May 2014.

Esposito, John L., ed., *The Oxford Encyclopedia of the Modern Islamic World,* New York: Oxford University Press, 1995.

Esposito, John L., John O. Voll, Osman Bakar, eds., *Asian Islam in the 21st Century,* New York: Oxford University Press, 2008.

Euben, Roxanne L., "Contingent Borders, Syncretic Perspectives: Globalization, Political Theory, and Islamizing Knowledge", *International Studies Review,* Vol. 4, No. 1, Spring, 2002.

"Europa wird islamisch", *Die Welt,* 19 April 2006, http://www.welt.de/print-welt/article211310/Europa-wird-islamisch.html, viewed 16 May 2014.

"Europe Will Be Islamic By End Of This Century Says Princeton Prof", *Free Republic,* 28 July 2008.

European Court of Human Rights, "Refah Partisi (The Welfare Party) and Others v. Turkey (Applications nos. 41340/98, 41342/98, 41343/98 and 41344/98) Judgement Strasbourg 13 February 2003", http://hudoc.echr.coe.int/sites/eng/pages/search.aspx?i=001-60936# {"itemid":["001-60936"]}, viewed 14 May 2014.

Evans, Hajj Abdalhamid, Senior Analyst, Imarat Consultants, *Halal: Identity, Opportunity & Influence,* a presentation at the Islamic Society of North America's Convention, July 2009, Washington DC, http://www.imarat-consultants.com/Imarat_Consultants/Downloads_files/AH%20ISNA%20talk%2007%3A09.pdf, viewed 16 May 2014.

al-Faruqi, Ismail Raji, *Al Tawhid: Its Implications for Thought and Life,* Herndon, Virginia: International Institute of Islamic Thought, 1983.

al-Faruqi, Ismail Raji, *Islam,* Brentwood, Maryland: International Graphics, 1984.

al-Faruqi Ismail Raji, *Islamization of Knowledge: General Principles and Work Plan,* Herndon, Virginia: International Institute of Islamic Thought, 1982.

Faruqi, Ismail R., *The Path of Da'wah In The West,* London: The UK Islamic Mission, 1986.

"Federal Shariat Court 1990", http://khatm-e-nubuwwat.org/lawyers/data/english/8/fed-shariat-court-1990.pdf, viewed 13 May 2014.

The Federation of Islamic Associations of New Zealand: Working Divisions webpage, http://www.fianz.co.nz/divisions, viewed 15 May 2014.

FIANZ NEWS, The Federation of Islamic Associations of New Zealand, April 2010, p. 1, http://archive-nz.com/page/2029655/2013-05-06/ http://www.fianz.co.nz/download/FIANZNEWSapril2010.pdf, viewed 15 May 2014.

Fischer, Johan, "'Cast The Net Wider': How A Vision Of Global Halal Markets Is Overcoming Network Envy", Copenhagen: Danish Institute for International Studies (DIIS), Working Paper No 2008/28, 2008, http://subweb.diis.dk/graphics/Publications/WP2008/WP2008-28_Cast_the_Net_Wider.pdf, viewed 15 May 2014.

Fishman, Shammai, "Some Notes on Arabic Terminology as a Link Between Tariq Ramadan and Sheikh Dr. Taha Jabir al-Alwani, Founder of the Doctrine of "Muslim Minority Jurisprudence" (*Fiqh al-Aqaliyyat al-Muslimah*)", Project for the Research of Islamist Movements (PRISM), Herzliya, Israel, [2003], http://www.e-prism.org/articlesbyotherscholars.html, viewed 6 May 2014.

Frier. Colin "Muslims torn between belief and finance", *The Observer,* 18 June 2000.

The Future of the Global Muslim Population, Pew Research Religion & Life Project, January 2011, http://features.pewforum.org/muslim-population, viewed 16 May 2014.

"Gaza: Halt Morality Enforcement Campaign", *Human Rights Watch,* 2 March 2011. http://www.hrw.org/news/2011/03/02/gaza-halt-morality-enforce ment-campaign, viewed 4 February 2014.

"Gaza: Hamas Should Stop Executions", *Human Rights Watch,* 1 August 2011. http://www.hrw.org/news/2011/08/01/gaza-hamas-should-stop-executions viewed 4 February 2014.

"Gaza: Lift Restrictions on Books, Newspapers", *Human Rights Watch,* 8 March 2011. http://www.hrw.org/news/2011/03/07/gaza-lift-restrictions-books-newspapers, viewed 4 February 2014.

GhaneaBassiri, Kambiz, *A History of Islam in America: From the New World to the New World Order*, New York: Cambridge University Press, 2010.

Geaves, Ron, *Aspects of Islam*, London: Darton, Longman and Todd, 2005.

Ghani, Dr Anwar-ul, "Halal Certification of New Zealand Food Products", Presentation, "NZ in Global Halal Economy", 12 July 2012; Auckland Business School, New Zealand, http://docs.business.auckland.ac.nz/ Doc/NZin-Halal-Economy-Dr-Ghani.pdf, viewed 6 February 2014.

Ghani, Dr Anwar-ul, "Message from the President of FIANZ", FIANZ News, April 2010. p. 1, http://www.fianz.co.nz/download/FIANZ NEWSapril2010.pdf; viewed 15 May 2014.

Glees, Anthony and Chris Pope, *When Students Turn to Terror: Terrorist and Extremist Activity on British Campuses*, London: The Social Affairs Unit, 2005.

Glickman, Harvey, "Islamism in Sudan's Civil War", *Orbis*, Vol. 44. No. 2, Spring 2000.

"Global Islamic banking assets set to top $2 tn", *Oman Observer*, 1 October 2013. http://main.omanobserver.om/?p=17701 viewed 6 February 2014.

Greene, Jay P., "Arabian Gulf Money and US Universities", *Campus Watch*, 7 May 2008, http://www.campus-watch.org/article/id/5077, viewed 6 February 2014.

Guillaume, A., *The Life of Muhammad: a translation of Sirat Rasul Allah*, Karachi: Oxford University Press, 1967.

Habib Hourani, Albert, *Minorities In The Arab World*, London: Oxford University Press, 1947.

"Halal - General Definition", Halal Accreditation, AFIC, http://web.archive .org/web/20100801015757/http://www.afic.com.au/ ?p=465, viewed 15 May 2014.

"Halal menu 'should appeal to all'", *BBC News*, 8 May 2006, http://news.bbc.co.uk/1/hi/world/asia-pacific/4752081.stm, viewed 15 May 2014.

"Halal movement can lead Muslims to rule world economy – Dr Ceric", *The Daily Mail* (Pakistan), 11 December 2010.

Hamid, Abdul Wahid and Jamil Sherif, eds., *The Quest for Sanity: Reflections on September 11 and the Aftermath*, The Muslim Council of Britain, 2002.

Haqqani, Husain, "The Role of Islam in Pakistan's Future", *The Washington Quarterly*, Winter 2004-05.

Haque, Mozammel, "No Place Of Radicalism In Islam", http://www.iccuk.org/media/reports/no_place_of_radicalism_in_islam.htm, viewed 21 December 2005.

Hassan, Riaz, "Globalization's Challenge to Islam", *Yale Global,* 17 April 2003, http://yaleglobal.yale.edu/content/globalizations-challenge-islam, viewed 13 May 2014.

Hefner, Robert W., ed., *The Politics of Multiculturalism: Pluralism and Citizenship in Malaysia, Singapore, and Indonesia,* Honolulu: University of Hawai'i Press, 2001.

Hick, John, ed., *The Myth of God Incarnate,* London: SCM Press, 1977.

Hippler, Jochen, *War, Repression, Terrorism: Political Violence and Civilisation in Western and Muslim Societies,* Stuttgart: Institut fur Auslandsbeziehungen, 2006.

Houben, Vincent J. H., "Southeast Asia and Islam", *The Annals of the American Academy of Political and Social Science,* July 2003; Vol. 588, pp. 149-170.

Hu, Michelle M., and Justin C. Worland, "Saudi Prince Who Funded Harvard Program Visits", *The Harvard Crimson,* 8 February 2012, http://www.thecrimson.com/article/2012/2/8/prince-alwaleed-centers-islam/, viewed 15 May 2014.

Hugeux, Vincent, "Côte d'Ivoire: Ouattara veut 'protéger les minorité'", *L'Express,* 25 January 2012, http://www.lexpress.fr/actualite/monde/afrique/cote-d-ivoire-ouattara-veut-proteger-les-minorites_1075076.html, viewed 15 May 2014.

Hussaini, Mohammad Mazhar, *Islamic Dietary Concepts & Practices,* Bedford Park, Illinois: The Islamic Food & Nutrition Council of America, 1993.

"Ibn Baaz: Using the mass-media for dawah", Quran Sunnah Educational Programs, http://www.qsep.com/modules.php?name=ilm&d_op=article&sid=501, viewed 7 February 2014.

ibn Baaz, 'Abdul 'Azeez ibn 'Abdullah, *Words of Advice Regarding Da'wah: from the noble Shaykh,* Birmingham: Al Hidaayah, 1998.

Ibrahim, Raymond, "How 'Religious Defamation' Laws would ban Islam", *Middle East Forum,* 26 September 2012, http://www.meforum.org/3345/islam-religious-defamation-laws, viewed 15 May 2014.

Idiz, Semih, "Erdogan Takes Islamist Stance, Snubs West at AKP Congress", *Al-Monitor,* 1 October 2012, http://www.al-monitor.com/pulse/politics/2012/09/erdogan-shuns-west-woos-islamists-at-akp-congress.html, viewed 14 May 2014.

Idris, Jaafar Sheikh, "The Process of Islamization", The Islamic Society of North America (ISNA), Plainfield, ndiana, 1976., Fourth Printing - January 1983, http://www.jaafaridris.com/the-process-of-islamization/, viewed 6 May 2014.

"Indonesia ensures Islamisation of the Moluccas", *Nederlands Dagblad,* October 16, 2008.

International Crisis Group, "Hizbollah And The Lebanese Crisis", Middle East Report No. 69, 10 October 2007.

International Crisis Group, "Islamic parties in Pakistan", Asia Report No. 216, 12 December 2011.

International Crisis Group, "Philippines Terrorism: The Role of Militant Islamic Converts", Asia report No. 110, 19 December 2005.

International Crisis Group, "The State of Sectarianism in Pakistan", Asia Report No. 95, 18 April 2005.

International Crisis Group, "Sudan's Southern Kordofan Problem: The Next Darfur?", Africa Report No. 145, 21 October 2008, p. 9 http://www.crisisgroup.org/~/media/Files/africa/horn-of-africa/sudan/Sudans%20Southern%20Kordofan%20Problem%20The%20Next%20Darfur, viewed 15 May 2014.

International Institute of Islamic Thought webpage, http://www.iiit.org/AboutUs/AboutIIIT/tabid/66/Default.aspx, viewed 9 May 2014.

International Islamic Council for Daw'a and Relief: *Coordination System of The International Islamic Council for Daw'a and Relief: 1414 AH.*1993 AD.,* Cairo: International Islamic Council for Daw'a and Relief, 1993, 1995, pp. 1-27.

International Islamic Council for Daw'a and Relief: *Guide to The International Islamic Council for Daw'a and Relief,* Cairo: International Islamic Council for Daw'a and Relief, 1994, pp. 1-22.

International Islamic Council for Daw'a and Relief: *Resolution on the By-Laws for The International Islamic Council for Daw'a and Relief,* Cairo: International Islamic Council for Daw'a and Relief, 1994, pp. 1-27.

"Iran: A legal System that Fails to Protect Freedom of Expression and Association", *Amnesty International,* AI-index: MDE 13/045/2001, http://www.amnesty.org/en/library/asset/MDE13/045/2001/en/73a8bc2a-d8ae-11dd-ad8c-f3d4445c118e/mde130452001en.html, viewed 15 May 2014.

Ishak, Mohd, Shuhaimi Bin Haji and Sohirin Mohammad Solihin, "Islam and Media", Kulliyyah of Islamic Revealed Knowledge and Human

Sciences, International Islamic University Malaysia, June 1, 2012, http://dx.doi.org/ 10.5539/ass.v8n7p263, viewed 7 February 2014.

"Islam, Secularism and the Battle for Turkey's Future", *STRATFOR* Special Report, August 2010.

Islamic Broadcasting Network - Islamic Media Foundation, Homepage, http://www.imf-ibn.net/, viewed 16 May 2014.

Islamic Conference of Foreign Ministers, "Cairo Declaration on Human Rights in Islam", Organization of the Islamic Conference (OIC), http://www.refworld.org/docid/3ae6b3822c.html, viewed 13 May 2014.

Islamic Media Agency webpage, http://www.islamicmedia.co.za/about.htm, viewed 7 February 2014.

Ismail, Salwa, "The Paradox of Islamist Politics", *Middle East Report,* No. 221, Winter, 2001.

"Islamic sect refused permission to build mega-mosque with four times the capacity of St Paul's Cathedral", *The Daily Mail,* 6 December 2012, http://www.dailymail.co.uk/news/article-2243800/East-London-mega-mosque-4-times-capacity-St-Pauls-Cathedral-rejected-local-council.html#ixzz2sHG06y1m, viewed 15 May 2014.

Jamail, Dahr, "Hezbollah's transformation", *Asia Times Online,* 20 July 2006, viewed 13 May 2014.

al-Jarbu, Sheikh Abd al-'Aziz bin Salih, "A Call to Migrate from the Lands of the Disbelievers to the Lands of the Muslims", At-Tibyan Publications, 2008 or 2009, http://www.archive.org/download/guidebooks/call_migrate.pdf viewed 12 May 2014.

al-Jarbu, Abd al-'Aziz bin Salih, "Clarifying the Obligation of Migration", quoted in Muhammad Qasim, "Destroying the Country Idol", *Azan,* Issue 3, 24 August 2013.

Jivanda, Tomas, "One in ten children under five in England and Wales is from a Muslim family, census figures show", *The Independent,* 9 January 2014.

Johnson, Stephen James, South Park' cuts image of Mohammed after threat, AFP, 22 April 2010, http://www.chargerbulletin.com/2010/04/22/south-park-cuts-image-of-mohammed-after-threat/, viewed 13 May 2014.

"Jordan", *International Religious Freedom Report for 2012,* United States Department of State, Bureau of Democracy, Human Rights and Labor, 2012, http://www.state.gov/j/drl/rls/irf/religiousfreedom/index.htm?year=2012&dlid=208396, viewed 14 May 2014.

"Judge rules in favour of fully clad Muslim witness – "free exercise of religion" is guaranteed under our Fundamental Rights", *Kaieteur News Online*, 12 January 2014, http://www.kaieteurnewsonline.com/2014/01/12/judge-rules-in-favour-of-fully-clad-muslim-witness-free-exercise-of-religion-is-guaranteed-under-our-fundamental-rights/, viewed 15 May 2014.

Kannun, Sheikh 'Abdallah, article in *Al-Umma*, No. 3, January 1981.

al-Kattani, 'Ali ibn al-Muntasir, *al-Muslimun fi Urubba wa Amrika*, 2 vols, Bayrut: Dar al-Kutub al-Ilmiyya, 2005.

al-Kattani, 'Ali ibn al-Muntasir, "Muslims in America", *al-Ittihad*, 11. No. 3, Spring 1974, reprinted as excerpt from *Muslim World*, 13 April 1974.

"Keep Islamism out of the classroom", *The Sunday Times*, 13 April 2014.

Kelso, Paul, "Banking on the common good", *The Guardian*, 18 June 2002.

Kerbaj, Richard and Sian Griffiths, "Gove in war on Islamic takeover of schools", *The Sunday Times*, 13 April 2014.

Kern, Soeren, "European 'No-Go' Zones for Non-Muslims Proliferating", *Gatestone Institute*, 22 August 2011, http://www.gatestoneinstitute.org/2367/european-muslim-no-go-zones, viewed 14 May 2014.

Kern, Soeren, "The Islamization of Germany in 2013", *Gatestone Institute*, 15 January 2014, http://www.gatestoneinstitute.org/4130/Islamization-germany, viewed 14 May 2014.

Kettani, M. Ali, *The Muslim Minorities*, Leicester: The Islamic Foundation, 1979.

Kettani, M. Ali, "Problems of Muslim Minorities", in *Muslim Communities in Non-Muslim States,* London: Islamic Council of Europe, 1980.

Khalid, 'Amr, in an interview on Dream 2 TV, 10 May 2008, quoted in *MEMRI Special Dispatch Series*, No. 2003, 27 July 2008.

Khamenei, Ali, *Essence of Tawhid: Denial of Servitude but to God*, Tehran: Foundation of Islamic Thought, 1991.

Kifner, John, "Egypt's New Islamic Schools: Setting an Example", Special to *The New York Times*, 29 September 1986.

Kimball, Sam, "Whose Side Is Yemen On?" *Foreign Policy*, 29 August 2012, http://www.foreignpolicy.com/articles/2012/08/29/whose_side_is_yemen_on, viewed 13 May 2014.

Knight, Sam, "Universities given 'how-to' guide for fighting violent Islam", *The Times,* 17 November 2006.

Kuran, Timur, *Islam & Mammon: The Economic Predicaments of Islamism*, Princeton, New Jersey: Princeton University Press, 2004.

Laessing, Ulf, "Christians grow anxious in "100 percent" Islamic Sudan", *Reuters*, 27 February 2013, http://uk.reuters.com/article/2013/02/27/uk-sudan-christians-idUKBRE91Q0QE20130227, viewed 16 May 2014.

Lal, K. S., *The Legacy of Muslim Rule in India*, New Delhi: Aditya Prakashan, 1992.

"Language Reform: From Ottoman to Turkish", http://countrystudies.us/turkey/25.htm, viewed 16 May 2014.

Lee, Raymond L. M., "Patterns of Religious Tension in Malaysia", *Asian Survey*, Vol. 28, No. 4, Apr. 1988.

Leong, Trinna, "Sabah Christians band together to stop conversions to Islam", *The Malaysian Insider*, 23 January 2014, http://www.the-malaysianinsider.com/malaysia/article/sabah-christians-band-together-to-stop-conversions-to-Islam?utm_source=feedburner&utm_medium=feed&utm_campaign=Feed%3A+tmi%2Fnews%2Fmalaysia+(TMI+-+Malaysia), viewed 30 January 2014.

Lester, Toby, "Tracking India's Bandit Queen: A conversation with Mary Anne Weaver", *Atlantic Unbound*, 1 November 1996, http://www.theatlantic.com/magazine/archive/1996/11/tracking-indias-bandit-queen/304892/, viewed 13 May 2014.

"Lexical Purification", Kurdish Academy of Language, http://www.kurdishacademy.org/?q=node/443, viewed 16 May 2014.

Lewis, B., Ch. Pellat and J. Schacht, eds., *The Encyclopaedia of Islam*, Leiden, Netherlands: Brill, 1983.

Lewis, Bernard, "Europe Will Be Islamic By End Of This Century Says Princeton Prof", *Free Republic*, 28 July 2008, reporting an interview given by Bernard Lewis to the German newspaper *Die Welt*. "Europa wird islamisch", *Die Welt*, 19 April 2006, http://www.welt.de/print-welt/article211310/Europa-wird-islamisch.html, viewed 16 May 2014.

Lewis, Bernard, *Islam: From the Prophet Muhammad to the capture of Constantinople, Vol. 1, Politics and War*, New York: Oxford University Press, 1987.

Lewis, Bernard, *The Political Language of Islam*, Chicago: University of Chicago Press, 1988.

Longva, Anh Nga, "The Apostasy Law in the Age of Universal Human Rights and Citizenship: Some Legal and Political Implications", paper delivered at the Fourth Nordic Conference on Middle Eastern Studies: The Middle East in a Globalizing World, Oslo, 13-16 August 1998. http://www.hf.uib.no/smi/pao/longva.html , viewed 13 May 2014.

MacLeod, Daniel, "Middle East crisis", *The Guardian,* 18 June 2002.

Machlis, David and Tovah Lazaroff, "Muslims are 'about to take over Europe'", *Jerusalem Post,* 29 January 2007.

McAmis, Robert Day, *Malay Muslims: The History and Challenge of Resurgent Islam in Southeast Asia,* Grand Rapids, Michigan: William B. Eerdmans, 2002.

McVeigh, Karen and Amelia Hill, "Bill limiting sharia law is motivated by 'concern for Muslim women'", *The Guardian,* 8 June 2011, http://www.theguardian.com/law/2011/jun/08/sharia-bill-lords-muslim-women, viewed 12 May 2014.

Maddy-Weitzman, Bruce, "The Arab League Comes Alive", *Middle East Quarterly,* 19:3, Summer 2012.

Mahmoud, Mohamed, "When Shari'a Governs: The Impasse of Religious Relations in Sudan", *Islam and Christian-Muslim Relations,* Vol. 18, No. 2, April 2007.

Malik, Brigadier S. K., *The Quranic Concept of War,* Lahore, Pakistan: Associated Printers, 1979.

Maqni, Nizar, "Tunisia: A New Home for Jihadi Salafis?" *Al Akhbar English,* 3 March 2012, http://english.al-akhbar.com/node/4772, viewed 14 May 2014.

Mashhour, Mustafa, *On the Path of Da'wah,* Cairo: Al-Falah Foundation, 1999, pp. 56–57, quoted in Egdunas Racius, *The Multiple Nature of the Islamic Da'wa,* Helsinki: Valopaino Oy, 2004.

Matthews, Daud R., *Presenting Islam in the West: (Introduction),* Leicester: UK Islamic Academy, 2004.

Mauro, Ryan, "Islamists Demand Counterterrorism Training Censor Ideology", *FrontPageMagazine,* 13 December 2011, http://www.front pagemag.com/2011/ryan-mauro/islamists-demand-counterterrorism-training-censor-ideology/, viewed 12 May 2014.

Maussen, Marcel, "The governance of Islam in Western Europe: A state of the art report", *IMISCOE Working Paper,* No. 16, June 2007.

A'la Mawdudi, Sayyid Abul, *The Islamic Movement: Dynamics of Values, Power and Change,* Khurram Murad, ed., London: The Islamic Foundation, 2007.

A'la Mawdudi, Sayyid Abul, *Jihad fi Salilillah: (Jihad in Islam),* transl. Khurshid Ahmad, Birmingham: U.K. Islamic Mission Dawah Centre, 1977.

Mayberry, Kate, "'Un-Islamic' book trial opens in Malaysia", *Aljazeera,* 6 August 2012, http://www.aljazeera.com/indepth/features/2012/08/2012 867105109271.html, viewed 13 May 2014.

"The Methodology of UKIM", UK Islamic Mission Sisters Wing, webpage, http://www.ukimsisters.org/ukim/methodology/, viewed 9 May2014.

Ministry of the Interior and Kingdom Relations, *From dawa to jihad: The various threats from radical Islam to the democratic legal order,* The Hague: General Intelligence and Security Service, December 2004.

Modood, Tariq, *Multicultural Politics: Racism, Ethnicity and Muslims in Britain,* Edinburgh: Edinburgh University Press, 2005.

Mohsin, Jugnu (e-mail correspondence 27 December 2003), quoted in Isobel Coleman, "Gender Disparities, Economic Growth and Islamization in Pakistan", *Council on Foreign Relations,* July 2004, http://www.cfr.org/asia-and-pacific/gender-disparities-economic-growth-islamization-pakistan/p7217, viewed 12 May 2014.

Molloy, Antonia, "Islamic law to be enshrined in British law as solicitors get guidelines on 'Sharia compliant' wills", *The Independent,* 23 March 2014, http://www.independent.co.uk/news/uk/home-news/islamic-law-to-be-enshrined-in-british-law-as-solicitors-get-guidelines-on-sharia-compliant-wills-9210682.html, viewed 14 May 2014.

Morris, Nigel, "Terror suspects could be banned from worshipping in mosques after burka escape by Mohammed Ahmed Mohamed, *The Independent,* 12 November 2013.

Morsy, Soheir A., " Islamic Clinics in Egypt: The Cultural Elaboration of Biomedical Hegemony", *Medical Anthropology Quarterly,* New Series, Vol. 2, No. 4, Dec. 1988.

Moussalli, Ahmad S., *The Islamic Quest for Democracy, Pluralism and Human Rights,* Gainesville, Florida: University Press of Florida, 2001.

Moya, Sebastian, "The History of Arabic Loanwords in Turkish", 9 December 2008, http://www.swarthmore.edu/SocSci/Linguistics/Theses09/smoya1%20LingThesis%20final%20pdf.pdf, viewed 16 May 2014.

Murad, Khurram, *Da'wah Among Non-Muslims in the West: Some Conceptual and Methodological Aspects,* Leicester: The Islamic Foundation, 1986

Murad, Khurram, "Editor's Preface", in Abul Hasan Ali Nadwi, *Muslims in the West: The Message and Mission,* Leicester: The Islamic Foundation, 1983.

Muslim Communities in Non-Muslim States, London: Islamic Council of Europe, 1980.

Muslim Council of Britain, *The Quest for Sanity: Reflections on September 11 and the Aftermath,* Wembley, Middlesex: The Muslim Council of Britain, 2002.

Muslim Council of Britain, "Towards Greater Understanding: Meeting the needs of Muslim pupils in state schools", 2007, http://www.crin.org/docs/Muslim_Council_Guidance_Schools.pdf, viewed 15 May 2014.

Muslim World League, "New Media and Communication Technology in the Muslim World: Challenge and Opportunity", The Second International Conference on Islamic Media, Jakarta, Indonesia: The Muslim World League, 12-16 December 2011.

Muslim World League, *Resolutions and Recommendations of the Message of the Mosque Conference: Held in Mecca at the Invitation of the Muslim World League, from 15th to 18th Ramadan, 1395, 10th to 23rd September, 1975,* Mecca: Muslim World League, 1976.

Muslim World League: World Supreme Council for Mosques webpage, http://en.themwl.org/node/46, viewed 15 May 2014.

Nadwi, Abul Hasan Ali, *Muslims in the West: The Message and Mission,* Leicester: The Islamic Foundation, 1983.

An-Na'im, Abdullahi Ahmed, "Application of Shari'ah (Islamic Law) and Human Rights Violations in the Sudan", in *Religion and Human Rights: Proceedings of the Conference Convened by the Sudan Human Rights Organization,* 1992.

Najjar, Fauzi M., "Book Banning in Contemporary Egypt", *The Muslim World,* Vol. 91, Nos. 3&4, Fall 2001, pp. 399-424.

Najjar, Fauzi M., "Islamic Fundamentalism and the Intellectuals: The Case of Nasr Hamid Abu Zayd", *British Journal of Middle Eastern Studies,* Vol. 27, No. 2, November 2000.

ibn Naqib al-Misri, Ahmad, *Reliance of the Traveller: The Classic Manual of Islamic Sacred Law 'Umdat al-Salik by Ahmad ibn Naqib al-Misri (d. 769/1368) in Arabic with facing English Text, Commentary and Appendices,* ed. and transl. Nuh Ha Mim Keller, Beltsville, Maryland: Amana Publications, 1997.

Naqshbandi, Mehmood, *Islam and Muslims in Britain: A Guide for Non-Muslims,* London: City of London Police, 2006.

Nardin, Terry, ed., *The Ethics of War and Peace: Religious and Secular Perspectives*, Princeton, New Jersey: Princeton University Press, 1996.

Nasr, Vali, "Pakistan after Islamization: Mainstream and Militant Islamism in a Changing State", in John L. Esposito, John O. Voll, Osman Bakar, eds., *Asian Islam in the 21st Century*, New York: Oxford University Press, 2008, pp. 31-48.

Nasry, Wafik, *"al-da'wah in Islam": Muḥammad Rašīd Riḍā's Tafsīr al-Qur'ān al-Ḥakīm al-Šahīr bi-Tafsīr al-Manār on the qur'ānic verse 3:104*, Rome: Unpublished Master's Thesis, Pontificio Instituto di Studi Arabie d'Islamistica, 2003.

Nawara, Wael and Feyzi Baban "Future of political islam: lessons from Turkey, Egypt", *Al-Monitor*, 29 January 2014, http://www.al-monitor.com/pulse/originals/2014/01/islam-turkey-egypt-ideology-islamist-law.html?utm_source=Al-Monitor+Newsletter+%5BEnglish%5D&utm_campaign=32d3bc2c8c-January_9_20141_8_2014&utm_medium=email&utm_term=0_28264b27a0-32d3bc2c8c-93088337#ixzz2ruJPcjm3, viewed 13 May 2014.

En Nawawi, Mahiudin Abu Zakaria Yahya Ibn Sharif, *Minhaj et Talibin: A manual of Muhammadan Law according to the School of Shafai*, transl. E. C. Howard, New Delhi: Adam Publishers & Distributors, 2005.

Nazeer, Zubaidah, "Indonesian ex-MP gets 16 years for corruption", *The Straits Times*, 12 December 2013, http://news.asiaone.com/news/asia/indonesian-ex-mp-gets-16-years-corruption, viewed 14 May 2014.

Negus, Steve, "The Muslim Brothers Keep a Low Profile, But Their Main Activity—Charity Work—Still Goes On," *Cairo Times*, Vol. 1, No. 3, 3 April 1997.

New Vision (Uganda), "House Approves Six Judges, *Pesa Times*, 20 January 2014, http://pesatimes.co.tz/news/legal-environment/house-approves-six-judges, viewed 15 May 2014.

Nietschmann, Bernard, "Transmigration: Annexation by Occupation", http://www.michr.net/moluccas-genocide-on-the-sly-ndash-indonesia rsquos-transmigration-and-islamisation-program.html, viewed 15 May 2014.

"Nigeria: Sect Leader Vows Revenge", *Daily Trust*, 27 July 2009, http://wwrn.org/articles/31419/?&place=nigeria, viewed 13 February 2014.

"Official indifference to other abuses of minority rights" in: "Pakistan: Insufficient Protection of Religious Minorities", *Amnesty International*, May 2001, ASA 33/008/2001.

"On a mat and a prayer", *The Economist*, 7 April 2011.

Organisation of Islamic Cooperation, "About OIC", http://www.oic-oci.org/oicv2/page/?p_id=52&p_ref=26&lan=en, viewed 9 May 2014.

Organisation of the Islamic Conference, *Dakar Declaration*, Sixth Islamic Summit Conference, (Session Of Al-Quds Al-Sharif, Concord And Unity), Dakar, Republic of Senegal, 3-5 Jumada II, 1412H (9-11 December, 1991), p. 8, http://www.ifrc.org/docs/ idrl/I643EN.pdf, viewed 9 May 2014.

"Oritsejafor raises alarm over 'intended extermination of Christians and Christianity from northern Nigeria'", *News Express* (Nigeria), 19 March 2013, http://www.newsexpressngr.com/news/detail.php?news=1274& title=Oritsejafor-raises-alarm-over-"intended-extermination-of-Christians-and-Christianity-from-northern-Nigeria" viewed 16 May 2014.

Ormeci, Ozan, *Assessing Current Developments in Turkey*, 27 August 2013, http://danielpipes.org/13322/turkey-developments, viewed 9 May 2014.

"Our Vision", Islam Channel webpage, http://www.islamchannel.tv/ pagesv4/OurVision.aspx, viewed 16 May 2014.

Parsa, Ali, *Shariah property investment: developing an international strategy*, London: Royal Institution of Chartered Surveyors, 2005.

Pascal, Blaise, *Pascal's Pensées*, New York: E.P. Dutton & Co., Inc., 1958.

Perry, John R., "Language Reform in Turkey and Iran", *International Journal of Middle East Studies*, 17: 3, August 1985.

"Persecuted Church News - Sudan: 'Religious Freedom'? Not Really!", *World Evangelical Alliance, Religious Liberty Prayer List*, No. 158, Wed 6, March, 2002, http://web.archive.org/web/20020617170740/http://worldevangelical.org/persec_sudan_06mar02.html, viewed 16 May 2014.

"Persecution Under the Blasphemy Laws in Pakistan", *Jubilee Campaign* Information Sheet, http://web.archive.org/web/20071019014952/ http://www.jubileecampaign.co.uk/world/pak25.htm, viewed 13 May 2014.

"The politics of mosque-building: constructing conflict", *The Economist*, 30 August 2007, http://www.economist.com/node/9725332, viewed 14 May 2014.

Pollard, Stephen, "Libya and the LSE: Large Arab gifts to universities lead to 'hostile' teaching," *The Telegraph*, 3 March 2011, http://www.telegraph .co.uk/news/worldnews/africaandindianocean/libya/8360103/Libya-

and-the-LSE-Large-Arab-gifts-to-universities-lead-to-hostile-teaching.html, viewed 15 May 2014.

"Population and Housing Census of Malaysia 2010", Department of Statistics, Malaysia. 28 January 2011, http://www.statistics.gov.my/portal /download_Population/files/census2010/Taburan_Penduduk_dan_Ciri-ciri_Asas_Demografi.pdf, viewed 12 May 2014.

"President Obama's Advisory Council on Faith-Based and Neighborhood Partnerships", *Pew Research Religion & Life Project*, 9 September 2009, http://www.pewforum.org/2009/08/18/president-obamas-advisory-council-on-faith-based-and-neighborhood-partnerships/, viewed 14 May 2014.

Price, Susannah, "Pakistani court frees 'blasphemer' ", *BBC News*, Thursday 15 August 2002, http://news.bbc.co.uk/1/low/world/south_asia/ 2196275.stm, viewed 13 May 2014.

Prince, Rob, "Tunisia culture wars: the case of Habib Kazdaghli, Dean of the University of Tunis-Manouba", *openDemocracy*, 26 July 2012, http://www.opendemocracy.net/rob-prince/tunisia-culture-wars-case-of-habib-kazdaghli-dean-of-university-of-tunis-manouba, viewed 13 May 2014.

Purves, Libby, "Third World Reveals Miss World Ugliness", *The Times*, 26 November 2002.

Putz, Ulrike, "Christians flee from radical rebels in Syria", *Spiegel Online International*, 25 July 2012, http://www.spiegel.de/international/ world/christians-flee-from-radical-rebels-in-syria-a-846180.html, viewed 15 May 2014.

Al-Qaradawi, Dr Yusuf, *Fiqh al-jihad : dirasah muqaranah li-ahkamih wa-falsafatih fi daw al-Qur an wa-al-Sunnah*, al-Qahirah (Cairo): Maktabat Wahbah, 2009.

Al-Qaradawi, Yusuf, "Muslim Minorities and Politics", *OnIslam.net*, 30 April 2012, http://www.onislam.net/english/shariah/contemporary-issues/ critiques-and-thought/456871-muslim-minorities-and-politics.html ?Thought=, viewed 6 May 2014.

Al-Qaradawi, Yusuf, *Priorities of the Islamic Movement in the Coming Phase*, Swansea: Awakening Publications, 2000.

Qasim, Muhammad, "Destroying the Country Idol", *Azan*, Issue 3, 24 August 2013 excerpts in MEMRI Special Dispatch No. 5428, 30 August 2013, http://www.memri.org/report/en/print7385.htm, viewed 13 May 2014.

Racius, Egdunas, *The Multiple Nature of the Islamic Da'wa,* Helsinki: Valopaino Oy, 2004.

Ramachandran, Sudha, "India lost in 'love jihad'", *Asia Times Online,* 28 October 2009, http://www.atimes.com/atimes/South_Asia/KJ28Df05.html, viewed 12 May 2014.

Readings, George, James Brandon and Richard Phelps," Islamism and Language: How Using the Wrong Words Reinforces Islamist Narratives", *Quilliam,* Concept Series 3, 7 December 2010.

Resolutions On Dawa Activities And Reactivation Of The Committee On Coordination Of Joint Islamic Action, Adopted By The Thirty-First Session Of The Islamic Conference Of Foreign Ministers (Session Of Progress And Global Harmony), Istanbul, Republic Of Turkey, 26-28 Rabiul Thani 1425h, 14-16 June 2004.

"Response of British Muslims for Secular Democracy (BMSD) to the Information and Guidance Published by Muslim Council of Britain: Meeting the Needs of Muslim Pupils in State Schools", BMSD Press Release 23 February 2007, http://www.siawi.org/article4.html, viewed 15 May 2014.

Rida, Muhammad Rashid, *Tafsīr al-Qur'ān al-Ḥakīm al-Šahīr bi-Tafsīr al-Manār on the qur'ānic verse 3:104,* transl. by Wafik Nasry in,"*al-da'wah in Islam": Muḥammad Rašīd Riḍā's Tafsīr al-Qur'ān al-Ḥakīm al-Šahīr bi-Tafsīr al-Manār on the qur'ānic verse 3:104,* Rome: Unpublished Master's Thesis, Pontificio Instituto di Studi Arabie d'Islamistica, 2003.

Rogers, Paul, "Syria, al-Qaida, and the future", *openDemocracy,* 2 August 2012, http://www.opendemocracy.net/paul-rogers/syria-al-qaida-and-future, viewed 13 May 2014.

Rose, Richard. B., "Islam and The Development of Personal Status Laws Among Christian Dhimmis: Motives, Sources, Consequences," *The Muslim World,* Vol. LXXII, Nos. 3-4, 1982.

Rubin, Barry, "Tunisia: Goodbye Democracy? Islamists Start to Take Over Media", *PJ Media,* 5 July 2012, http://pjmedia.com/barryrubin/2012/07/05/tunisia-same-old-same-old/, viewed 13 May 2014.

Rudolph, Ekkehard, Summary of the position of the Sudanese Islamist Hasan al-Turabi as described by al-Turabi in *Akhbar al-'Alam al-Islami,* No. 908 (Jan 14, 1985).

Rudolph, Ekkehard, "The Debate on Muslim-Christian Dialogue as Reflected in Muslim Periodicals in Arabic (1970-1991)" in Jacques

Waardenburg ed., *Muslim Perceptions of Other Religions: A Historical Survey*, New York: Oxford University Press, 1999.

Rusin, David J., "Western Courts Bend to Islamic Practices", *PJ Media*, 28 September 2012.

Safran, Janina M., "Rules of Purity and Confessional Boundaries: Maliki Debates about the Pollution of the Christian", *History of Religions*, Vol. 42, No. 3 Feb., 2003, pp. 197-212.

Sahih Al-Bukhari, The Translation of the Meanings of: Arabic-English, transl. M. Muhsin Khan, Riyadh: Darussalam, 1997.

Salkida, Ahmad, "Nigeria: Sect Leader Vows Revenge", *Daily Trust*, 27 July 2009.

Sardar, Ziauddin, *Desperately Seeking Paradise: Journeys of a Sceptical Muslim*, London: Granta Books, 2004.

Sarwar, Ghulam, "Challenges Facing Islam and the Muslim Ummah", http://www.defencejournal.com/feb-mar99/challenges-islam.htm, viewed 12 May 2014.

Sarwar, Ghulam, "Compulsory Christian Collective Worship and Christian Religious Education (RE) in UK Schools: What Can Muslims Do?", *Islam 4u*, http://islam4u.montadamoslim.com/t157-compulsory -christian-collective-worship-and-christian-religious-education-re-in-uk-schools-what-can-muslims-do, viewed 15 May 2014.

Saunders, Robert A., "The ummah as nation: a reappraisal in the wake of the 'Cartoons Affair'", *Nations and Nationalism*, Vol. 14, No. 2, 2008.

Schmedding, Anne, "New mosques in Germany – religious architecture as a symbol of integration", Goethe Institut, July 2012, http://www.goethe .de/kue/arc/nba/en9538251.htm, viewed 15 May 2014.

Schmidt, Susan, "Lobbying through the Silver Screen", *The National Interest*, 23 October 2012, http://nationalinterest.org/commentary/lobbying-through-the-silver-screen-7647?page=1, viewed 7 February 2014.

Schmidt, Susan, "Saudi Money Shaping U.S. Research", *The National Interest*, 11 February 2013, http://nationalinterest.org/commentary/ saudi-money-shaping-us-research-8083, viewed 10 February 2014.

Scruton Roger, *The West and the Rest: Globalization and the Terrorist Threat*, London: Continuum, 2002.

Sepehr, Houshang, "A Caliphate disguised as a republic", *IV Online magazine*, 382, 7 October 2006, http://www.internationalviewpoint.org/ spip.php?article1148, viewed 13 May 2014.

Sewall, Gilbert T., *Islam and Textbooks: A Report of the American Textbook Council*, New York: American Textbook Council, 2003.

Shahine, Gihan, "'A Muslim need not break or burn': Angry Muslims are finding guidance from Moderate Preachers in the Row over the US-film made against Islam", *Al-Ahram Weekly*, No. 1115, 20-26 September 2012.

Shari'ati Ali, *On The Sociology Of Islam,* transl. by Hamid Algar, Oneonta, New York: Mizan Press, 1979.

Sharp, Jeremy M., "U.S. Democracy Promotion Policy in the Middle East: The Islamist Dilemma", *CRS Report for Congress,* 15 June 2006, http://www.fas.org/sgp/crs/mideast/RL33486.pdf, viewed 14 May 2014.

Shavit, Uriya and Frederic Wiesenbach, "Muslim Strategies to Convert Western Christians", *Middle East Quarterly*, Vol. XVI, No. 2, Spring 2009.

Siddiqi, Muhammad Iqbal, *The Penal Law of Islam,* Lahore: Kazi Publications, 1979.

Siddiqui, Kalim in Zafar Bangash, ed., *In Pursuit of the Power of Islam: Major Writings of Kalim Siddiqui,* London: The Open Press, 1996.

Siddiqui, Kalim, *The Muslim Manifesto – a strategy for survival,* London: The Muslim Institute, 1990.

"Silent Scream; The Sudan Ethnically Cleanses Its Christians", 3 April 2012, http://joshuapundit.blogspot.co.uk/2012/04/silent-screamthe-sudan-ethnically.html, viewed 16 May 2014.

Simcox, Robin, *A Degree of Influence: The Funding of Strategically Important Subjects in UK Universities,* London: The Centre for Social Cohesion, 2009.

Simcox, Robin, "Yemen Beyond Saleh: Problems and Prospects for the U.S. and its Allies", The Henry Jackson Society, May 2011.

Solagberu, Abdur-Razzaq Mustapha Balogun, "Islamization or Re-Islamization of Knowledge?", http://i-epistemology.net/islamization-of-knowledge/64-islamization-or-re-islamization-of-knowledge.html, viewed 9 May 2014.

Sookhdeo, Patrick, *Global Jihad: The Future in the Face of Militant Islam,* McLean, Virginia: Isaac Publishing, 2007.

Sookhdeo, Patrick, *Is the Muslim Isa the Biblical Jesus?,* McLean, Virginia: Isaac Publishing, 2012.

Sookhdeo, Patrick, *Islam in our Midst: The Challenge to our Christian Heritage,* McLean, Virginia: Isaac Publishing, 2011.

Sookhdeo, Patrick, *Understanding Shari'a Finance,* McLean, Virginia: Isaac Publishing, 2008.

Sookhdeo, Rosemary, *Why Christian Women Convert to Islam*. McLean, Virginia: Isaac Publishing, 2007.

Soufan, Ali, "How Al Qaeda Made Its Comeback", *Wall Street Journal,* 7 August 2013, http://online.wsj.com/news/articles/SB10001424127 887324653004578651952240608788, viewed 12 May

"Special Representative to Muslim Communities", U.S. Department of State webpage, http://www.state.gov/s/srmc/ viewed 14 May 2014.

"Spreading Islam through the media", The Dawah Project, http://www.thedawahproject.com/about-us/, viewed 16 May 2014.

Spyer, Jonathan, "Hizballah And The Arab Revolutions: The Contradiction Made Apparent?" *Middle East Review of International Affairs,* 27 April 2012, http://www.gloria-center.org/2012/04/hizballah-and-the-arab-revolutions-the-contradiction-made-apparent/, viewed 13 May 2014.

" 'Stop using political power to convert bumis to Islam' ", *Malaysiakini,* 25 January 2014,http://beta.malaysiakini.com/news/252732?utm_source =dlvr.it&utm_medium=twitter, viewed 9 May 2014.

Strasbourg Consortium's webpage, http://www.strasbourgconsortium.org/ index.php?pageId=9&linkId=164&contentId=1627&blurbId=778, viewed 12 May 2014.

Succarieh, Mouna, "Rise of Radical Islam in Yemen Altering Its Tribalism, Book Finds" *Al-Monitor,* 22 September 2012, http://www.al-monitor.com/pulse/fa/politics/2012/09/weekenda-detailed-look-at-islamism-in-yemen.html#, viewed 13 May 2014.

Sudan Human Rights Organization, *Religion and Human Rights: Proceedings of the Conference Convened by the Sudan Human Rights Organization,* 1992 http://wwrn.org/articles/31419/?&place=nigeria, viewed 13 February 2014.

Sylvester, Rachel and Alice Thomson, "'Some parts of Britain have their own form of justice'", *The Times,* 18 January 2014.

Tadros Samuel, "Victory or Death: The Muslim Brotherhood in the Trenches", http://www.hudson.org/research/9687-victory-or-death-the-muslim-brotherhood-in-the-trenches, viewed 13 May 2014.

Tafsir al-Jalalayn: Great Commentaries on the Holy Qur'an, transl. Feras Hamza, Vol. 1, Louisville, Kentucky: Fons Vitae, 2008.

Tafsir Ibn Kathir : (Abridged) Vol. 2 Parts 3,4, & 5 (Surat Al-Baqarah, verse 253-Surat An-Nisa, Verse 147), abridged by Shaykh Safiur-Rahman Al-Mubarakpuri, Riyadh: Darussalam, 2000.

Taheri, Amir, "Who Rules Iran?" *Iran Press Service,* http://www.iran-press-service.com/articles_2004/Mar_04/who_rules_iran_29304.htm, viewed 13 May 2014.

Tamimi, Azzam, "Human Rights – Islamic and Secular Perspectives", in Abdul Wahid Hamid and Jamil Sherif, eds., *The Quest for Sanity: Reflections on September 11 and the Aftermath,* Wembley, UK: The Muslim Council of Britain, 2002.

Tarhuni, Omar, "Khutbah: Community", Royal Holloway University Khutbahs, http://www.khutbahbank.org.uk/Royal_Holloway_khutbahs/Omar_Tarhuni/community.htm, viewed 9 May 2014.

Tauqir, M. Ahmad, "Death the only punishment for blasphemer: FSC", *Pakistan Today,* 4 December 2013, http://www.pakistantoday.com.pk/2013/12/04/national/death-the-only-punishment-for-blasphemer-fsc/, viewed 16 May 2014.

de Teran, Natasha, "Islamic Finance in London: The City Makes a Head Start for Hub Status", *The Banker,* 1 September 2007, http://www.the-banker.com/World/Middle-East/The-City-makes-a-head-startfor-hub-status, viewed 16 May 2014.

"Third Islamic Summit Conference: The Mecca Declaration", http://jang.com.pk/important_events/oic2003/3rd.htm, viewed 12 May 2014.

Tibenderana, Kasenga P., *Islamic Fundamentalism: The Quest for the Rights of Muslims in Uganda,* Kampala: Fountain Publishers, 2006.

Tibi, Bassam, "War and Peace in Islam", in Terry Nardin, ed., *The Ethics of War and Peace: Religious and Secular Perspectives,* Princeton, New Jersey: Princeton University Press, 1996, pp. 128-145.

Thompson, Michael J., "Islam, Rights, and Ethical Life: The Problem of Political Modernity in the Islamic World", *Theoria, A Journal of Social and Political Theory,* Vol. 57, No. 123, June 2010.

Trifkovic, Serge, "Islam's Immigrant Invasion of Europe", *FrontPageMagazine,* 6 January 2003, http://archive.frontpagemag.com/readArticle.aspx?ARTID=20545, viewed 12 May 2014.

Tyan, E., "Da'wa", in B. Lewis, Ch. Pellat and J. Schacht, eds., *The Encyclopaedia of Islam,* Vol. 2, pp. 170-172, Leiden, Netherlands: Brill, 1983.

"United Nations Human Rights Committee 48th Session: Summary Record of the 1251st Meeting, 2nd Periodic Report of the Islamic Republic of Iran, 29 July 1993", *United Nations, International Covenant on Civil and*

Political Rights (CCPR), http://www.bayefsky.com/summary/iran _ccpr_c_sr _1251_1993.php, viewed 13 May 2014.

United Nations Human Rights Committee, "General Comment No. 34, Article 19: Freedoms of opinion and expression", 102nd session, http://www2 .ohchr.org/english/bodies/hrc/docs/gc34/pdf, viewed 16 May 2014.

United Nations Human Rights Council, Resolution 16/18, adopted 12/04/11 by the UN Human Rights Council, http://daccess-dds-ny.un.org/doc/RESOLUTION/GEN/G11/127/27/PDF/G1112727 .pdf?OpenElement, viewed 16 May 2014.

United Nations Office of the High Commissioner for Human Rights, "Defamation of Islam: Commission on Human Rights resolution 1999/82", ap.ohchr.org/Documents/E/CHR/.../E-CN_4-RES-1999-82.doc, viewed 2 April 2012.

United Nations Office of the High Commissioner for Human Rights, Summary Record of the 61st Meeting, 29 April 1999, http://www.unhchr.ch/huridocda/huridoca.nsf/3d1134784d618e28c 1256991004b7950/4e605bd4d096c6958025681f00587847?OpenDoc ument, viewed 9 February 2012.

United States Commission on International Religious Freedom, *Annual Report of the United States Commission on International Religious Freedom May 2011*, Washington DC: US Commission on International Religious Freedom, 2011.

United States Commission on International Religious Freedom, "Press Release: USCIRF Calls for New Efforts to Address Statelessness on Second Anniversary of South Sudan's Independence", 9 July 2013, http://uscirf1.rssing.com/chan-7335254/all_p3.html#item54, viewed 16 May 2014.

United States Department of State, "Sudan, International Religious Freedom Report", released by the Bureau of Democracy, Human Rights, and Labor, 26 October 2001.

United States Holocaust Memorial Museum, "Warning: Sudan", http://www.ushmm.org/genocide/take_action/atrisk/region/sudan, viewed 16 May 2014.

Vidino, Lorenzo, ed., *The West and the Muslim Brotherhood After the Arab Spring*, Al Mesbar Studies & Research Centre in collaboration with The Foreign Policy Research Institute, February 2013.

Waardenburg, Jacques, ed., *Muslim Perceptions of Other Religions: A Historical Survey*, New York: Oxford University Press, 1999.

Waldman, Matt, "The Sun In The Sky: The Relationship Between Pakistan's ISI And Afghan Insurgents", *Crisis States Discussion Paper*, No. 18, London: LSE DESTIN Crisis States Research Centre, 2010.

Wan-Hassana, Wan Melissa and Khairil Wahidin Awang, "Halal Food in New Zealand Restaurants: An Exploratory Study", *International Journal of Economics and Management*, 3(2): 385 – 402 (2009), http://econ.upm.edu.my/ijem/vol3no2/bab11.pdf, viewed 6 May 2014.

"The war for Muslim minds: an interview with Gilles Kepel", openDemocracy, 11 November 2004, http://www.opendemocracy.net/faith-europe_islam/article_2216.jsp, viewed 13 May 2014.

Weiss, Deborah, "OIC Ramps Up 'Islamophobia' Campaign", *FrontPageMagazine*, 28 February 2013. http://www.frontpagemag.com/2013/deborah-weiss/oic-ramps-up-islamophobia-campaign/, viewed 12 May 2014.

Werbner Pnina, *Imagined Diasporas Among Manchester Muslims: The Public Performance of Pakistani Transnational Identity Politics*, Oxford: James Currey, 2002.

Westrop Samuel, *The Interfaith Industry*, London: Stand for Peace, 2013.

"What's gone wrong with democracy: Democracy was the most successful political ideal of the 20th century. Why has it run into trouble, and what can be done to revive it?", *The Economist*, Vol. 410 No. 8876, 1-7 March 2014.

Wiedl, Nina, "Dawa and the Islamist Revival in the West", *Current Trends in Islamist Ideology*, Vol. 9, December 14, 2009.

Winsor, Tom, interviewed by Rachel Sylvester and Alice Thomson, "'Some parts of Britain have their own form of justice'", *The Times*, 18 January 2014.

World Almanac of Islamism 2014: American Foreign Policy Council, Lanham, Maryland: Rowman & Littlefield, 2014.

"The World's Billionaires", *Forbes Magazine*, 9 March 2006, http://www.forbes.com/2006/03/07/06billionaires_worlds-richest-people_land.html, viewed 15 May 2014.

World Halal Forum, "6th World Halal Forum Creates a Notable Paradigm Shift: The introduction of Halal 2.0 - the convergence of Islamic Finance and Halal", 4 April 2011, http://www.worldhalalforum.org/download/WHF2011_OC_Press_Release.doc, viewed 16 May 2014.

Yakan, Fathi, *Problems Faced by the Da'wah and the Da'iyah*, Singapore: International Islamic Federation of Student Organisations, 1985.

Yilmaz, Ihsan, "Law as Chameleon: The Question of Incorporation of Muslim Personal Law into the English Law", *Journal of Muslim Minority Affairs*, Vol. 21, No. 2, October 2001.

Yusuf, Badmas Lanre, "Islamic Dawah in Nigeria Today", *The Muslim World League Journal*, Vol. 21, No. 8, February 1994, http://www.unilorin.edu.ng/publications/yusufbo/Islamic%20Dawah%20in%20Nigeria%20Today.pdf, viewed 8 February 2014.

Abu Zaid, Nasr Hamid, "Brutality and civilisation – violence and terrorism?", in Jochen Hippler, *War, Repression, Terrorism: Political Violence and Civilisation in Western and Muslim Societies*, Stuttgart: Institut fur Auslandsbeziehungen, 2006.

al-Zein, Jihad, "What Will Be the Real Costs of Turkey's Involvement in Syria?" *Al-Monitor*, 18 September 2012, http://www.al-monitor.com/pulse/politics/2012/09/what-will-turkeys-involvement-in-syria-cost-its-leaders.html, viewed 14 May 2014.

NOTES AND SOURCES

[1] Muhammad Rashid Rida, Tafsīr al-Qur'ān al-Ḥakīm al-Šahīr bi-Tafsīr al-Manār on the qur'ānic verse 3:104, transl. Wafik Nasry in *"al-da'wah in Islam": Muḥammad Rašīd Riḍā's Tafsīr al-Qur'ān al-Ḥakīm al-Šahīr bi-Tafsīr al-Manār on the qur'ānic verse 3:104*, Rome: Unpublished Master's Thesis, Pontificio Instituto di Studi Arabie d'Islamistica, 2003, p. 25.

[2] Jaafar Sheikh Idris, "The Process of Islamization", The Islamic Society of North America (ISNA), Plainfield, Indiana, 1976, Fourth Printing - January 1983, http://www.jaafaridris.com/the-process-of-islamization/, viewed 6 May 2014.

[3] Pakistani journalist Jugnu Mohsin (e-mail correspondence 27 December 2003), quoted in Isobel Coleman, "Gender Disparities, Economic Growth and Islamization in Pakistan", *Council on Foreign Relations*, July 2004, http://www.cfr.org/asia-and-pacific/gender-disparities-economic-growth-islamization-pakistan/p7217, viewed 12 May 2014.

[4] Sayyid Abul A'la Mawdudi, *Jihad fi Salilillah: (Jihad in Islam)*, transl. Khurshid Ahmad, Birmingham, U.K. Islamic Mission Dawah Centre, 1977 p. 4.

[5] Muhammad Qasim, "Destroying the Country Idol", *Azan*, Issue 3, 24 August 2013. (*Azan* is a magazine published by the Taliban in Pakistan and Afghanistan. Key excerpts from the article are available in MEMRI Special Dispatch No. 5428, 30 August 2013 at http://www.memri.org/report/en/print7385.htm, viewed 6 May 2014.

[6] Blaise Pascal, *Pascal's Pensées*, New York: E.P. Dutton & Co., Inc., 1958.

[7] Rida in: Wafik Nasry, *«al-da'wah in Islam»: Muḥammad Rašīd Riḍā's Tafsīr al-Qur'ān* pp. 24-25, 40. On p. 45 Rashid Rida implies that *dawa* includes the duty of

hisba, i.e. the duty of Muslim individuals and state to ensure Allah's commands (sharia) are implemented by all in society.

[8] Khurram Murad, *Da'wah Among Non-Muslims in the West: Some Conceptual and Methodological Aspects,* Leicester: The Islamic Foundation, 1986, p. 8.

[9] Based in Egypt, Abduh tried to make Islam compatible with the modern age by reinterpreting traditional Islamic concepts in modern terms. He called for a return to the Quran and *sunna* as the true sources of Islam, rather than following the teaching of the chain of great Islamic scholars through the ages. He wanted to reform Islam by selectively adapting the best of Western scientific, political, philosophical and cultural thought. He saw Islam as a religion of reason, totally in harmony with science, but weakened by centuries of blind imitation and superstition. He wanted to draw a distinction between the unchangeable core of Islam (*ibadat*) and the flexible social rules (*muamalat*).

[10] Rida in: Wafik Nasry, *«al-da'wah in Islam»: Muḥammad Rašīd Riḍā's Tafsīr al-Qur'ān* p. 71.

[11] Rida in: Wafik Nasry, *«al-da'wah in Islam»: Muḥammad Rašīd Riḍā's Tafsīr al-Qur'ān* p. 54.

[12] Rida in: Wafik Nasry, *«al-da'wah in Islam»: Muḥammad Rašīd Riḍā's Tafsīr al-Qur'ān* pp. 24,26, 54.

[13] M. Manazir Ahsan, "Dawa and Its Significance for the Future" in Merryl Wyn Davies and Adnan Khalil Pasha, eds., *Beyond Frontiers: Islam and Contemporary Needs,* London: Mansell Publishing 1989, pp. 13-14.

[14] *Resolutions and Recommendations of the Message of the Mosque Conference: Held in Mecca at the Invitation of the Muslim World League, from 15th to 18th Ramadan, 1395, 10th to 23rd September, 1975*, Mecca: Muslim World League, 1976.

[15] Ozan Ormeci, *Assessing Current Developments in Turkey*, 27 August 2013, http://danielpipes.org/13322/turkey-developments, viewed 9 May 2014.

[16] "The War Cry of the Sabahans", Statement issued 25 January 2014. "'Stop using political power to convert bumis to Islam'", *Malaysiakini*, 25 January 2014,http://beta.malaysiakini.com/news/252732?utm_source=dlvr.it&utm_medium= twitter, viewed 9 May 2014.

[17] *Tafsir al-Jalalayn*, transl. Feras Hamza, Amman, Jordan: Royal Aal al-Bayt Institute for Islamic Thought, 2013; *Tafsir Ibn Kathir , (Abridged) Vol. 2 Parts 3,4, & 5 (Surat Al-Baqarah, verse 253-Surat An-Nisa, Verse 147)*, abridged by Shaykh Safiur-Rahman Al-Mubarakpuri, Riyadh: Darussalam, 2000, pp 237-239.

[18] Nina Wiedl, "Dawa and the Islamist Revival in the West", *Current Trends in Islamist Ideology,* Vol. 9, 14 December 2009, pp. 120-150.

[19] *The Translation of the Meanings of Sahih Al-Bukhari: Arabic-English*, transl. M. Muhsin Khan, Riyadh: Darussalam, 1997, Volume 1, Book 1 Number 6, pp. 50-54 A.

Guillaume, *The Life of Muhammad: a translation of Sirat Rasul Allah*, Karachi: Oxford University Press, 1967, pp. 652-66, 658.

20 E. Tyan, "Da'wa", in B. Lewis, Ch. Pellat and J. Schacht, eds., *The Encyclopaedia of Islam*, Vol. 2, pp. 170-172, Leiden, Netherlands: Brill, 1983.

21 K.S. Lal, *The Legacy of Muslim Rule in India,* New Delhi: Aditya Prakashan, 1992, pp. 93-105.

22 Wiedl, "Dawa and the Islamist Revival in the West", 120-150.

23 Kalim Siddiqui in Zafar Bangash, ed., *In Pursuit of the Power of Islam: Major Writings of Kalim Siddiqui,* London: The Open Press, 1996, p. 125.

24 Kalim Siddiqui in Zafar Bengash, ed., *In Pursuit of the Power of Islam: Major Writings of Kalim Siddiqui,* pp. 125-126.

25 Rida in: Nasry, Wafik, *«al-da'wah in Islam»: Muḥammad Rašīd Riḍā's Tafsīr al-Qur'ān* pp. 42-54.

26 Abdul Azeez ibn Abdullaah ibn Baaz, *Words of Advice Regarding Da'wah: from the Noble Shaykh,* Birmingham: Al-Hidaayah, 1998, p. 18.

27 Mustafa Mashhour, *On the Path of Da'wah,* Cairo: Al-Falah Foundation, 1999, pp. 56–57, quoted in Egdunas Racius, *The Multiple Nature of the Islamic Da'wa,* Helsinki: Valopaino Oy, 2004, p. 75.

28 *Resolutions and Recommendations of the Message of the Mosque Conference,* 1976. See also "Dawah", Oxford Islamic Studies Online, http://www.oxfordislamic studies.com/articles/opr/t236/e0182, viewed 14 January 2014.

29 Racius, *The Multiple Nature of the Islamic Da'wa,* p. 100.

30 The Organisation of Islamic Cooperation, About OIC - http://www.oic-oci.org/oicv2/page/?p_id=52&p_ref=26&lan=en, viewed 9 May 2014.

31 Abdullah al-Ahsan, *OIC The Organization of the Islamic Conference: (An Introduction to an Islamic Political Institution)*, Herndon, VA: The International Institute of Islamic Thought, 1988, p. 106.

32 "Third Islamic Summit Conference: The Mecca Declaration", http://jang.com.pk/important_events/oic2003/3rd.htm, viewed 12 May 2014.

33 Dakar Declaration, Sixth Islamic Summit Conference, (Session Of Al-Quds Al-Sharif, Concord And Unity), Dakar, Republic Of Senegal, 3-5 Jumada II, 1412H (9-11 December, 1991), p. 8, http://www.ifrc.org/docs/idrl/I643EN.pdf, viewed 9 May 2014.

34 Resolutions On Dawa Activities And Reactivation Of The Committee On Coordination Of Joint Islamic Action, Adopted By The Thirty-First Session Of The Islamic Conference Of Foreign Ministers (Session Of Progress And Global Harmony), Istanbul, Republic Of Turkey, 26-28 Rabiul Thani 1425h, 14-16 June 2004.

[35] Abdullah al-Ahsan, *OIC The Organization of the Islamic Conference: (An Introduction to an Islamic Political Institution)*, p. 110.

[36] Mozammel Haque, "No Place Of Radicalism In Islam", http://www.iccuk.org /media/reports/no_place_of_radicalism_in_islam.htm, viewed 21 December 2005.

[37] International Crisis Group, "Philippines Terrorism: The Role of Militant Islamic Converts", Asia report No. 110, 19 December 2005, pp. 4-5.

[38] See its website, http://web.archive.org/web/20091027111403/http://www .geocities.com/mnjilani/WICS22.htm, viewed 13 May 2014.

[39] Rida in: Nasry, Wafik, «al-da'wah in Islam»: *Muḥammad Rašīd Riḍā's Tafsīr al-Qur'ān*, pp. 54-58.

[40] Dr Yusuf Al-Qaradawi, Fiqh al-jihād : dirāsah muqāranah li-aḥkāmih wa-falsafatih fī ḍaw' al-Qur'ān wa-al-Sunnah, al-Qāhirah (Cairo): Maktabat Wahbah, 2009.

[41] Ekkehard Rudolph's summary of the position of the Sudanese Islamist Hasan al-Turabi as described by al-Turabi in *Akhbar al-'Alam al-Islami*, No. 908 (January 14, 1985). See Ekkehard Rudolph, "The Debate on Muslim-Christian Dialogue as Reflected in Muslim Periodicals in Arabic (1970-1991)" in Jacques Waardenburg ed., *Muslim Perceptions of Other Religions: A Historical Survey*, New York, Oxford University Press, 1999, pp. 300-301.

[42] Racius, *The Multiple Nature Of The Islamic Da'wa*, pp. 103-105.

[43] Abuhuraira Abdurrahman, *Method of Islamic Da'wah*, Johor Baru, Malaysia: Perniagaan Jahabersa, 2003.

[44] Abuhuraira Abdurrahman, *Method of Islamic Da'wah*, pp. 148-156.

[45] 'Abdul 'Azeez ibn 'Abdullah ibn Baaz, *Words of Advice Regarding Da'wah*, pp. 96-97.

[46] "The Methodology of UKIM", UK Islamic Mission Sisters Wing, webpage, http://www.ukimsisters.org/ukim/methodology/, viewed 9 May 2014.

[47] Confidential personal communication about Yumbe District, February 2009.

[48] Confidential personal source, 2012.

[49] "The War Cry of the Sabahans", Statement issued 25 January 2014. "'Stop using political power to convert bumis to Islam'", *Malaysiakini*, 25 January 2014, http://beta.malaysiakini.com/news/252732?utm_source=dlvr.it&utm_medium= twitter, viewed 9 May 2014.

[50] "The War Cry of the Sabahans"; Trinna Leong, "Sabah Christians band together to stop conversions to Islam", *The Malaysian Insider*, 23 January 2014, http://www .themalaysianinsider.com/malaysia/article/sabah-christians-band-together-to-stop-conversions-to-Islam?utm_source=feedburner&utm_medium=feed&utm_campaign= Feed%3A+tmi%2Fnews%2Fmalaysia+(TMI+-+Malaysia), viewed 30 January 2014.

[51] "As part of an organized campaign, young Muslim men are deliberately luring women from different faiths into marriage so they will convert to Islam, say radical Indian Hindu and Christian groups in south India. The alleged plot has been dubbed "love jihad". It first surfaced in September, when two Muslim men from Pathanamthitta town in the southwestern state of Kerala reportedly enticed two women - a Hindu and a Christian - into marriage and forced them to convert to Islam." Sudha Ramachandran, "India lost in 'love jihad'", *Asia Times Online*, 28 October 2009, http://www.atimes.com/atimes/South_Asia/KJ28Df05.html, viewed 12 May 2014.

[52] Confidential personal source, 9 June 2012.

[53] *The State of Human Rights in Pakistan in 2012*, Asian Human Rights Commission, 2012, p. 8. http://www.humanrights.asia/resources/hrreport/2012/ahrc-spr-008-2012.pdf/view viewed 7 March 2014.

[54] Reported by the Christian organisation, Association of Victims of Abduction and Enforced Disappearance, Myles Collier, "Abduction of Christian Girls Increased in Egypt Since Regime Change", *The Christian Post*, 17 April 2013, http://global.christianpost.com/news/abductions-of-christian-girls-increased-in-egypt-since-regime-change-94130/, viewed 9 May 2014.

[55] Mary Abdelmassih, "Egyptian Muslim Ring Uses Sexual Coercion to Convert Christian Girls: Report", *Assyrian Christian News Agency*, 13 July 2011, http://aina.org/news/20110712201559.htm, viewed 9 May 2014.

[56] Rosemary Sookhdeo, *Why Christian women convert to Islam*, McLean, Virginia: Isaac Publishing, 2007.

[57] Carl Ellis, personal communication, 8 February 2014. Carl Ellis is the author of S.O.S *Saving Our Sons: Confronting the Lure of Islam With Truth, Faith & Courage*, Chicago, Illinois: Imani Books, 2007.

[58] Confidential personal source, Tbilisi, Georgia, 19 February 2014.

[59] Kathy Dobie, "Black, Female and Muslim: The Premiere Statewide Islamic Sisters' Friendship Conference, the Malcolm Shabazz Mosque, 116th Street, Harlem", *The Village Voice*, 28 May 1991, pp. 25-29.

[60] Mona Abul-Fadl, *Where East Meets West: Appropriating the Islamic Encounter for a Spiritual-Cultural Revival,* Herndon, Virginia: The International Institute of Islamic Thought, 1992, p. 3.

[61] International Institute of Islamic Thought webpage, http://www.iiit.org/AboutUs/AboutIIIT/tabid/66/Default.aspx, viewed 9 May 2014.

[62] Abul-Fadl, *Where East Meets West*, 1992, p. 1.

[63] Abul-Fadl, *Where East Meets West*, pp. 8-9.

[64] See Patrick Sookhheo, *Islam in our Midst*: *The Challenge to Our Christian Heritage,* McLean, Virginia: Isaac Publishing, 2011, pp. 11-17.

[65] Abul-Fadl, *Where East Meets West*, p. 3. Abul-Fadl's sentence finishes "not to its subversion". She is clearly aware that from the Western point of view what the IIIT is attempting to do is neatly summed up by the word "subversion". But in the Islamist view, to Islamise Western culture is not to subvert it but to sanctify it.

[66] Abdur-Razzaq Mustapha Balogun Solagberu, "Islamization or Re-Islamization of Knowledge?", http://i-epistemology.net/islamization-of-kowledge/64-islamization-or-re-islamization-of-knowledge.html, viewed 9 May 2014.

[67] Bernard Lewis, *Islam: From the Prophet Muhammad to the capture of Constantinople, Vol. 1, Politics and War*, New York: Oxford University Press, 1987, pp. xvi-xvii.

[68] Ali Khamenei, *Essence of Tawhid: Denial of Servitude but to God*, Tehran, Foundation of Islamic Thought, 1991, pp. 24-25.

[69] Robert A. Saunders, "The ummah as nation: a reappraisal in the wake of the 'Cartoons Affair'", *Nations and Nationalism*, Vol. 14, No. 2, 2008 (303-321), pp. 306-307.

[70] Ahmad S. Dallal, "Ummah", in John L. Esposito, ed., *The Encyclopedia of the Modern Muslim World*, Vol. 4, pp. 267-270, New York: Oxford University Press, 1995.

[71] Omar Tarhuni, "Khutbah: Community", Royal Holloway University Khutbahs, http://www.khutbahbank.org.uk/Royal_Holloway_khutbahs/Omar_Tarhuni/community.htm, viewed 9 May 2014. (Omar Tarhuni was a Harvard-trained international lawyer from Libya who lived in the UK.)

[72] Rida in: Nasry, Wafik, *«al-da'wah in Islam»: Muḥammad Rašīd Riḍā's Tafsīr al-Qur'ān*, p. 46.

[73] Ziauddin Sardar, *Desperately Seeking Paradise: Journeys of a Sceptical Muslim*, London: Granta Books, 2004, p. 132.

[74] Ron Geaves, *Aspects of Islam*, London: Darton, Longman and Todd, 2005, p. 79.

[75] Ziauddin Sardar, *Desperately Seeking Paradise*, p. 132.

[76] Bernard Lewis, *The Political Language of Islam*, Chicago: University of Chicago Press, 1988, pp. 4-5.

[77] Ziauddin Sardar, *Desperately Seeking Paradise*, pp. 183-184.

[78] Tariq Modood, *Multicultural Politics: Racism, Ethnicity and Muslims in Britain*, Edinburgh: Edinburgh University Press, 2005, pp. 160-167, 199; Humayun Ansari, *'The Infidel Within': Muslims in Britain Since 1800*, London, Hurst & Co., 2004, pp. 18-19.

[79] Ali Soufan, "How Al Qaeda Made Its Comeback", *Wall Street Journal*, 7 August 2013, http://online.wsj.com/news/articles/SB10001424127887324653004578651952240608788, viewed 12 May 2014.

[80] Pnina Werbner, *Imagined Diasporas Among Manchester Muslims: The Public Performance of Pakistani Transnational Identity Politics*, Oxford: James Currey, 2002, pp. 180-181.

[81] Center for Security Policy, "Muslim Brotherhood Strategy for North America: An Explanatory Memorandum on the General Strategic Goal for the Group in North Americahttp://www.centerforsecuritypolicy.org/wp-content/uploads/2014/05/Explanatory_Memoradum.pdf, viewed 13 May 2014.

[82] Samuel P. Huntington, *The Clash of Civilizations and the Remaking of World Order,* New York, Simon & Shuster, 1996.

[83] Ghulam Sarwar, "Challenges Facing Islam and the Muslim Ummah", http://www.defencejournal.com/feb-mar99/challenges-islam.htm, viewed 12 May 2014.

[84] Abdulaziz Othman Altwaijri, "The Civilizational Role of the Muslim Umma in Tomorrow's World", *Islamic Educational, Scientific and Cultural Organization (ISESCO),* 2007. http://www.isesco.org.ma/english/publications/Islamtoday/18/P4.php, viewed 19 January 2009.

[85] Ziauddin Sardar, *Desperately Seeking Paradise*, p. 194.

[86] Roxanne L. Euben, "Contingent Borders, Syncretic Perspectives: Globalization, Political Theory, and Islamizing Knowledge", *International Studies Review*, Vol. 4, No. 1, Spring, 2002, pp. 23-48.

[87] For example, Sheikh Abd al-'Aziz bin Salih al-Jarbu, "A Call to Migrate from the Lands of the Disbelievers to the Lands of the Muslims", At-Tibyan Publications, 2008 or 2009, http://www.archive.org/download/guidebooks/call_migrate.pdf, viewed 12 May 2014.

[88] Humayun Ansari, *'The Infidel Within': Muslims in Britain Since 1800,* p. 205.

[89] Constitution of the Federation of Islamic Associations in the United States and Canada quoted in Abdo A. Elkholy, *The Arab Moslems in the United States: Religion and Assimilation*, New Haven, Connecticut: College & University Press, 1966, p. 154.

[90] Khurram Murad, "Editor's Preface", in Abul Hasan Ali Nadwi, *Muslims in the West: The Message and Mission,* Leicester: The Islamic Foundation, 1983, p. 7.

[91] M. Ali Kettani, *The Muslim Minorities*, Leicester: The Islamic Foundation, 1979, pp. 24-25.

[92] Yusuf Al-Qaradawi "Muslim Minorities and Politics", *OnIslam.net*, 30 April 2012, http://www.onislam.net/english/shariah/contemporary-issues/critiques-and-thought/456871-muslim-minorities-and-politics.html?Thought=, viewed 6 May 2014.

[93] Khurram Murad, "Editor's Preface", in Abul Hasan Ali Nadwi, *Muslims in the West: The Message and Mission,* p. 11.

[94] Isma'il Raji al-Faruqi, *Al Tawhid: Its Implications for Thought and Life,* Herndon, VA: International Institute of Islamic Thought, 1983, p. 142.

[95] Yusuf Al-Qaradawi "Muslim Minorities and Politics", *OnIslam.net*, 30 April 2012, viewed 6 May 2014.

[96] Ismail R. Faruqi, *The Path of Da'wah In The West*, London: The UK Islamic Mission, 1986, pp. 19-26.

[97] Tomas Jivanda, "One in ten children under five in England and Wales is from a Muslim family, census figures show", *The Independent*, 9 January 2014.

[98] Serge Trifkovic, "Islam's Immigrant Invasion of Europe", *FrontPageMagazine*, 6 January 2003, http://archive.frontpagemag.com/readArticle.aspx?ARTID=20545, viewed 12 May 2014.

[99] Some Western European Muslim populations in 2010, according to the Pew Forum were: Austria 5.7% 475,000; Belgium 6.0% 638,000; Denmark 4.1% 226,000; France 7.5% 4,704,000; Germany: 5.0% 4,119,000; Netherlands 5.5% 914,000; Norway 3.0% 144,000; Spain 2.3% 1,021,000; Sweden 4.9% 451,000; Switzerland 5.7% 433,000; UK 4.6% 2,869,000. Source: *The Future of the Global Muslim Population*, Pew Research, January 2011, http://features.pewforum.org/muslim-population. These figures are very conservative and in all probability the numbers of Muslims are considerably higher.

[100] Amr Khalid, in an interview on Dream 2 TV, 10 May 2008, quoted in *MEMRI Special Dispatch Series*, No. 2003, 27 July 2008.

[101] Christopher Caldwell, "Islamic Europe?", *The Weekly Standard*, 4 October 2004, http://www.weeklystandard.com/Content/Public/Articles/000/000/004/685ozxcq.asp, viewed 16 May 2014; "Europe Will Be Islamic By End Of This Century Says Princeton Prof", *Free Republic*, 28 July 2008, reporting an interview given by Bernard Lewis to the German newspaper *Die Welt*. "Europa wird islamisch", *Die Welt*, 19 April 2006, http://www.welt.de/print-welt/article211310/Europa-wird-islamisch.html, viewed 16 May 2014.

[102] David Machlis and Tovah Lazaroff, "Muslims are 'about to take over Europe'", *Jerusalem Post*, 29 January 2007.

[103] Bernard Nietschmann, "Transmigration: Annexation by Occupation", http://www.michr.net/moluccas-genocide-on-the-sly-ndash-indonesiarsquos-transmigration-and-islamisation-program.html, viewed 15 May 2014.

[104] "Indonesia ensures Islamisation of the Moluccas", *Nederlands Dagblad*, October 16, 2008.

[105] Kee Thuan Chye, "Will There Be Justice for Sabah?" *MSN Malaysia*, http://news.malaysia.msn.com/community/blogs/blog-will-there-be-justice-for-sabah,viewed 12 May 2014.

[106] "'Stop using political power to convert bumis to Islam'", *Malaysiakini*, 25 January 2014, http://beta.malaysiakini.com/news/252732?utm_source=dlvr.it&utm_medium=twitter, viewed 25 January 2014.

107 "Population and Housing Census of Malaysia 2010", Department of Statistics, Malaysia. 28 January 2011, p. 92, http://www.statistics.gov.my/portal/download_ Population/files/census2010/Taburan_Penduduk_dan_Ciri-ciri_Asas_ Demografi.pdf, viewed 12 May 2014.

108 "Warning: Sudan", United States Holocaust Memorial Museum, http://www.ushmm.org/genocide/take_action/atrisk/region/sudan, viewed 16 May 2014; Alan Boswell, "Darfur Redux: Is 'Ethnic Cleansing' Occurring in Sudan's Nuba Mountains?", *TIME World*, 14 June 2011, http://www.time.com/ time/world/article/0,8599,2077376,00.html, viewed 16 May 2014; "Silent Scream; The Sudan Ethnically Cleanses Its Christians", 3 April 2012, http://joshuapundit.blogspot.co.uk/2012/04/silent-screamthe-sudan-ethnically.html, viewed 16 May 2014.

109 International Crisis Group, "Sudan's Southern Kordofan Problem: The Next Darfur?", Africa Report No. 145, 21 October 2008, p. 9 http://www.crisisgroup.org/~/ media/Files/africa/horn-of-africa/sudan/Sudans%20Southern%20Kordofan%20 Problem%20The%20Next%20Darfur, viewed 15 May 2014.

110 Sayyid Abul A'la Mawdudi, *The Islamic Movement: Dynamics of Values, Power and Change,* Khurram Murad, ed., London: The Islamic Foundation, 2007, p. 79.

111 M. Ali Kettani, *The Muslim Minorities*, p. 25.

112 "Bangladesh coalition party vows Islamic state", *Reuters*, 10 April 2001.

113 "Bangladesh SC rejects Jamaat's plea against disqualification", *The Hindu*, 5 August 2013.

114 Yusuf Al-Qaradawi "Muslim Minorities and Politics", *OnIslam.net*, 30 April 2012, viewed 6 May 2014. .

115 Faisal Bodi, "Koranic codes", *The Guardian,* 24 July 1999, http://www .theguardian.com/comment/story/0,,279722,00.html, viewed 12 May 2014.

116 Humayun Ansari, *Muslims in Britain,* London: Minorities Rights Group International, 2002, p. 22.

117 Roger Scruton, *The West and the Rest: Globalization and the Terrorist Threat,* London: Continuum, 2002, p. viii.

118 Michael J. Thompson, "Islam, Rights, and Ethical Life: The Problem of Political Modernity in the Islamic World", *Theoria, A Journal of Social and Political Theory,* Vol. 57, No. 123, June 2010.

119 European Court of Human Rights, "Refah Partisi (The Welfare Party) and Others v. Turkey (Applications nos. 41340/98, 41342/98, 41343/98 and 41344/98) Judgement Strasbourg 13 February 2003", http://hudoc.echr.coe.int/sites/eng/pages/ search.aspx?i=001-60936#{"itemid":["001-60936"]}, viewed 14 May 2014.

[120] Islamic Conference of Foreign Ministers, "Cairo Declaration on Human Rights in Islam", Organization of the Islamic Conference (OIC), full text can be found at http://www.refworld.org/docid/3ae6b3822c.html, viewed 15 January 2014.

[121] Ihsan Yilmaz, "Law as Chameleon: The Question of Incorporation of Muslim Personal Law into the English Law", *Journal of Muslim Minority Affairs*, Vol. 21, No. 2, October 2001, pp. 299.

[122] Humayun Ansari, *Muslims in Britain,* p. 22.

[123] Clive Coleman, "One UK legal system? Think again", *The Times,* 2 December 2006.

[124] Bootie Cosgrove-Mather, "Many British Muslims Put Islam First, NRO: Survey Shows Many More Loyal To Fellow Muslims Outside U.K.", CBS News, 14 August 2006, http://www.cbsnews.com/stories/2006/08/14/opinion/main1893879.shtml, viewed 16 May 2014.

[125] "Sharia Courts in the UK: what do they mean?", *Barnabas Aid*, March/April 2009, pp. 12-13.

[126] Karen McVeigh and Amelia Hill, "Bill limiting sharia law is motivated by 'concern for Muslim women'", *The Guardian,* 8 June 2011, http://www.theguardian .com/law/2011/jun/08/sharia-bill-lords-muslim-women, viewed 12 May 2014.

[127] Antonia Molloy, "Islamic law to be enshrined in British law as solicitors get guidelines on 'Sharia compliant' wills", *The Independent,* 23 March 2014, http://www.independent.co.uk/news/uk/home-news/islamic-law-to-be-enshrined-in-british-law-as-solicitors-get-guidelines-on-sharia-compliant-wills-9210682.html, viewed 14 May 2014.

[128] Tom Winsor, interviewed by Rachel Sylvester and Alice Thomson, "'Some parts of Britain have their own form of justice'", *The Times*, 18 January 2014.

[129] David J. Rusin, "Western Courts Bend to Islamic Practices", *PJ Media,* 28 September 2012.

[130] Timur Kuran, *Islam & Mammon: The Economic Predicaments of Islamism,* Princeton, NJ, Princeton University Press, 2004, pp. 2-3, 38, 84-89.

[131] Khurshid Ahmad, "Economic Development in an Islamic Framework" in Khurshid Ahmad (ed.), *Studies in Islamic Economics*, Leicester,:The Islamic Foundation, 1980, pp. 182, 188.

[132] Colin Frier, "Muslims torn between belief and finance", *The Observer*, 18 June 2000; Paul Kelso, "Banking on the common good", *The Guardian*, 18 June 2002.

[133] For example, in a speech in October 2013, Prime Minister David Cameron declared that he wanted to make London "one of the great capitals of Islamic finance". David Cameron, "Why I Want London To Be One Of The Great Capitals of Islamic Finance", *Linkedin*, 29 October 2013. http://www.linkedin.com/today/post/article/20131029170632-146036479-why-i-want-london-to-be-one-of-the-great-capitals-of-islamic-finance, viewed 16 May 2014.

134 Ali Parsa, *Shariah property investment: developing an international strategy*, London: Royal Institution of Chartered Surveyors, 2005.

135 Natasha de Teran, "Islamic Finance in London: The City Makes a Head Start for Hub Status", *The Banker,* 1 September 2007, http://www.thebanker.com/World/ Middle-East/The-City-makes-a-head-startfor-hub-status, viewed 16 May 2014.

136 For more on this subject, see Patrick Sookhdeo, *Understanding Shari'a Finance*, McLean, Virginia: Isaac Publishing, 2008.

137 6th World Halal Forum Creates a Notable Paradigm Shift The introduction of Halal 2.0 - the convergence of Islamic Finance and Halal, World Halal Forum, 4 April 2011, http://www.worldhalalforum.org/download/WHF2011_OC_Press_Release .doc, viewed 16 May 2014.

138 Hajj Abdalhamid Evans, Senior Analyst, Imarat Consultants, *Halal: Identity, Opportunity & Influence*, a presentation at the Islamic Society of North America's Convention, July 2009, Washington DC, http://www.imaratconsultants.com/Imarat_ Consultants/Downloads_files/AH%20ISNA%20talk%2007%3A09.pdf, viewed 16 May 2014.

139 Janina M. Safran , "Rules of Purity and Confessional Boundaries: Maliki Debates about the Pollution of the Christian", *History of Religions,* Vol. 42, No. 3 Feb., 2003, pp. 197-212.

140 Wan Melissa Wan-Hassana and Khairil Wahidin Awang, "Halal Food in New Zealand Restaurants: An Exploratory Study", *International Journal of Economics and Management,* 3(2): 385 – 402 (2009), http://econ.upm.edu.my/ijem/vol3no2/ bab11.pdf, viewed 6 May 2014.

141 Wan-Hassana and Awang, "Halal Food in New Zealand Restaurants".

142 Wan-Hassana and Awang, "Halal Food in New Zealand Restaurants"p. 389.

143 "Halal - General Definition", Halal Accreditation, AFIC, http://web.archive.org /web/20100801015757/http://www.afic.com.au/?p=465, viewed 15 May 2014.

144 Mohammad Mazhar Hussaini, *Islamic Dietary Concepts & Practices,* Bedford Park, Illinois: The Islamic Food & Nutrition Council of America, 1993, pp. 15-16.

145 "Halal movement can lead Muslims to rule world economy – Dr Ceric", *The Daily Mail* (Pakistan), 11 December 2010.

146 "Halal movement can lead Muslims to rule world economy – Dr Ceric", *The Daily Mail* (Pakistan), 11 December 2010.

147 "Halal menu 'should appeal to all'", *BBC News,* 8 May 2006, http://news.bbc.co.uk/1/hi/world/asia-pacific/4752081.stm, viewed 15 May 2014.

148 Johan Fischer, "'Cast The Net Wider': How A Vision Of Global Halal Markets Is Overcoming Network Envy", Copenhagen: Danish Institute for International Studies (DIIS), Working Paper No 2008/28, 2008, http://subweb.diis.dk/graphics/ Publications/WP2008/WP2008-28_Cast_the_Net_Wider.pdf, viewed 15 May 2014.

149 Zaher Bitar, "Dubai Chamber to attract world Islamic business anchors", *Gulf News*, 29 September 2013, http://gulfnews.com/business/general/dubai-chamber-to-attract-world-islamic-business-anchors-1.1237067, viewed 6 February 2014; "Global Islamic banking assets set to top \$2 tn", *Oman Observer*, 1 October 2013. http://main.omanobserver.om/?p=17701, viewed 6 February 2014.

150 Fischer, "'Cast The Net Wider' : How A Vision Of Global Halal Markets Is Overcoming Network Envy"

151 Wan-Hassana and Awang, "Halal Food in New Zealand Restaurants"

152 The Federation of Islamic Associations of New Zealand: Working Divisions, http://www.fianz.co.nz/divisions, (see the section Investment and Funding) viewed 15 May 2014; FIANZ NEWS, The Federation of Islamic Associations of New Zealand, April 2010, p. 1, http://archive-nz.com/page/2029655/2013-05-06/http://www.fianz.co.nz/download/FIANZNEWSapril2010.pdf, viewed 15 May 2014.

153 Dr Anwar-ul Ghani, "Halal Certification of New Zealand Food Products", Presentation, "NZ in Global Halal Economy", 12 July 2012; Auckland Business School, New Zealand, http://docs.business.auckland.ac.nz/Doc/NZin-Halal-Economy-Dr-Ghani.pdf, viewed 15 May 2014; Dr Anwar-ul Ghani, "Message from the President of FIANZ", FIANZ News, April 2010. p. 1, http://www.fianz.co.nz/download/FIANZNEWSapril2010.pdf; viewed 15 May 2014.

154 Catch the Fire Ministries Inc & Ors v Islamic Council of Victoria Inc [2006] VSCA 284 (14 December 2006), Supreme Court of Victoria - Court of Appeal, 14 December 2006, http://www.austlii.edu.au/au/cases/vic/VSCA/2006/284.html, viewed 15 May 2014.

155 Raymond Ibrahim, "How 'Religious Defamation' Laws would ban Islam", *Middle East Forum,* 26 September 2012, http://www.meforum.org/3345/islam-religious-defamation-laws, viewed 15 May 2014. Ibrahim points out that Islam itself, in its source texts and common practice, actively defames other religions, including Christianity and Judaism.

156 Commission on Human Rights – Summary Record of the 61st Meeting, 29 April 1999, http://www.unhchr.ch/huridocda/huridoca.nsf/3d1134784d618e28c125699 1004b7950/4e605bd4d096c6958025681f00587847?OpenDocument, viewed 9 February 2012.

157 See text of the 1999 Resolution "Defamation of Islam: Commission on Human Rights resolution 1999/82", Office of the High Commissioner for Human Rights, ap.ohchr.org/Documents/E/CHR/.../E-CN_4-RES-1999-82.doc, viewed 2 April 2012.

158 Michael Curtis, Islam and Free Speech: OIC vs. Universal Declaration of Human Rights, *The Gatestone Institute*, 8 February 2012, http://www.gatestoneinstitute.org/2828/islam-free-speech-oic, viewed 3 April 2012.

159 For a full list see Strasbourg Consortium's webpage, http://www.strasbourg consortium.org/index.php?pageId=9&linkId=164&contentId=1627&blurbId=778, viewed 12 May 2014.

160 Resolution 16/18, adopted 12/04/11 by the UN Human Rights Council, http://daccess-dds-ny.un.org/doc/RESOLUTION/GEN/G11/127/27/PDF/G1112727 .pdf?OpenElement, viewed 16 May 2014.

161 "General Comment No. 34, Article 19: Freedoms of opinion and expression", United Nations Human Rights Committee 102nd session, Geneva, 11–29 July 2011, http://www2.ohchr.org/english/bodies/hrc/docs/gc34/pdf, viewed 16 May 2014.

162 Gihan Shahine, "'A Muslim need not break or burn': Angry Muslims are finding guidance from Moderate Preachers in the Row over the US-film made against Islam", *Al-Ahram Weekly,* No. 1115, 20-26 September 2012, pp. 8-9.

163 Citizens for National Security, *Council on American-Islamic Relations: Its Use of Lawfare and Intimidation*, Boca Raton, Florida, Citizens for National Security, October 2013.

164 Jason Burke, "Britain stops talk of 'war on terror', *The Observer,* 10 December 2006.

165 Martin E. Dempsey, Memorandum for Chiefs of the Military Services, Commanders of the Combatant Commands, Chief, National Guard Bureau, Subject: Review of Military Education and Training Curriculum, CM-0098-12 in *Responses to 30-Day Review of Military Education and Training Programs*, 24 April 2012, http://www.dod.mil/pubs/foi/joint_staff/jointStaff_jointOperations/12F1160_FINAL _RESPONSE_DOCSs_30Day_review_militaryEducation_and_training_programs-6- 1-12.pdf, viewed 16 May 2014.

166 Ryan Mauro, "Islamists Demand Counterterrorism Training Censor Ideology", *FrontPageMagazine*13 December 2011, http://www.frontpagemag.com/2011/ryan-mauro/islamists-demand-counterterrorism-training-censor-ideology/, viewed 12 May 2014.

167 Taha Jabir al-Alwani, "Settling-down of Islam after the Settlement of Muslims in the West" (Tawtin al-Islam ba'ad Istitan al-Muslimin fi al-Gharb), *Al-Sharq al-Awsat*, 18 January 2000 http://www.alhramain.com/text/alraseed/958/qazaya/2.htm. quoted in Shammai Fishman, "Some Notes on Arabic Terminology as a Link Between Tariq Ramadan and Sheikh Dr. Taha Jabir al-Alwani, Founder of the Doctrine of "Muslim Minority Jurisprudence" (*Fiqh al-Aqaliyyat al-Muslimah*)", Project for the Research of Islamist Movements (PRISM), Herzliya, Israel, 2003, http://www.e-prism.org/ articlesbyotherscholars.html, viewed 6 May 2014.

168 Fishman, "Some Notes on Arabic Terminology", pp. 1-3, 5.

169 Islamic Media Agency webpage, http://www.islamicmedia.co.za/about.htm, viewed 7 February 2014.

170 Mohd. Shuhaimi Bin Haji Ishak and Sohirin Mohammad Solihin, "Islam and Media", Kulliyyah of Islamic Revealed Knowledge and Human Sciences, International Islamic University Malaysia, June 1, 2012, http://dx.doi.org/10.5539/ ass.v8n7p263, viewed 7 February 2014.

171 Badmas Lanre Yusuf, "Islamic Dawah in Nigeria Today", *The Muslim World League Journal*, Vol. 21, No. 8, February 1994, http://www.unilorin.edu.ng/publications/yusufbo/Islamic%20Dawah%20in%20Nigeria%20Today.pdf, viewed 8 February 2014.

172 "Ibn Baaz: Using the mass-media for dawah", Quran Sunnah Educational Programs, http://www.qsep.com/modules.php?name=ilm&d_op=article&sid=501, viewed 7 February 2014.

173 Uriya Shavit and Frederic Wiesenbach, "Muslim Strategies to Convert Western Christians", *Middle East Quarterly*, Vol. XVI, No.2, Spring 2009, pp. 3-14.

174 "Channel 4 to broadcast Call to Prayer during Ramadan, Channel 4", 2 July 2013, http://www.channel4.com/info/press/news/channel-4-to-broadcast-call-to-prayer-during-ramadan, viewed 14 May 2014.

175 Susan Schmidt, "Lobbying through the Silver Screen", *The National Interest*, 23 October 2012, http://nationalinterest.org/commentary/lobbying-through-the-silver-screen-7647?page=1, viewed 7 February 2014.

176 Shavit and Wiesenbach, "Muslim Strategies to Convert Western Christians", pp. 3-14.

177 Shavit and Wiesenbach, "Muslim Strategies to Convert Western Christians", pp. 3-14.

178 Phrases like "rectifying the image of Islam" and "removing misconceptions about Islam" are Islamic ways of referring to *dawa*.

179 "New Media and Communication Technology in the Muslim World: Challenge and Opportunity", The Second International Conference on Islamic Media, Jakarta, Indonesia: The Muslim World League, 12-16 December 2011.

180 "Our Vision", Islam Channel webpage, http://www.islamchannel.tv/pagesv4/OurVision.aspx, viewed 16 May 2014.

181 "Spreading Islam through the media", The Dawah Project, http://www.thedawahproject.com/about-us/, viewed 16 May 2014.

182 Islamic Broadcasting Network - Islamic Media Foundation, Homepage, http://www.imf-ibn.net/, viewed 16 May 2014.

183 Islamic Broadcasting Network - Islamic Media Foundation, Homepage, viewed 16 May 2014.

184 Terri DeYoung, "Arabic Language and Middle East/North African Studies, University of Indiana, 1999, http://www.indiana.edu/~arabic/arabic_history.htm, viewed 17 August 2011.

185 Deborah Weiss, "OIC Ramps Up 'Islamophobia' Campaign", *FrontPageMagazine*, 28 February 2013. http://www.frontpagemag.com/2013/deborah-weiss/oic-ramps-up-islamophobia-campaign/, viewed 12 May 2014.

[186] Sebastian Moya, "The History of Arabic Loanwords in Turkish", 9 December 2008, http://www.swarthmore.edu/SocSci/Linguistics/Theses09/smoya1%20Ling Thesis%20final%20pdf.pdf, viewed 16 May 2014.

[187] John R. Perry, "Language Reform in Turkey and Iran", *International Journal of Middle East Studies*, 17: 3, Aug. 1985, pp. 295-311.

[188] "Language Reform: From Ottoman to Turkish", http://countrystudies.us/ turkey/25.htm, viewed 16 May 2014.

[189] "Lexical Purification", Kurdish Academy of Language, http://www.kurdish academy.org/?q=node/443, viewed 16 May 2014.

[190] George Readings, James Brandon and Richard Phelps, "Islamism and Language: How Using the Wrong Words Reinforces Islamist Narratives", *Quilliam*, Concept Series 3, 7 December 2010.

[191] See Patrick Sookhdeo, *Is the Muslim Isa the Biblical Jesus?*, McLean, Virginia: Isaac Publishing, 2012.

[192] James Brandon and Salam Hafez, *Crimes of the Community: Honour-Based Violence in the UK*, London: Centre for Social Cohesion, 2008, pp. 94-96, 105-106.

[193] M. A. Zaki Badawi, *Islam in Britain: a Public Lecture 1981,* London: Ta-Ha Publishers, 1981, pp. 25-27.

[194] Kambiz GhaneaBassiri, *A History of Islam in America: From the New World to the New World Order*, New York: Cambridge University Press, 2010, pp. 258-59.

[195] 'Ali ibn al-Muntasir al-Kattani, "Muslims in America", *al-Ittihad,* 11. No. 3, Spring 1974, pp. 15-16, reprinted as excerpt from *Muslim World*, 13 April 1974; 'Ali ibn al-Muntasir al-Kattani, *al-Muslimun fi Urubba wa Amrika*, 2 vols, Bayrut: Dar al-Kutub al-Ilmiyya, 2005, p. 5.

[196] Kalim Siddiqui, *The Muslim Manifesto – a strategy for survival,* London: The Muslim Institute, 1990, pp. 2-3.

[197] Kalim Siddiqui in Zafar Bangash, ed., *In Pursuit of the Power of Islam: Major Writings of Kalim Siddiqui,*,pp. 253-255.

[198] M. Ali Kettani, "Problems of Muslim Minorities", in *Muslim Communities in Non-Muslim States,* London: Islamic Council of Europe, 1980, pp. 96-105; Siddiqui, *The Muslim Manifesto,* pp. 2-3.

[199] An interesting study by the Gatestone Institute provides a detailed chronology of all the gains made by Islam in Germany in one year. Soeren Kern, *The Islamization of Germany in 2013*, Gatestone Institute, 15 January 2014, http://www.gatestone institute.org/4130/Islamization-germany, viewed 14 May 2014.

200 "Bishop attacks 'Muslim hypocrisy'", *BBC News,* 5 November 2006, http://news.bbc.co.uk/1/hi/uk/6117912.stm, viewed 15 May 2014.

201 *Muslim Communities in Non-Muslim States,* London: Islamic Council of Europe, 1980, p. xi.

202 Kettani, "Problems of Muslim Minorities", in *Muslim Communities in Non-Muslim States,* p. 105.

203 Interview with Tariq Ramadan, 10 September 2013 http://www.islamonline.net/Arabic/Daawa/2003/09/article05.shtml quoted in Shammai Fishman, "Some Notes on Arabic Terminology as a Link Between Tariq Ramadan and Sheikh Dr. Taha Jabir al-Alwani, Founder of the Doctrine of "Muslim Minority Jurisprudence" (*Fiqh al-Aqaliyyat al-Muslimah*)", Project for the Research of Islamist Movements (PRISM), Herzliya, Israel, [2003], http://www.e-prism.org/articlesbyotherscholars.html, viewed 6 May 2014.

204 Ziauddin Sardar, *Desperately Seeking Paradise*, pp. 193-203.

205 Mona Abul-Fadl, "Islamization as a Force of Global Cultural Renewal or: The Relevance of the Tawḥīdī Episteme to Modernity", *The American Journal of Islamic Social Sciences,* Vol. 5, No. 2, 1988, p.165.

206 Mona Abul-Fadl, *Rethinking Culture, Renewing The Academy: Tawhidi Perspectives,* Contrasting Episteme Collection Mona M. Abul-Fadl © Draft under Review Restricted Circulation/ GSISS Library/ In House Collection 1, http://muslimwomenstudies.com/Rethinking%20Culture-part%20A%20&%20B-cpy.pdf, viewed 28 April 2014.

207 Abul-Fadl, *Where East Meets West*, pp. 3-5.

208 Ali Shari'ati, *On The Sociology Of Islam,* transl. by Hamid Algar, Oneonta, New York: Mizan Press, 1979, p. 82.

209 Shari'ati, *On The Sociology of Islam*, p. 86.

210 Abul-Fadl, *Where East Meets West*, pp. 3-5.

211 Sardar, *Desperately Seeking Paradise*, pp. 193-203.

212 Sardar, *Desperately Seeking Paradise*, pp. 193-203.

213 Ismail Raji al-Faruqi, *Islamization of Knowledge: General Principles and Work Plan,* Herndon, Virginia: International Institute of Islamic Thought, 1982, pp. 39-47.

214 Including *Introducing Islam from Within: Alternative Perspectives; Where East Meets West: Appropriating the Islamic Encounter for a Spiritual-Cultural Revival; Contrasting Epistemics;* and *Rethinking Culture, Renewing The Academy: Tawhidi Perspectives.*

215 Abul-Fadl, *Where East Meets West*, pp. 3-5.

216 Abul-Fadl, *Where East Meets West,* pp. 4-6, 7, 56-69.

217 Kazenga P. Tibenderana, *Islamic Fundamentalism: The Quest for the Rights of Muslims in Uganda*, Kampala: Fountain Publishers, 2006, p. 80.

218 Abul-Fadl, *Where East Meets West*, p. 2.

219 Abul Fadl, *Where East Meets West*, pp. 1-3.

220 Abul-Fadl, *Rethinking Culture, Renewing The Academy*.

221 Abul-Fadl, *Where East Meets West*, pp. 9-11.

222 Abul-Fadl, *Where East Meets West*, pp. 26-29.

223 Abul-Fadl, *Where East Meets West*, pp. 28-48.

224 Ghulam Sarwar, "Compulsory Christian Collective Worship and Christian Religious Education (RE) in UK Schools: What Can Muslims Do?", *Islam 4u*, http://islam4u.montadamoslim.com/t157-compulsory-christian-collective-worship-and-christian-religious-education-re-in-uk-schools-what-can-muslims-do, viewed 15 May 2014.

225 Gilbert T. Sewall, *Islam and Textbooks: A Report of the American Textbook Council*, New York: American Textbook Council, 2003, pp. 9-11.

226 The Muslim Council of Britain, "Towards Greater Understanding: Meeting the needs of Muslim pupils in state schools, Information & Guidance for Schools", 2007, http://www.crin.org/docs/Muslim_Council_Guidance_Schools.pdf, viewed 15 May 2014.

227 Woman's headscarf, covering hair and neck but not face.

228 Full-length outer garment for women.

229 "Response of British Muslims for Secular Democracy (BMSD) to the Information and Guidance Published by Muslim Council of Britain: Meeting the Needs of Muslim Pupils in State Schools", BMSD Press Release 23 February 2007, http://www.siawi.org/article4.html, viewed 15 May 2014.

230 Confidential personal source, 2012.

231 Richard Kerbaj and Sian Griffiths, "Gove in war on Islamic takeover of schools", *The Sunday Times*, 13 April 2014; "Keep Islamism out of the classroom", *The Sunday Times*, 13 April 2014.

232 Anthony Glees and Chris Pope, *When Students Turn to Terror: Terrorist and Extremist Activity on British Campuses*, London: The Social Affairs Unit, 2005.

233 Sam Knight, "Universities given 'how-to' guide for fighting violent Islam", *The Times*, 17 November 2006.

234 Glees and Pope, *When Students Turn to Terror*.

235 Opaque veil covering the full face except the eyes.

[236] Mehmood Naqshbandi, *Islam and Muslims in Britain: A Guide for Non-Muslims*, London: City of London Police, 2006.

[237] Akbar S. Ahmed, *Postmodernism and Islam: Predicament and Promise*, London: Routledge, 1992, p. 168.

[238] Daniel MacLeod, "Middle East crisis", *The Guardian,* 18 June 2002.

[239] Robin Simcox, *A Degree of Influence: The Funding of Strategically Important Subjects in UK Universities,* London: The Centre for Social Cohesion, 2009, pp. 11-12; Stephen Pollard, "Libya and the LSE: Large Arab gifts to universities lead to 'hostile' teaching," *The Telegraph,* 3 March 2011, http://www.telegraph.co.uk/news/worldnews/africaandindianocean/libya/8360103/Libya-and-the-LSE-Large-Arab-gifts-to-universities-lead-to-hostile-teaching.html, viewed 15 May 2014.

[240] "All Foreign Gifts", Federal Student Aid, an office of the US Department of Education, 5 April 2013, http://studentaid.ed.gov/sites/default/files/fsawg/datacenter/library/ForeignGift04052013.xls, viewed 15 May 2014.

[241] Opened in 2009 with a $20 billion endowment from King Abdullah of Saudi Arabia.

[242] Susan Schmidt, "Saudi Money Shaping U.S. Research", *The National Interest,* 11 February 2013, http://nationalinterest.org/commentary/saudi-money-shaping-us-research-8083, viewed 10 February 2014.

[243] Jay P. Greene, "Arabian Gulf Money and US Universities", *Campus Watch,* 7 May 2008, http://www.campus-watch.org/article/id/5077, viewed 6 February 2014.

[244] "The World's Billionaires", *Forbes Magazine,* 9 March 2006, http://www.forbes.com/2006/03/07/06billionaires_worlds-richest-people_land.html, viewed 15 May 2014. Saudi Arabia had eleven billionaires in 2006.

[245] Michelle M. Hu and Justin C. Worland, "Saudi Prince Who Funded Harvard Program Visits", *The Harvard Crimson,* 8 February 2012, http://www.thecrimson.com/article/2012/2/8/prince-alwaleed-centers-islam/, viewed 15 May 2014.

[246] New Vision (Uganda), "House Approves Six Judges, *Pesa Times,* 20 January 2014, http://pesatimes.co.tz/news/legal-environment/house-approves-six-judges, viewed 15 May 2014.

[247] Confidential personal source, July 2013.

[248] Tanzanian government figures from 2009 but disputed by Muslims who say the Christian figure is inflated. There has been no religious question in the census since 1967 (when Christians were 34% and Muslims 31%) because the subject is so sensitive.

[249] According to the 2012 census the total population of Tanzania was about 44.9 million, of whom 1.3 million lived in Zanzibar.

[250] Vincent Hugeux, "Côte d'Ivoire: Ouattara veut 'protéger les minorité'", *L'Express,* 25 January 2012, http://www.lexpress.fr/actualite/monde/afrique/cote-d-ivoire-ouattara-veut-proteger-les-minorites_1075076.html,, viewed 15 May 2014.

251 Confidential personal source, 25 January 2014.

252 Tibenderana, *Islamic Fundamentalism,* pp. 113-117.

253 Although on the South American mainland, Suriname (formerly Dutch Guiana) and Guyana (formerly British Guiana) tend to align themselves with the Dutch- and English-speaking Caribbean islands rather than the Spanish- and Portuguese-speaking South American nations. They are members of CARICOM, the 15-nation Caribbean Community.

254 "Judge rules in favour of fully clad Muslim witness – "free exercise of religion" is guaranteed under our Fundamental Rights", *Kaieteur News Online,* 12 January 2014, http://www.kaieteurnewsonline.com/2014/01/12/judge-rules-in-favour-of-fully-clad-muslim-witness-free-exercise-of-religion-is-guaranteed-under-our-fundamental-rights/, viewed 15 May 2014.

255 *Resolutions and Recommendations of the Message of the Mosque Conference,* 1976.

256 Muslim World League: World Supreme Council for Mosques webpage, http://en.themwl.org/node/46, viewed 15 May 2014.

257 Marcel Maussen, "The governance of Islam in Western Europe: A state of the art report", *IMISCOE Working Paper,* No. 16, June 2007.

258 Maussen, "The governance of Islam in Western Europe".

259 Nigel Morris, "Terror suspects could be banned from worshipping in mosques after burka escape by Mohammed Ahmed Mohamed, *The Independent,* 12 November 2013; Anne Schmedding, "New mosques in Germany – religious architecture as a symbol of integration", Goethe Institut, July 2012, http://www.goethe.de /kue/arc/nba/en9538251.htm, viewed 15 May 2014; "On a mat and a prayer", *The Economist,* 7 April 2011.

260 "Islamic sect refused permission to build mega-mosque with four times the capacity of St Paul's Cathedral", *Daily Mail,* 6 December 2012, http://www.daily mail.co.uk/news/article-2243800/East-London-mega-mosque-4-times-capacity-St-Pauls-Cathedral-rejected-local-council.html#ixzz2sHG06y1m, viewed 15 May 2014.

261 Maussen, "The governance of Islam in Western Europe".

262 "The politics of mosque-building: constructing conflict", *The Economist,* 30 August 2007.

263 Confidential personal source, 25 January 2014.

264 Confidential personal source, February 2009.

265 Kate Connolly, "Row threatens Cologne's mega mosque", *The Guardian,* 5 March 2012, http://www.theguardian.com/world/2012/mar/05/row-over-cologne-mega-mosque, viewed 14 May 2014.

266 Reuven Erlich, "The Use of Mosques for Military and Political Purposes by Hamas and other Terrorist Organisations and Islamic Groups", *Think-Israel*, 1 March 2009, http://www,think-israel.org/erlich.terroristsmosques.html, viewed 6 May 2014.

267 Soeren Kern, "European 'No-Go' Zones for Non-Muslims Proliferating" *Gatestone Institute*, 22 August 2011, http://www.gatestoneinstitute.org/2367/european-muslim-no-go-zones, viewed 14 May 2014.

268 Daud R. Matthews, *Presenting Islam in the West: (Introduction)*, Leicester: UK Islamic Academy, 2004, p. 12.

269 *Akhbar al-'Alam al-Islami*, No. 908 (January 14, 1985), summarised in Rudolph, "The Debate on Muslim-Christian Dialogue as Reflected in Muslim Periodicals in Arabic (1970-1991)" in Waardenburg ed., *Muslim Perceptions of Other Religions*, p. 300.

270 Ahmad Deedat writing in *Akhbar al-'Alam al-Islami*, No. 1115, 27 March 1989.

271 For example, the Moroccan Sheikh 'Abdallah Kannun wrote in the Qatari monthly *Al-Umma*, No. 3, January 1981, pp. 24ff. of how critical theology from liberal Christian theologians, such as John Hick's 1977 book *The Myth of God Incarnate*, was a step towards Islam and a good foundation for Muslim-Christian dialogue.

272 "Barnabas Aid Response to the Yale Center for Faith and Culture Statement", 30 January 2008,http://www.barnabasfund.org/US/News/Archives/Barnabas-Fund-Response-to-the-Yale-Center-for-Faith-and-Culture-Statement.html?p=7, viewed 12 May 2014.

273 Samuel Westrop, *The Interfaith Industry*, London: Stand for Peace, September 2013, p. 2 and *passim*.

274 "Special Representative to Muslim Communities", U.S. Department of State webpage, http://www.state.gov/s/srmc/ viewed 14 May 2014.

275 Pew Forum, "President Obama's Advisory Council on Faith-Based and Neighborhood Partnerships", *Pew Research Religion & Life Project*, 9 September 2009, http://www.pewforum.org/2009/08/18/president-obamas-advisory-council-on-faith-based-and-neighborhood-partnerships/, viewed 14 May 2014.

276 Sarah Baxter, "Obama reaches out to Muslims", *The Sunday Times,* 18 January 2009.

277 Tom Baldwin, "Barack Obama offers open hand to Muslims", *The Times*, 28 January 2009.

278 Bat Ye'or, *Islam and Dhimmitude: Where Civilizations Collide*, Madison, New Jersey: Fairleigh Dickinson University Press, 2002, pp. 96-98.

279 Mahiudin Abu Zakaria Yahya Ibn Sharif En Nawawi, *Minhaj et Talibin: A manual of Muhammadan Law according to the School of Shafai,*transl. E. C. Howard, Book 58, Chapter 1, Section 3, New Delhi, Adam Publishers & Distributors, 2005, p. 469.

280 Ahmad ibn Naqib al-Misri, *Reliance of the Traveller: The Classic Manual of Islamic Sacred Law 'Umdat al-Salik by Ahmad ibn Naqib al-Misri (d. 769/1368) in Arabic with facing English Text, Commentary and Appendices,* ed. and transl. Nuh Ha Mim Keller, Beltsville, MD: Amana Publications, 1997,p. 609.

281 Ann Elizabeth Mayer, *Islam and Human Rights: Tradition and Politics,* Boulder, Colorado: Westview Press, 1991, pp. 148-149.

282 Yusuf Al-Qaradawi, *Priorities of the Islamic Movement in the Coming Phase,* Swansea: Awakening Publications, 2000, pp. 192-197.

283 Abdelmassih, "Two Christians Murdered in Egypt for Refusing to pay Jizya to Muslims

284 Albert Habib Hourani, *Minorities In The Arab World,* London: Oxford University Press, 1947, p. 17.

285 Richard. B. Rose, "Islam and The Development of Personal Status Laws Among Christian Dhimmis: Motives, Sources, Consequences," *The Muslim World,* Vol. LXXII, Nos. 3-4, 1982, pp. 159, 174-175.

286 Bat Ye'or, *Islam and Dhimmitude: Where Civilizations Collide*, Madison, New Jersey: Fairleigh Dickinson University Press, 2002.

287 Libby Purves, "Third World Reveals Miss World Ugliness", *The Times,* 26 November 2002; 'Stephen James Johnson, South Park' cuts image of Mohammed after threat, AFP, 22 April 2010, http://www.chargerbulletin.com/2010/04/22/south-park-cuts-image-of-mohammed-after-threat/, viewed 13 May 2014.

288 Tibenderana, *Islamic Fundamentalism,* pp. 38-67, 79-80, 93, 118-119, 120-127.

289 Dr Ahmad K. Sengendo, Foreword to Kazenga P. Tibenderana, *Islamic Fundamentalism: The Quest for the Rights of Muslims in Uganda,* Kampala: Fountain Publishers, 2006, p. xix.

290 Kampala: Fountain Publishers, 2006.

291 Tibenderana, *Islamic Fundamentalism,* pp. 93, 122.

292 Azzam Tamimi, "Human Rights – Islamic and Secular Perspectives", in *The Quest for Sanity:Reflections on September 11 and the Aftermath,* Wembley, Middlesex: The Muslim Council of Britain, 2002, pp. 229-235.

293 For instance, in Egypt (prior to the "Arab Spring" in 2011) certain high public positions were closed to Christians by an unwritten rule, while churches needed special permits for the minutest renovations. In Pakistan religious minorities suffer from "arbitrary denial of social and economic rights as well as the rights to preach, practice and propagate minority beliefs" as well as being subject to a wide range of harassment and humiliation. "Official indifference to other abuses of minority rights" in: "Pakistan: Insufficient Protection of Religious Minorities", *Amnesty International,* May 2001, ASA 33/008/2001, pp. 25-28.

294 "Human Rights Committee 48th Session: Summary Record of the 1251st Meeting, 2nd Periodic Report of the Islamic Republic of Iran, 29 July 1993", *United Nations, International Covenant on Civil and Political Rights (CCPR)*, http://www.bayefsky.com/summary/iran_ccpr_c_sr_1251_1993.php, viewed 13 May 2014.

295 Salwa Ismail, "The Paradox of Islamist Politics", *Middle East Report*, No. 221, Winter, 2001, pp. 34-39.

296 Riaz Hassan, "Globalization's Challenge to Islam", *Yale Global*, 17 April 2003, http://yaleglobal.yale.edu/content/globalizations-challenge-islam, viewed 13 May 2014.

297 Ismail, "The Paradox of Islamist Politics", pp. 34-39.

298 Ismail, "The Paradox of Islamist Politics", pp. 34-39.

299 "The Islamization of Tanzania is on the rise" email from confidential personal source, 16 January 2014.

300 Cameron S. Brown, "Waiting For The Other Shoe To Drop: How Inevitable Is An Islamist Future?", *The Middle East Review of International Affairs*, Vol. 10, No. 2, June 2006, pp. 108-119.

301 Sheri Berman, "Islamism, Revolution, and Civil Society", *Perspectives on Politics*, Vol. 1, No. 2, June 2003, pp. 257-72, https://docs.google.com/a/barnard.edu/viewer?a=v&pid=sites&srcid=YmFybmFyZC5lZHV8c2hlcmktYmVybWFufGd4Oj E1OGYzOGI5MTljZjUzNWU, viewed 13 May 2014.

302 Toby Lester, "Tracking India's Bandit Queen: A conversation with Mary Anne Weaver", *Atlantic Unbound*, 1 November 1996, http://www.theatlantic.com/magazine/archive/1996/11/tracking-indias-bandit-queen/304892/, viewed 13 May 2014.

303 Lester, "Tracking India's Bandit Queen".

304 Soheir A. Morsy, "Islamic Clinics in Egypt: The Cultural Elaboration of Biomedical Hegemony", *Medical Anthropology Quarterly*, New Series, Vol. 2, No. 4, Dec. 1988, pp. 355-369.

305 John Kifner, "Egypt's New Islamic Schools: Setting an Example", Special to *The New York Times*, 29 September 1986, Section A, p.2.

306 Berman, "Islamism, Revolution, and Civil Society" pp. 257-72.

307 Berman, "Islamism, Revolution, and Civil Society", pp. 257-72.

308 Berman, "Islamism, Revolution, and Civil Society", pp. 257-72.

309 Fauzi M. Najjar, "Book Banning in Contemporary Egypt", *The Muslim World*, Vol. 91, Nos. 3 & 4, Fall 2001, pp. 399-424.

310 Steve Negus, "The Muslim Brothers Keep a Low Profile, But Their Main Activity—Charity Work—Still Goes On," *Cairo Times*, Vol. 1, No. 3, 3 April 1997.

311 Berman, "Islamism, Revolution, and Civil Society", pp. 257-72.

312 Lorenzo Vidino, ed., *The West and the Muslim Brotherhood After the Arab Spring,* Al Mesbar Studies & Research Centre in collaboration with The Foreign Policy Research Institute, February 2013, p. 1.

313 Wael Nawara and Feyzi Baban "Future of political islam: lessons from Turkey, Egypt", Al-Monitor, 29 January 2014, http://www.al-monitor.com/pulse/ originals/2014/01/islam-turkey-egypt-ideology-islamist-law.html?utm_source= Al-Monitor+Newsletter+%5BEnglish%5D&utm_campaign=32d3bc2c8c- January_9_20141_8_2014&utm_medium=email&utm_term=0_28264b27a0- 32d3bc2c8c-93088337#ixzz2ruJPcjm3, viewed 13 May 2014.

314 "What's gone wrong with democracy: Democracy was the most successful political ideal of the 20th century. Why has it run into trouble, and what can be done to revive it?", *The Economist*, Vol. 410, No. 8876, 1-7 March 2014, pp. 47-52.

315 Samuel Tadros, "Victory or Death: The Muslim Brotherhood in the Trenches", http://www.hudson.org/research/9687-victory-or-death-the-muslim-brotherhood-in- the-trenches, viewed 13 May 2014.

316 Dahr Jamail, "Hezbollah's transformation", *Asia Times Online*, 20 July 2006, viewed 13 May 2014.

317 Mouna Succarieh, "Rise of Radical Islam in Yemen Altering Its Tribalism, Book Finds" *Al-Monitor*, 22 September 2012, http://www.al-monitor.com/pulse/fa/ politics/2012/09/weekenda-detailed-look-at-islamism-in-yemen.html#, viewed 13 May 2014.

318 Bruce Maddy-Weitzman, "The Arab League Comes Alive", *Middle East Quarterly*, 19:3, Summer 2012, pp. 71-78.

319 Jeb Boone, "Yemen's Transition: Who's Who in the Yemeni Opposition", The Jamestown Foundation, *Militant Leadership Monitor (MLM)*, Vol. 2, Issue 12, 30 December 2011.

320 Robin Simcox, *Yemen Beyond Saleh: Problems and Prospects for the U.S. and its Allies*, The Henry Jackson Society, May 2011.

321 Boone, "Yemen's Transition: Who's Who in the Yemeni Opposition".

322 "Blast kills dozens as Yemen violence rages", CBS News, May 21, 2012. http://www.cbsnews.com/news/blast-kills-dozens-as-yemen-violence-rages/, viewed 13 May 2014.

323 Sam Kimball, "Whose Side Is Yemen On?" *Foreign Policy*, 29 August 2012, http://www.foreignpolicy.com/articles/2012/08/29/whose_side_is_yemen_on, viewed 13 May 2014.

324 International Crisis Group, "Islamic parties in Pakistan", Asia Report No. 216, 12 December 2011.

325 Vali Nasr, "Pakistan after Islamization: Mainstream and Militant Islamism in a Changing State", in John L. Esposito, John O. Voll, Osman Bakar, eds., *Asian Islam in the 21st Century*, New York: Oxford University Press, 2008, pp. 31-48.

326 Nazih N. Ayubi, "Islamic State", in John L. Esposito, ed., *The Oxford Encyclopedia of the Modern Islamic World*, New York; Oxford University Press, 1995, Vol. 2., pp. 323-324.

327 Husain Haqqani, "The Role of Islam in Pakistan's Future", *The Washington Quarterly*, Winter 2004-05, pp. 85-96.

328 International Crisis Group, "The State of Sectarianism in Pakistan".

329 Haqqani, "The Role of Islam in Pakistan's Future", pp. 85-96.

330 "Annual Report of the United States Commission on International Religious Freedom May 2011", Washington DC: United States Commission on International Religious Freedom, 2011, pp. 104-117.

331 Points 67 and 69 of a judgment given by Gul Muhammad Khan in a case against Muhammad Ismail Qureshi (Shariat Petition No. 6/L of 1987) Federal Shariat Court, 30 October 1990, *All Pakistan Legal Decisions* Vol. XLIII (1991) FSC35, "Federal Shariat Court 1990", http://khatm-e-nubuwwat.org/lawyers/data/english/8/fed-shariat-court-1990.pdf, viewed 13 May 2014.

332 "Death only penalty for blasphemer: Shariat Court", *The International News* [Pakistan], 5 December 2013, http://www.thenews.com.pk/Todays-News-13-27076-Death-only-penalty-for-blasphemer-Shariat-Court, viewed 16 May 2014; M. Ahmad Tauqir, "Death the only punishment for blasphemer: FSC", *Pakistan Today*, 4 December 2013, http://www.pakistantoday.com.pk/2013/12/04/national/death-the-only-punishment-for-blasphemer-fsc/, viewed 16 May 2014.

333 Judgment in the Court of Khan Talib Hussain Baloch, Additional Sessions Judge, Sargodha, Sessions Case No. 6 of 1992, Sessions Trial No. 6 of 1992, the State vs. Gul Masih s/o Dolat Masih caste Christian r/o Chak No. 46 N.B. City Sarghoda, pp. 10-11.

334 "Persecution Under the Blasphemy Laws in Pakistan", *Jubilee Campaign* Information Sheet, http://web.archive.org/web/20071019014952/http://www.jubilee campaign.co.uk/world/pak25.htm, viewed 13 May 2014.

335 Susannah Price, "Pakistani court frees 'blasphemer' ", *BBC News*, Thursday 15 August 2002, http://news.bbc.co.uk/1/low/world/south_asia/2196275.stm, viewed 13 May 2014.

336 Harvey Glickman, "Islamism in Sudan's Civil War", *Orbis*, Vol. 44. No. 2, Spring 2000, pp. 267-282.

337 Abdullahi Ahmed An-Na'im, "Application of Shari'ah (Islamic Law) and Human Rights Violations in the Sudan", in *Religion and Human Rights: Proceedings of the Conference Convened by the Sudan Human Rights Organization*, 1992, p. 101; "Sudan, International Religious Freedom Report", US Department of State, Released

by the Bureau of Democracy, Human Rights, and Labor, 26 October 2001; "Persecuted Church News - Sudan: 'Religious Freedom'? Not Really!", *World Evangelical Alliance, Religious Liberty Prayer List,* No. 158, Wed 6, March, 2002, http://web.archive.org/web/20020617170740/http://worldevangelical.org/persec_sudan_06mar02.html, viewed 16 May 2014.

338 Mohamed Mahmoud, "When Shari'a Governs: The Impasse of Religious Relations in Sudan", *Islam and Christian-Muslim Relations,* Vol. 18, No. 2, April 2007, pp. 275-286.

339 Abdul Rahman Embong, "The Culture and Practice of Pluralism in Postcolonial Malaysia" in Robert W. Hefner, ed., *The Politics of Multiculturalism: Pluralism and Citizenship in Malaysia, Singapore, and Indonesia,* Honolulu: University of Hawai'i Press, 2001, p. 59.

340 Robert W. Hefner, "Introduction" in Robert W. Hefner, ed., *The Politics of Multiculturalism: Pluralism and Citizenship in Malaysia, Singapore, and Indonesia,* pp. 22-24.

341 Osman Bakar, "Islam, Ethnicity, Pluralism and Democracy: Malaysia's Unique Experience", in: "Islam, Democracy and the Secularist State in the Post-Modern Era", Burtonsville, MD: Center for the Study of Islam & Democracy (CSID), 2001, pp. 48-53.

342 Raymond L. M. Lee, "Patterns of Religious Tension in Malaysia", *Asian Survey,* Vol. 28, No. 4, Apr. 1988, pp. 400-418.

343 Vincent J. H. Houben, "Southeast Asia and Islam", *The Annals of the American Academy of Political and Social Science,* July 2003; Vol. 588, pp. 149-170.

344 Kate Mayberry, " 'Un-Islamic' book trial opens in Malaysia", *Aljazeera,* 6 August 2012, http://www.aljazeera.com/indepth/features/2012/08/2012867105 109271.html, viewed 13 May 2014.

345 Zainah Anwar, "What Islam, Whose Islam? Sisters in Islam and the Struggle for Women's Rights" in Robert Hefner, ed., *The Politics of Multiculturalism,* pp. 235-236; Embong, "The Culture and Practice of Pluralism in Post-Colonial Malaysia" in Hefner, ed., *The Politics of Multiculturalism,* pp.74-75.

346 Bakar, "Islam, Ethnicity, Pluralism and Democracy: Malaysia's Unique Experience", in *Islam, Democracy and the Secularist State in the Post-Modern Era",* pp. 48-53.

347 Sholto Byrnes, "Creeping Islamisation: Observations on Malaysia", *New Statesman,* 6 September 2007, http://www.newstatesman.com/society/2007/09/malaysia-religious-muslim, viewed 13 May 2014.

348 Robert Day McAmis, *Malay Muslims: The History and Challenge of Resurgent Islam in Southeast Asia,* Grand Rapids, Michigan: William B. Eerdmans, 2002, pp. 86-90; Embong, "The Culture and Practice of Pluralism in Post-Colonial Malaysia"

in Hefner, ed., *The Politics of Multiculturalism: Pluralism and Citizenship in Malaysia*, pp. 74-75.

349 Byrnes, "Creeping Islamisation"

350 Mayberry, "'Un-Islamic' book trial opens in Malaysia".

351 Amir Taheri, "Who Rules Iran?" *Iran Press Service*, http://www.iran-press-service.com/articles_2004/Mar_04/who_rules_iran_29304.htm, viewed 13 May 2014.

352 Ahmad S. Moussalli, *The Islamic Quest for Democracy, Pluralism and Human Rights*, Gainesville, FL: University Press of Florida, 2001, p. 56.

353 Houshang Sepehr, "A Caliphate disguised as a republic", *IV Online magazine*, 382, 7 October 2006, http://www.internationalviewpoint.org/spip.php?article1148, viewed 13 May 2014.

354 Moussalli, *The Islamic Quest for Democracy, Pluralism and Human Rights*, p. 56.

355 Ladan Boroumand, "The Untold Story of the Fight for Human Rights", *Journal of Democracy*, Vol. 18, No. 4, October 2007, p. 67.

356 "Human Rights Committee 48th Session: Summary Record of the 1251st Meeting"

357 "Iran: A legal System that Fails to Protect Freedom of Expression and Association", *Amnesty International*, AI-index: MDE 13/045/2001, http://www.amnesty.org/en/library/asset/MDE13/045/2001/en/73a8bc2a-d8ae-11dd-ad8c-f3d4445c118e/mde130452001en.html, viewed 15 May 2014.

358 United States Commission on International Religious Freedom, "Annual Report of the United States Commission on International Religious Freedom May 2011", Washington DC: US Commission on International Religious Freedom, 2011, pp. 68-81.

359 United States Commission on International Religious Freedom, "Annual Report of the United States Commission on International Religious Freedom May 2011", pp. 68-81.

360 Qasim, "Destroying the Country Idol".

361 Abd al-'Aziz bin Salih al-Jarbu, "Clarifying the Obligation of Migration", quoted in Muhammad Qasim, "Destroying the Country Idol", *Azan*, Issue 3, 24 August 2013. (*Azan* is a magazine published by the Taliban in Pakistan and Afghanistan. Key excerpts from the article are available in MEMRI Special Dispatch No. 5428, 30 August 2013 at http://www.memri.org/report/en/print7385.htm, viewed 6 May 2014.

362 Fathi Yakan, *Problems Faced by the Da'wah and the Da'iyah*, Singapore: International Islamic Federation of Student Organisations, 1985, p. 231.

363 'Abdul 'Azeez ibn 'Abdullaah ibn Baaz, *Words of Advice Regarding Da'wah,* p. 27.

364 Ministry of the Interior and Kingdom Relations, *From dawa to jihad: The various threats from radical Islam to the democratic legal order*, The Hague: General Intelligence and Security Service, December 2004, p. 27.

365 Yusuf Al-Qaradawi "Muslim Minorities and Politics", *OnIslam.net*, 30 April 2012, viewed 6 May 2014.

366 Dr Yusuf Al-Qaradawi, *Fiqh al-jihād : dirāsah muqāranah li-aḥkāmih wa-falsafatih fī ḍawawatih fī ḍaw. 27.nnah*, al-Qāhirah (Cairo): Maktabat Wahbah, 2009.

367 Summary by Rajab Abu Maleeh, "Al-Qaradawi's Fiqh of Jihad (Book Review 7/11", *OnIslam.net* viewed 29 April 2014, http://www.onislam.net/english/shariah/contemporary-issues/interviews-reviews-and-events/448773-al-qaradawis-fiqh-of-jihad-book-review-911.html?Events=

368 Brigadier S. K. Malik, *The Quranic Concept of War,* Lahore, Pakistan: Associated Printers, 1979, p. 54.

369 Sayyid Abul A'la Mawdudi, *Jihad fi Salilillah: (Jihad in Islam),* transl. Khurshid Ahmad, Birmingham, U.K. Islamic Mission Dawah Centre, 1977, p. 4.

370 Isma'il Raji al-Faruqi, *Islam*, Brentwood, Maryland: International Graphics, 1984, p. 60.

371 Qasim, "Destroying the Country Idol".

372 Bernard Lewis, *The Political Language of Islam,* Chicago: University of Chicago Press, 1988, p. 92.

373 Nasr Hamid Abu Zaid, "Brutality and civilisation – violence and terrorism?", in Jochen Hippler, *War, Repression, Terrorism: Political Violence and Civilisation in Western and Muslim Societies,* Stuttgart: Institut fur Auslandsbeziehungen, 2006, pp. 301-329.

374 For more information on jihad in the Quran, *hadith*, sharia and Islamic history as well as for a range of Muslim interpretations of these sources, see Patrick Sookhdeo, *Global Jihad: The Future in the Face of Militant Islam*, McLean, Virginia: Isaac Publishing, 2007.

375 Bassam Tibi, "War and Peace in Islam", in Terry Nardin, ed., *The Ethics of War and Peace: Religious and Secular Perspectives,* Princeton, New Jersey: Princeton University Press, 1996, pp. 128-145.

376 Ayatollah Khomeini of Iran issued a *fatwa* demanding the death penalty for author Salman Rushdie whose book *The Satanic Verses* Khomeini said had blasphemed Muhammad.

377 Pope Benedict XVI, speaking on the subject of "Faith, Reason and the University" at the University of Regensburg in September 2006 made an appeal to reason, quoting from a 14th century Byzantine emperor, Manuel II (Paleologus), who,

during a discussion about religion with an important Muslim scholar, said it was unreasonable to spread a faith by the sword and violence as Muhammad had commanded Muslims to do. Pope Benedict presented the emperor's argument that violence is incompatible with the nature of God and the nature of the soul.

378 Winsor, "'Some parts of Britain have their own form of justice'".

379 Paul Rogers, "Syria, al-Qaida, and the future", *openDemocracy*, 2 August 2012, http://www.opendemocracy.net/paul-rogers/syria-al-qaida-and-future, viewed 13 May 2014.

380 Rowan Callick, "Christians 'emptied from the Middle East", *The Australian,* 6 October 2012, http://www.theaustralian.com.au/news/world/christians-emptied-from-middle-east/story-e6frg6so-1226489418086, viewed 15 May 2014.

381 Ulrike Putz, "Christians flee from radical rebels in Syria", *Spiegel Online International,* 25 July 2012, http://www.spiegel.de/international/world/christians-flee-from-radical-rebels-in-syria-a-846180.html, viewed 15 May 2014.

382 Adamu Adamu and Michelle Faul, "Few voters in Nigerian state amid Islamic uprising", *Associated Press*, 28 December 2013, http://news.yahoo.com/few-voters-nigerian-state-amid-islamic-uprising-094737998.html, viewed 20 January 2014; "Oritsejafor raises alarm over 'intended extermination of Christians and Christianity from northern Nigeria'", *News Express* (Nigeria), 19 March 2013, http://www.newsexpressngr.com/news/detail.php?news=1274&title=Oritsejafor-raises-alarm-over-"intended-extermination-of-Christians-and-Christianity-from-northern-Nigeria" viewed 16 May 2014; "Boko Haram raid kills dozens in Nigeria", *Al-Jazeera*, 12 February 2014, http://www.aljazeera.com/news/africa/2014/02/boko-haram-raid-kills-dozens-nigeria-201421221431015516.html, viewed 13 February 2014; Ahmad Salkida, "Nigeria: Sect Leader Vows Revenge", *Daily Trust*, 27 July 2009, http://wwrn.org/articles/31419/?&place=nigeria, viewed 13 February 2014; Martin Barillas, "Nigeria: Islamist terrorists threaten to abduct Christian women to teach fear of Islam", *Spero News,* 9 March 2012; "Boko Haram issues three-day ultimatum to Christians", *AFP*, 2 January 2012, http://www.vanguardngr.com/2012/01/boko-haram-spokesman-threatens-christians-troops/#sthash.1VvYWuqo.dpuf, viewed 13 February 2014.

383 United States Commission on International Religious Freedom, "Press Release: USCIRF Calls for New Efforts to Address Statelessness on Second Anniversary of South Sudan's Independence", 9 July 2013, http://uscirf1.rssing.com/chan-7335254/all_p3.html#item54, viewed 16 May 2014; "Warning: Sudan", United States Holocaust Memorial Museum; Alan Boswell, "Darfur Redux: Is 'Ethnic Cleansing' Occurring in Sudan's Nuba Mountains; "Silent Scream; The Sudan Ethnically Cleanses Its Christians".

384 Ulf Laessing, "Christians grow anxious in "100 percent" Islamic Sudan", *Reuters*, 27 February 2013, http://uk.reuters.com/article/2013/02/27/uk-sudan-christians-idUKBRE91Q0QE20130227, viewed 16 May 2014; "Christian proselytizing activities in Sudan are limited, says minister", *Sudan Tribune*, 17 April 2013,

http://www.sudantribune.com/spip.php?article46270, viewed 16 May 2014; "Canada Condemns Sudan's Deteriorating Human Rights Situation", *International Business Times*, 4 March 2013, http://ca.ibtimes.com/articles/441741/20130304/sharia law-canada-sudan-amputation-humanrightswatch.htm, viewed 16 May 2014.

385 Pierre Conesa, "Background to Washington's War on Terror: Al-Qaida, the sect", *Le Monde Diplomatique,* January 2002, http://mondediplo.com/2002/01/07sect, viewed 13 May 2014; "The war for Muslim minds: an interview with Gilles Kepel", openDemocracy, 11 November 2004, http://www.opendemocracy.net/faith-europe_islam/article_2216.jsp, viewed 13 May 2014.

386 al-Qaradawi, *Priorities of the Islamic Movement in the Coming Phase*, pp. 165-166.

387 "Catherine Samba-Panza chosen as CAR's new interim President", *AFP*, 21 January 2014, http://www.the-star.co.ke/news/article-151614/catherine-samba-panza-chosen-cars-new-interim-president#sthash.7VHXxiXc.dpuf, viewed 10 March 2014.

388 Anh Nga Longva, "The Apostasy Law in the Age of Universal Human Rights and Citizenship: Some Legal and Political Implications", paper delivered at the Fourth Nordic Conference on Middle Eastern Studies: The Middle East in a Globalizing World, Oslo, 13-16 August 1998. http://www.hf.uib.no/smi/pao/longva.html , viewed 13 May 2014.

389 Jordan, *International Religious Freedom Report for 2012*, United States Department of State, Bureau of Democracy, Human Rights and Labor, 2012, http://www.state.gov/j/drl/rls/irf/religiousfreedom/index.htm?year=2012&dlid=2083 96, viewed 14 May 2014.

390 Fauzi M. Najjar, "Islamic Fundamentalism and the Intellectuals: The Case of Nasr Hamid Abu Zayd", *British Journal of Middle Eastern Studies*, Vol. 27, No. 2, November 2000, pp. 177-200.

391 al-Jarbu, "A Call to Migrate from the Lands of the Disbelievers to the Lands of the Muslims", p. 8.

392 Jacquelyn K. Davis and Charles M. Perry, "Rethinking the War on Terror, Developing a Strategy to Counter Extremist Ideologies: A Workshop Report", March 2007, http://www.ifpa.org/pdf/Rethink_WOT.pdf, viewed 14 May 2014.

393 *World Almanac of Islamism 2014: American Foreign Policy Council*, Lanham, MD: Rowman & Littlefield, 2014, pp. 259-271.

394 Jeremy M. Sharp, "U.S. Democracy Promotion Policy in the Middle East: The Islamist Dilemma", *CRS Report for Congress*, 15 June 2006, http://www.fas.org/sgp/crs/mideast/RL33486.pdf, viewed 14 May 2014.

[395] Valentina Bartolucci, "Morocco's silent revolution", *openDemocracy,* 17 January 2012, http://www.opendemocracy.net/valentina-bartolucci/moroccos-silent -revolution, viewed 13 May 2014.

[396] Berman, "Islamism, Revolution, and Civil Society pp. 257-72.

[397] Barry Rubin, "Tunisia: Goodbye Democracy? Islamists Start to Take Over Media", PJ Media, 5 July 2012, http://pjmedia.com/barryrubin/2012/07/05/ tunisia-same-old-same-old/, viewed 13 May 2014.

[398] Nizar Maqni, "Tunisia: A New Home for Jihadi Salafis?" *Al Akhbar English,* 3 March 2012, http://english.al-akhbar.com/node/4772, viewed 14 May 2014.

[399] Rob Prince, "Tunisia culture wars: the case of Habib Kazdaghli, Dean of the University of Tunis-Manouba", *openDemocracy,* 26 July 2012, http://www.open-democracy.net/rob-prince/tunisia-culture-wars-case-of-habib-kazdaghli-dean-of -university-of-tunis-manouba, viewed 13 May 2014.

[400] Brown, "Waiting For The Other Shoe To Drop: How Inevitable Is An Islamist Future?", pp. 108-119.

[401] Gamal Essam El-Din, "Dogma rules: Islamists on the Constitutional Assembly are steamrolling through constitutional drafts that will turn Egypt into a non-civil state", *Al-Ahram Weekly*, Issue No. 1108, 26 July - 1Aug 2012, p. 3.

[402] Peter Beaumont, "Mohamed Morsi signs Egypt's new constitution into law", *The Guardian,* 26 December 2012, http://www.theguardian.com/world/2012/dec/ 26/mohamed-morsi-egypt-constitution-law, viewed 14 May 2014.

[403] Hamas is an Arabic acronym for the Islamic Resistance Movement (Harakat Al-Muqawama Al-Islamia) but also means "zeal" in Arabic.

[404] "Gaza: Hamas Should Stop Executions", *Human Rights Watch*, 1 August 2011. http://www.hrw.org/news/2011/08/01/gaza-hamas-should-stop-executions viewed 14 May 2014; "Gaza: Lift Restrictions on Books, Newspapers", *Human Rights Watch,* 8 March 2011. http://www.hrw.org/news/2011/03/07/gaza-lift-restrictions-books-news papers viewed 14 May 2014; Gaza: Halt Morality Enforcement Campaign", *Human Rights Watch,* 2 March 2011. http://www.hrw.org/news/2011/03/02/gaza-halt -morality-enforcement-campaign, viewed 14 May 2014.

[405] International Crisis Group, "Hizbollah And The Lebanese Crisis", Middle East Report No. 69, 10 October 2007.

[406] Hussain Abdul-Hussain, "Hezbollah: The State within a State", *Current Trends in Islamist Ideology*, Vol. 8, 21 May 2009.

[407] Jonathan Spyer, "Hizballah And The Arab Revolutions: The Contradiction Made Apparent?" *Middle East Review of International Affairs,* 27 April 2012, http://www.gloria-center.org/2012/04/hizballah-and-the-arab-revolutions-the -contradiction-made-apparent/, viewed 13 May 2014.

408 Nathan J. Brown, "Jordan and its Islamic Movement: The Limits of Inclusion?" Carnegie Endowment for International Peace, Democracy And Rule Of Law Project, Number 74, November 2006, http://carnegieendowment.org/files/cp_74_brown_final.pdf, viewed 6 May 2014.

409 Senem Aydin and Ruşen Çakır, "Political Islam in Turkey", Centre European Policy Studies (CEPS) Working Document No. 265, April 2007.

410 "The AKP Government's Attempts to move Turkey from Secularism to Islamism (Part III): PM Erdogan: Islam is Turkey's Supra-Identity", *MEMRI,* Special Dispatch Series No. 1086, February 7, 2006, http://www.memri.org/report/en/print1600.htm, viewed 13 May 2014; Brown, "Waiting For The Other Shoe To Drop: How Inevitable Is An Islamist Future?", pp. 108-119.

411 Aydin and Çakır, "Political Islam in Turkey".

412 "Islam, Secularism and the Battle for Turkey's Future", *STRATFOR* Special Report, August 2010.

413 Jihad al-Zein, "What Will Be the Real Costs of Turkey's Involvement in Syria?" *Al-Monitor,* 18 September 2012, http://www.al-monitor.com/pulse/politics/2012/09/what-will-turkeys-involvement-in-syria-cost-its-leaders.html, viewed 14 May 2014; Semih Idiz, "Erdogan Takes Islamist Stance, Snubs West at AKP Congress", *Al-Monitor,* 1 October 2012, http://www.al-monitor.com/pulse/politics/2012/09/erdogan-shuns-west-woos-islamists-at-akp-congress.html, viewed 14 May 2014.

414 Matt Waldman, "The Sun In The Sky: The Relationship Between Pakistan's ISI And Afghan Insurgents", *Crisis States Discussion Paper,* No. 18, London: LSE DESTIN Crisis States Research Centre, 2010.

415 Haqqani, "The Role of Islam in Pakistan's Future", *The Washington Quarterly,* Winter 2004-05, pp. 85-96.

416 International Crisis Group, "Islamic parties in Pakistan".

417 International Crisis Group, "The State of Sectarianism in Pakistan", Asia Report No. 95, 18 April 2005.

418 Bathiar Effendy, Dean of the School of Social and Political Sciences at the State Islamic University, Jakarta, "PKS Fiasco and the End of the 'Da wah' Party?", *The Jakarta Post*, 19 August 2013, p. 46.

419 Zubaidah Nazeer, "Indonesian ex-MP gets 16 years for corruption", *The Straits Times*, 12 December 2013, http://news.asiaone.com/news/asia/indonesian-ex-mp-gets-16-years-corruption, viewed 14 May 2014.

420 Effendy, "PKS Fiasco and the End of the 'Da'wah' Party?", pp. 46-47.

INDEX